CRIME AND THE MIND

CRIME AND THE MIND

An Outline of Psychiatric Criminology

by Walter Bromberg, M.D.

Formerly Director, Psychiatric Clinic,
Court of General Sessions, New York, N.Y., and
Senior Psychiatrist, Bellevue Psychiatric
Hospital, New York

GREENWOOD PRESS, PUBLISHERS
WESTPORT, CONNECTICUT

Library of Congress Cataloging in Publication Data

Bromberg, Walter, 1900–
    Crime and the mind.

    Bibliography: p.
    1. Criminal psychology. 2. Psychiatry.
I. Title.
HV6080.B7 1972   364.3   77-170192
ISBN 0-8371-6249-1

Originally published in 1948 J. B. Lippincott Company,
Philadelphia

Reprinted with the permission of Walter Bromberg

Reprinted by Greenwood Press, Inc.

First Greenwood reprinting 1972
Second Greenwood reprinting 1973
Third Greenwood reprinting 1977

Library of Congress catalog card number 77-170192

ISBN 0-8371-6249-1

Printed in the United States of America

Preface

Crime and the activities of criminals have exerted a perennial fascination alike on the average citizen and those who deal professionally with crime. Universal concern with crime, with its effect on life and property, and its resistance to control, is based on weighty practical considerations. The obduracy of criminals to cure and the difficulty of eradicating crime constitute a challenge to thinking individuals in society. But there are deeper psychological forces active within men that move society to maintain a perpetual interest in crime. The unconscious participation of law-abiding individuals in criminal activity confers on every civilized person a degree of familiarity with the psychological aspects of wrongdoing. The same impulses which eventuate in crime among offenders are present in normal individuals, interwoven with their emotions and instinctive urges but controlled by conscience. The ever-present concern with crime arises from both practical and psychological sources. Unconscious motives as well as civilized interest in reducing criminal depredations account for the universal appeal which crime exerts. From both sources arises the stimulation for efforts to find a solution for the social plague of crime.

Biologic and sociologic sciences and the spirit of humanitarianism have been directed during the past century toward a solution of the riddle of the criminal. It has appeared obvious in this undertaking that exact knowledge should preface any informed attempt at treatment of the problem of crime. Psychiatry, which to some degree has opened the door to the causes of human misbehavior, is in a position to assess the force of human factors involved in antisocial behavior. The clinical study of criminals is an important step toward amassing such information, and the present work records a move in this direction.

The material in this volume was developed from clinical study of hundreds of convicted criminals. Its emphasis is on the phenomenology of crime, the psychology of the offender and the emotional interrelations between the latter and his society. Because crimes are committed preponderantly by legally sane individuals, albeit of distorted personality, the accent in this book has been placed on the large group of psychopathic, neurotic, emotionally immature and clinically normal individuals who have been involved occasionally or persistently in criminal activity. The viewpoint expressed herein and the selection of material and interpretations, both psychiatric and sociologic, are the sole responsibility of the author.

v

This book had its inception in a seminar on psychiatric criminology given under the auspices of the Department of Psychiatry, College of Medicine, New York University. The case material was derived from the Court of General Sessions, New York, and several U. S. naval activities, notably the U. S. Naval Prison, Portsmouth, New Hampshire. Permission was obtained for the use of the material from the Criminal Courts of New York from the Hon. George L. Donnellan, senior judge of the Court of General Sessions, and Mr. Irving W. Halpern, Chief Probation Officer of that Court. The material derived from naval activities was used with the permission of the Bureau of Medicine and Surgery, U. S. Navy. The cases quoted have been given fictitious names with rare and obvious exceptions.

A word must be said for the inspiration provided by the judges of the Court of General Sessions, particularly that of the Hon. Cornelius F. Collins, formerly senior judge, a devoted friend of the movement for the psychological investigation of crime. Of the judges presiding in the Court of General Sessions, each at some time gave valuable criticism to the work of psychiatry in crime and pointed out, by virtue of his legal knowledge and sociologic judgment, some of the areas of conflict between psychiatry and law. Among these were the late Hon. Morris Koenig, the Hon. John J. Freschi and the Hon. Jonah J. Goldstein.

Acknowledgment is due also to William B. Herlands, Commissioner of Investigation of New York City, for the use of material prepared under the direction of the Department of Investigation, New York City. I am indebted to Dr. Louis Wender, formerly Director of the Hillside Hospital, Hastings, New York, for permission to use a case treated by him in conjunction with the author. To Mr. George Tyson, Clerk of the Court, Eastville Courthouse, Eastville, Virginia, I am indebted for the opportunity to see the earliest existing American Criminal Court records. The author is indebted to his many colleagues and clinical associates with whom aspects of certain cases were developed. Prominent among these were Dr. Sylvan Keiser, Dr. John Frosch, Dr. Robert Symonds, Dr. Charles B. Thompson, Solomon Machover, psychologist, and Dr. Karl M. Bowman, then Director of the Bellevue Psychiatric Hospital. The many students from the Social Research Laboratory, College of the City of New York, the Department of Sociology, New York University, and the Graduate School, Columbia University, as well as members of the staff of the Probation Department, Court of General Sessions, are due thanks for their help in abstracting case material. The manuscript was given the benefit of several critical readings by my wife, Esther Boyd Bromberg. To others who faithfully assisted in the laborious work of assembling and typing this material, the author is grateful.

Reno, Nevada   WALTER BROMBERG, M. D.

Contents

vii

Contents

PART ONE

The Legal and Social Environment of the Criminal

1

The Approach to the Criminal

⌈ The criminal offender before the law is almost instinctively looked upon as an enemy of the law-abiding community. The average observer readily attributes many characteristics to the criminal which set the latter apart in an illegal social status. Thus the criminal is accredited with a manner of speech, a style of dress and living and a series of feelings which stamp him as being different from the mass of conforming individuals in society. Not only is the offender considered to possess certain outward indications of his variance from the group of lawful citizens, but he is perceived to have a specific criminal psychology. This psychological attitude is thought to be characterized by a disregard of the rights of others, a sense of cruelty and an intolerance for established standards of fair play and decency. The offender, furthermore, is commonly held to be a member of a group having identifiable physical, psychological and social peculiarities which place it outside the pale of civilized social life.⌋

Under scientific inquiry into the criminal offender as an individual, the casual assumption that he belongs to a group of differently constructed human beings becomes untenable. The notion of the criminal as a group-member fails to retain its apparent fixity when the inquirer probes beneath surface appearances. Exploration of the personality of individual offenders demonstrates differences within the antisocial group which vary almost as widely as those encountered among the law-abiding population. More remarkable is the discovery that the individual criminal is not generally cognizant of the essential antisociality of his attitude toward society. The offender does not admit the resemblance of his acts and inner feelings to those of other criminals. In contact with the police, when apprehended or in court, the criminal resents being included in the criminal "group." Lacking insight into the impression which his coalesced attitudes give to the

1

world about him, each offender insists on being considered closer to the law-abiding citizen than to another criminal.

Contact with the individual offender shows that he often reacts to the group into which his personality pattern has impelled him with the same aversion toward crime that inspires the lawful individual. In spite of the drama which has attached to a few publicized desperadoes, few offenders actually enjoy their exclusion from the pale of society. Each offender points with sincerity and conviction to virtues such as sentiment for family and friends, idealism which he finds obstructed by factors beyond his control, obedience to certain laws and customs and religious loyalty. There is rarely a conviction of personal wrongdoing and, if it is present, it is glossed over with ready rationalizations. Whereas the outside observer perceives the common characteristics of the group, those who are tinted cannot see their own discoloration. This protective mental blindness has developed automatically because the great majority of criminals are reacting to forces which keep them actively antagonistic to society. In reality, the criminal is struggling with a personal conflict, the essential features of which are only secondarily related to society.

The psychological conflict of the criminal is clearly demonstrated in his reaction to trial and conviction. He is so deeply preoccupied and involved with his rights under the law that, by his knowledge of these details, his active opposition to the spirit of the law is established. It is a common experience of the court and prison psychiatrist to hear convicted individuals review their cases, tacitly admitting the crime but going on to relate what they consider innumerable instances of unfairness and trickery on the part of the prosecution.

Extensive knowledge of his rights and a peculiar insistence in a feeling of persecution set the criminal apart from the individual who has no need for familiarity with this aspect of legal procedure. Clearly, preoccupation with safeguards of legal trials serves to support the offender's psychological position within himself far more than to aid his legal status. These maneuvers are in the nature of instinctive self-protective responses of which the criminal is largely unaware. On casual observation it appears inconceivable that those who flout laws should have so little apparent insight into the very obvious opposition they assume toward social mores. Close scrutiny of the tendency toward self-protection, however, reveals that the evident gap between feeling and knowledge is not comprehended by the criminal. He cannot see what is happening within himself because his reactions and counterreactions lie in the deeper recesses of his mind, as far beyond his consciousness as they are beyond his control.

For obvious reasons of self-protection, society has thought of crime as a group problem. With respect to ideas about personal safety for the individual and security of his property, society is a consolidated institution. The criminal violates universally accepted safeguards of both person and property. The results of criminals' malefactions, therefore, give their number the appearance of an organized group in action. This group idea has subtly dominated the thinking of those agents of society who deal with crime. Methods of treatment and the emotional feelings surrounding criminals reflect preoccupation with the notion that offenders are of a social class lying on the periphery of normal life. Such an orientation would naturally leave little room for study of the offender as a personality.

The "enlightened" school of criminologists, who stressed the social causes of crime, thought in terms of the criminal group. Their attention was riveted on the environment of the outlaw. Proponents of the theory of economic causation of crime, who insisted that poverty, underprivilege and the unequal distribution of wealth were the motives for crime, likewise kept far afield from the individual as the object of study. Those who followed Ferri, discussing telluric and broader sociocultural influences on crime, and spiritual leaders who called for moral awakening of society, similarly stressed the criminal as a member of the group. The inherent difficulty of these approaches to the problem of crime was the by-passing of the main point of interest, namely, the criminal as a man. It can be truthfully asserted that not until the entrance of psychiatry and psychology into the field of crime did interest in crime receive its present definitive form of stress upon the individual offender.

The entrance of medical science into the field of criminology during the nineteenth century had the effect of slowly modifying the long-held view of the criminal as a peculiar species of man. It is true that Lombroso hailed his discoveries of exaggerated body measurements among criminals as evidence of the existence of an atavistic type of humanity, a human subspecies. Nevertheless, the accent on specific biologic abnormalities found to exist in the criminal and urged by the school of medical anthropologists in the late nineteenth century, directed attention to the individual criminal as a man to be studied.

Psychiatry does not, by its emphasis on the individual, purport to minimize the influence of environmental factors. It does not attempt to argue the question of multiple causes of crime. The mental sciences seek to assess, as accurately as possible, the effect of social and environmental factors on the individual offender. In some cases, it is understandable that a youth from a broken home, without adequate parental supervision, lacking emotional security and overwhelmed by feelings of inferiority, is readily impelled into antisocial patterns. The question which psychiatry wishes to answer is: Why do some of those enmeshed in unwholesome environments develop into antisocial beings, while others become normal, law-abiding citizens? Psychiatry seeks its answer in a painstaking study of the personality as it develops through emotional vicissitudes of life to the point where it is in obvious disharmony with legally constituted society.

The orientation of this work is expressed in the idea that antisocial activity is one aspect of human behavior, rather than a specific human abnormality. Maladjustments in life, of which crime is one manifestation, come to attention through the impingement of a given personality on his environment. The most plausible approach to the understanding of criminal actions, therefore, is that espoused by psychological medicine, which points to the offender as a complex personality developing out of and living in his society. Psychiatry, by the same token, cannot neglect society, the medium in which its criminally inclined members function. The final picture which emerges is that of the criminal as a psychologically sick individual whose total life pattern is at odds with his social milieu and especially with the coalesced feelings of society as represented in law and legal institutions.

The objective of this work is the exposition of the emotional and intellectual attitudes of the criminal, together with the interplay of the universe of the individual offender with that of his society.

The psychological approach to crime does not minimize the extensive and valuable contributions from related fields of investigation in the evaluation of factors in crime. Sociology has not only traced and described the influence of unfavorable environmental and cultural factors in producing crime; it has as well supplied a mighty stimulus for the development of prevention and treatment technics. The sociologist will continue to demonstrate these potent environmental factors and to bring about further amelioration of situations which society cannot afford to neglect. It is the responsibility of the psychiatric criminologist, however, to describe and delineate the emotional mechanisms which play a specific role in the criminal reactions of maladjusted individuals to their social background. The functions of the psychiatrist and the sociologist must be clearly understood if futile debate over the relative importance of environment and the personality is to be kept at a minimum.

The psychiatrist, observing how antisocial psychological drives affect the individual, cannot wholly endorse the doctrine of free will in human behavior. It is equally difficult for the sociologist to favor this concept when he notes man's struggle in a frequently overwhelming environment. In viewing criminology, psychiatrists may not, however, overlook the legal viewpoint—that men not bereft of reason are responsible for their actions. Many persons concerned with the functioning of criminal law have perceived the force of unconscious determinants in individual criminal behavior, but the majority still believe that an individual has complete power to decide between good and evil conduct. Because current standards of ethical behavior are based on the theory that a man's conduct consists of a series of consciously selected actions, the psychiatrist must accept and work within present legal limitations until the mental sciences have amassed data conclusively demonstrating the new knowledge of human behavior.

Criminal law is primarily concerned with the protection of society. The charge that criminal law is anachronistic is sustained if one looks only at the cold letter of the law, particularly in areas where vestiges of the early spirit of vengeance find expression. The criminal courts and the large body of enforcement officers represent a tremendous financial investment for society. It is not unnatural, under this circumstance, that the people engaged in legal and judicial functions tend to be only as interested in the individual criminal as they are allowed to be by society's perennial demand for protection. In spite of its clearly defined mission to protect society, however, the law only *appears* to remain static with regard to the psychological problems of the criminal. The existence of social workers, probation officers, criminologic psychiatry, and an intelligent judiciary is evidence that justice is tempered with a consideration for the individual. In the last five decades society has become increasingly aware that its safety is assured as much by the rehabilitation of the criminal as by his punishment. More recently, crime prevention has become a major preoccupation with law enforcement officers throughout the country. Psychological knowledge of the nature of criminal behavior has become increasingly more potent in directing society's attention to the total mental hygiene program which necessarily must precede the eventual inclusion of its ideas in criminal codes.

Human ideas move slowly and in consonance with the emotional atmosphere of the time in which they evolve. Ideas of justice as enunciated in law are perhaps the most frequently cited instances of survival of archaic concepts. Our present-day laws are so strongly derivative that they embody little or none of what is currently known and felt about human behavior. Laws which were written to meet the needs of the past are not necessarily a codification of what society feels and wants in a later day; still the law, while anachronistic in precept, is less so in practice, particularly where it depends upon the liberality of judges, the type of offense and the enlightment of the community.

Seen in this perspective, the newer knowledge of the roots of human misbehavior reflected in criminal conduct cannot be expected to replace age-old attitudes toward wrongdoers or to melt overnight the prejudices and superstitions of man. Psychological principles can, however, be expected to illuminate a dark corner of behavior and to lay a scientific basis for plans to attack the oldest of social diseases. In this campaign, criminologic psychiatry stands in close relation to the law, since both disciplines deal, in the last analysis, with the same human realities.

The use of psychological thinking in the judicial process is not a recent development. Knowledge of human nature has always been employed in certain aspects of the judicial process. The distinction must be clear, however, between "psychology" as the common experience of introspective men and that body of special medical and biologic knowledge included under the term "psychiatry" or "medical psychology." Preference for a disciplined scientific psychology is dictated not only by reasons of accuracy and universality of application, but by the complexity of the human mind.

Although knowledge of human nature, legal logic and social reasoning has been the intellectual equipment of the judges, it has been obvious for almost two centuries that special technical knowledge was needed to assist the judiciary in the trial and disposition of certain criminals. The grosser situations which arose as a result of mental disease (insanity) or mental defects (feeble-mindedness) called for expert opinion beyond that which the court could exercise in these matters. Those who originally dealt with mental aberrations later became important adjuncts to the court in judging the manifold intricacies of erring human beings. It was not until a little more than a century ago that formal recognition was given to this need by making provisions for the use of accredited expert witnesses. The appreciation of the insight which the mental sciences can furnish legal institutions has grown steadily during the past fifty years. At the present time, psychiatrists as technical aides to administrators are widely employed in criminology, delinquency and penology, and are uilized by social agencies to help meet the problems imposed by socially maladjusted individuals.

2

The Criminal and His Society

SOCIAL ATTITUDES TOWARD THE CRIMINAL

It may appear unorthodox in a book devoted to the psychology of criminals to initiate the discussion with an examination of attitudes toward crime among members of society. But enough has been said in the preceding chapter to bring agreement from thoughtful persons that society cannot be neglected in a psychological estimate of the criminal. The current public attitude toward criminal offenders is virtually a recapitulation of the historical evolution of social sentiments centering around crime. The emotional reactions in the ordinary observer of a criminal offense portray in miniature the evolution of social viewpoints regarding criminals and their treatment during the past five thousand years.

The average citizen is content ordinarily to relegate his responsibility and participation in crime to duly authorized agents of the law, retaining perhaps a curious and journalistic interest in criminal actions. This is, however, merely a surface phenomenon. If the search into the mental occupation of the law-abiding person is pressed beyond the point of casualness, one meets immediately prejudices and feelings of great strength and considerable complexity. In the average person who is a victim or is closely related to a victim of a criminal act, rage is the earliest reaction after the crime is committed, accompanied by an immediate impulse toward revenge in kind. Slowly the overwhelming personal feeling for revenge subsides and is replaced by the conviction that the law will eventually achieve retribution for wrongs inflicted. A sense of satisfaction or even righteousness arises from the anticipation of that degree of justice, interpreted by the individual as revenge, to be brought about through the due course of the law. The psychological metamorphosis continues as the victim's vengeful feelings fade, and he falls to pondering over the criminal as a man and the reason lying behind his evil acts. When the potential emotional gratification consequent upon the law's eventual triumph is realized, there is often a spread of curiosity from the particular criminal case in hand to the over-all problem of crime as a human failing. Feelings of pity for the unfortunate offender gradually assume dominance, interrupted by returning impulses toward vengeance and surges of righteous anger. Pity and sympathy are followed by wider interest

7

in the criminal as a human being and humanitarian urges to offer succor or solace to the unhappy offender. Combined with such attitudes are reflections on the need for cure, through penitence, of the offender's unfortunate nature.

The observer's appreciation that penitence would relieve the criminal's guilty feelings springs, in part, from the observer's ever-present unconscious vengeance motive. Covered by more mature, altruistic considerations, the suppressed drive for retaliation is still powerfully active. While the invocation of repentance for the erring criminal may actually help the offender as a member of society, it is not realized that the proposed penitence is a vicarious experience for the observer, satisfying an emotional necessity for him. The observer of crime thus simultaneously gratifies the twin feelings of vengeance and relief of guilt in his reflections and fantasies covering the criminal. The public's emotional participation in a crime ordinarily ends with this gratification.

The psychological cycle which operates automatically in every interested person is the substrate of the perennial fascination for crime. The repetition of this individual reaction on each new contact with crime, whether that contact is real or portrayed for entertainment purposes, signalizes the cycle of primitive revenge feelings and humanitarianism. With it a secondary gratification arises in the ego of the observer derived (reflexly) from the supposed repentance of the offender. It is evident that public interest so continually demonstrated in criminals and crime is based on an unconscious participation in criminal feelings by society and, for that reason, its character is unperceived by the great majority.

The scientific inquirer who neglects no thread of psychological import in his scrutiny of crime breaks through the circuit of the public's unconscious reactions. The criminologic psychiatrist is aware of this sequence of unconscious motivations in studying the intricate interplay of emotion between the criminal, the victim and his society. At the same time the practical outcome of these psychological phenomena requires comment. The vengeance motive, which is known to persist inexorably in the unconscious feelings of the public toward wrongdoers, is covered by conscious impulses to improve the lot of the criminal and to make him "good." The practical effect of the rational wish to improve the criminal as a man, when this wish is consolidated into the mass sentiment of humanitarianism, is to outweigh the unconscious motive of revenge.

The mass of feeling which is invested in the criminal by members of society must be more generally understood before a practical application of the findings of modern criminologic psychiatry can be made. As the paradigm of reactions outlined above indicates, the emotions that arise in the victim or the observer of a criminal act approach the instinctual level, being at first automatic and only later modified by reason or sympathy. Behind society's resultant attitude toward the criminal, which determines the final success of programs for the treatment of criminals, are deeply based emotions. These feelings constitute a powerful influence to stimulate or retard a psychologically oriented treatment program for wrongdoers. Without an accounting of the ingrained reactions of society to crime, a psychological basis for a new criminology would be unsound. The psychological continuity of motives behind these attitudes is established by interpreting extant criminal records and the views of those who have dealt with the application of ethics to law. A reading of these attitudes has the value of illuminating the emotional atmosphere surrounding the criminal in the various periods of our civilization and points as well to unconscious components of current feeling toward the criminal which are present in today's law-abiding population.

HISTORICAL BACKGROUND

Among primitive peoples, crime, when it represented the breaking of a taboo, affected the entire social body. The expiation of idols or tribal gods was therefore required so that the community would not suffer the vengeance of the gods. It was the obligation of each member of the primitive tribe or clan to punish the wrongdoer. Punishment served as a protection for the entire community and was a direct appeasement of the gods whose taboos were violated. Sacrifice and death, hence, were a common punishment in revenge for injury done the tribe. The vengeance expressed in the "lex talionis," or "eye for an eye" doctrine, underlying the philosophy of criminal practice in ancient civilizations, had a similar derivation. Expiation of sin demanded reparation by punishment equal to the injury to the group. However, vengeance was combined with a final social purpose. The punishments decreed to wrongdoers by the ancient Hebrew law were based on the twofold purpose of deterring others from similar actions and of cleansing the social body. In the Judaic tradition the justification for severe punishment was a religious one. Crime was equivalent to sin. The ancient world shared Hebraic attitudes toward crime but did not share its rationalization. The Greeks mollified the severity of punishment by death by introducing exile as a sentence for major crimes.

The enlightened Greeks, in decreeing exile, stressed social reasons for criminal punishments. The notion that society was polluted by the offender was a reflection of their broader view of society's responsibility toward its members. On the other hand, the laws of the Roman Empire regarding crime and punishment were based on an attitude apparently divorced from rationalization or justification. Punishments were set down with positiveness. A spirit of martial briskness in correcting wrongs is evident in the Roman criminal code. The viewpoint seems clear. No tampering with conscience, no religio-spiritual concepts, but a stern legal code based upon the accepted class distinctions and social forms of the times. The death punishment was meted out for widely differing offenses. A criminal injury was viewed objectively as a hurt that required vengeance through the infliction of an equivalent injury to the transgressor.

Records of criminologic practice during the next millennium of history, though fragmentary, indicate the persistence of the basic attitude of the "lex talionis" during the Dark and Middle Ages. For example, the Anglo-Saxon law, based in part on the old German (Salic) code, held no exceptions to the universal primitive custom of decreeing death freely for numerous offenses. The heartlessness of punishment during this period, so shocking to modern sensibilities, fitted the prevailing social theory of equal retribution for crime inflicted.

Thus William the Conqueror ordained the alternative punishment of death by hanging: "plucking out the eyes or cutting off the feet, hands and testicles, so that . . . (he) will be a living sign to all of his crime and iniquity."

At the same time, a new spirit is discernible in the criminal law under King Alfred. His laws, which quoted the Ten Commandments, showed a beginning consideration for the moral state of the wrongdoer. The benign influence of some Anglo-Saxon kings was partly due to early church teachings and partly to the political organization of the royal courts.

Crimes of violence in the Middle Ages, although matters for private vengeance, frequently developed into feuds and later into private wars. Under these circumstances, the king found it expedient to appear among his warring lords as a peacemaker, not only to preserve life but also to conserve the armed forces of the kingdom. One result of the monarch's intervention in private wars and feuds, later superseded by the state as the legal authority, was to decrease the frequency of corporal punishment. In spite of this development with its resultant diminution of death as punishment for personal crime, nothing was visible in attitudes underlying punishment akin to a personal interest in the culprit as an antisocial individual. Crime in the Middle Ages was essentially a private war and for that reason was not a concern of the public. Crime, viewed as an injury to an individual demanding personal retribution, attached no dishonor to those who engaged in it and elicited no moral feelings on the part of society. Where reparation with the

payment of life was the final price for crime, no reason existed for speculation as to the motive involved in criminal acts.

The idea of searching for a motive behind crime, a commonplace
experience in present-day thinking, has a long history. The earliest indication of interest in the criminal mind and its content is found in the
Church's accent on moral responsibility as a force in daily life. The ecclesiastical concept of moral responsibility, which asserted that each man was
individually responsible before God and could attain a position of grace
only through constant examination of his conscience, was the stimulus that,
aided by intellectual interests, led to our present psychological concern with
the mind of the wrongdoer. The ecclesiastical attitude which exhorted meditation, penitence and repeated exploration of the inner mind, influenced the
thinking and attitudes of people toward criminals and tended to supplant
the instinctive archaic "lex talionis."

The practical effect of this reorientation was not evident for several centuries. In medieval times the influence of demonology, which the Church
espoused to aid in its struggle for the salvation of souls, was a factor in the
persistence of severe punishments. Since many legal problems fell into the
hands of ecclesiastic courts, both judges and bishops were frequently called
on to pass sentence on witches as part of their legal duties. This they did
with vigor. It was not uncommon for churchmen sitting as judges to con-
demn hundreds of women to the flames for criminal acts, as did a certain
bishop in Bamberg in the thirteenth century. Although essentially an ecclesiastical concept, demonology, the representative psychologic trend of the
Middle Ages, had a definite relationship to the then current attitudes on
crime. It was tacitly assumed that wrongdoing was the result of "possession"
by the Prince of Evil, and whatever was evil, fantastic or bizarre was imputed to Satan. Crime, mental disease (possession) or any human misdemeanor or catastrophe became the responsibility of the Dark Host and
beyond the realm of human intercession.

The original impetus toward concern with the mind and soul of the
criminal, as has been noted, arose from the stress placed on moral responsibility by the early Church. This concept was furthered to a tremendous
extent by the spirit of humanitarianism which influenced thought and action
in the eighteenth century. The perception of the worth of each human
being as a reflection of his Maker was brought to a sharp focus under the
powerful influence of the French humanists. The British deists and French
humanists reacted against the corruption and privilege in the Church and
bent their energies to improving the lot of man in practical ways. Rousseau
and Voltaire in France, Bentham in England, and Beccaria in Italy, imbued

with the new humanitarian concern for man, suggested sweeping alterations in the philosophy of criminal law. Referring to their writings, philosophers set in motion a movement to correct that state of affairs which permitted the death penalty as readily for the theft of a sheep or a loaf of bread as it did for murder. Out of this dissatisfaction with man's inhumanity to man came suggestions which eventually changed the entire spirit of penology.

The change in psychological attitudes was reflected in legal changes in English criminal practice. One such change which helped modify the harsh attitude prevalent toward offenders was the bar to "cruel or unusual punishment" embodied in the Bill of Rights presented to William and Mary on their accession to the English throne. Still another factor in reducing the number of death penalties was the "benefit of clergy" provision. This privilege, which grew out of the right of a member of the clergy to be relieved of trial in a secular court when he was suspected of a criminal offense, was gradually extended to any educated man. Until 1487, a literate man who committed murder could be excused from the death punishment on the grounds of a "clergyable offense."

A consequence of the influence of humanitarianism on the treatment of the criminal was the development of our present penitentiary system, which had its inception in the latter part of the eighteenth century. This system only recently introduced the principle of incarceration as punishment in contradistinction to physical injury (flogging, branding, mutilating) or death for convicted criminals. The penitentiary plan, basically a reform effort, had its greatest growth in America. Its proponents wished to cure criminals during their period of imprisonment through the salutary effect of meditation. The theory embodied education of the will through penitence, but the practical application was unwittingly harsh. In the hope that silence would lead to meditation, some institutions quartered prisoners in individual cells and forbade conversation. The Philadelphia Penitentiary became a model of the newer penology.

Stress on moral reformation of the individual while he was segregated from society was hailed as a true advance in criminology. Solitary work during the daylight period and silent meditation at night were the moral weapons which the advocates of this prison system hoped would achieve moral rehabilitation of the criminal. The life of enforced silence was a heritage from the religious practice of monastic solitude, wherein a person sought to attain a state of sinlessness.

So extreme became the practice of solitary confinement for convicts as a substitute for capital punishment that criticism quickly arose because of the mental and physical crippling wrought by solitude in prison. For example, the plan to replace capital punishment by life imprisonment, which was proposed for the state of Louisiana in 1821, called for the individual cells to be painted black inside and out and to bear in distinct white letters the name and offense of the convict with the following epitaph: "His bread is bread of the coarsest kind; his drink is water mingled with tears; he is dead to the world; this cell is his grave; his existence is prolonged that he may remember his crime and repent it."

The total effect of the penitentiary as a departure from older methods of corporal punishment was salutary. As the death penalty became a less common form of punishment, the vengeance motive lost some of its effect. But the concept of the convict as a doomed man, spurred by the requirement for everlasting penitence—an essential aspect of penitentiary theory and practice—was actually derived from the vengeance motive, disguised though that motive might be. Although progress from corporal punishment to imprisonment represented vast improvement over earlier social attitudes toward the individual criminal, preoccupation with the notion that crime was evil remained an active force in social feeling.

Inherent in the penitentiary theory was the Calvinistic note of man's predestination to sin, i.e., crime. Society's unconscious prejudice against wrongdoers was reflected in the idea of depravity as a characteristic of all criminals. The doctrine of moral depravity as the basic cause of social evil, of which more will be said later, had in it many elements of the outspoken vengeance motive implicit in ancient penology. The newer nineteenth-century approach to the handling of the criminal through incarceration satisfied ambivalent tendencies: the wish morally to improve the miscreant through meditation, and the primitive feeling for revenge. The evolution of penal institutions and practice shows how tenaciously man clings to his instinctive tendencies.

Science has exerted the strongest and most persistent influence on man's eternal struggle against the instinctive forces within himself. Objective science has been a strong ally in criminology as in other fields where prejudice and ingrained emotional bias must be fought to achieve betterment in human institutions. In the struggle against inhuman treatment of criminals, medical and psychological sciences joined forces with humanitarianism. Social reformers, spurred by the impetus of the humanist revolt, and physicians, drawn to the study of scientific riddles which the criminal presented, were active during the late eighteenth and the nineteenth century. Religion and humanism in different ways introduced society to moral obloquy in the criminal; biologic science studied his physical defects and subjective variations. The consequences of these activities were profound. The measurement and analysis of criminal individuals by medical anthropologists in time caused the development of an attitude of objectivity toward human behavior which exerted far-reaching influences on modern attitudes toward criminals.

SCIENTIFIC PIONEERS IN CRIMINOLOGY

The entrance of scientific medicine into criminology occurred, ironically, through the discoveries of phrenology, the charlatan of mental sciences. Franz Gall, the Viennese physician whose study of human skulls under the name of "craniology" later degenerated into the fakerism of phrenology, spent his first years of research among the inmates of Viennese jails and asylums. Gall's careful measurements of skulls led him to the belief that "faculties" of the mind corresponded to the knobs of the skull and that the larger a given knob, the more influential in determining behavior was the brain lobe that lay beneath. Gall described thirty-five of these "organs" of the mind and divided them into "affective" and "intellectual" faculties. Faculties of combativeness, secretiveness and acquisitiveness, which were "obviously" the cause of criminal behavior, were easily diagnosed. Gall and his followers noted how the higher "propensities" combated the lower or more depraved propensities and thus estimated the balance between the criminal and social faculties in their subjects. They spoke in clinical terms. Thus the organ of "destructiveness" would lead its possessor to murder unless the organs of "self-esteem" and "piety" should prove stronger.

For a time some practical use was made of phrenology by men in charge of asylums for the criminal insane. Dr. Brigham of the New York State Lunatic Asylum, an outstanding alienist in the 1840's, believed that criminals were the unfortunate victims of defective physical structures wherein the lower propensities were unduly preponderant without the counterbalance of appropriate higher faculties. A celebrated case in which phrenology was used in Europe occurred in the examination of Tardy, the pirate, in whom it was found that the organs of "combativeness, acquisitiveness," et cetera, were overdeveloped, while the bumps of "veneration" were smaller than normal.

The basic hypothesis used by phrenology in explaining crime fell into disuse until Lombroso, in 1876, startled the world with his discoveries of the physical structure of the criminal. The Lombrosian theory was the lineal descendant of Gall's phrenology, since it related mental function and specific criminal behavior to structural anomalies or deviations. Lombroso, in performing an autopsy, in 1870, on the cadaver of a vicious criminal, found a long series of atavistic anomalies in the skull of the brigand. He experienced the inner flash that often knits isolated facts into a scientific theory, and the enigma of the criminal problem suddenly appeared to him to be solved. In language rendered flamboyant by his enthusiasm, Lombroso described the criminal as an "atavistic being who reproduces in his person the ferocious instincts of primitive humanity and the inferior animals."

His belief was that the structural characteristics of inferior animals and the behavior of primitive men were reproduced anachronistically among living criminals. The criminal was an atavistic phenomenon. In addition to the skeletal peculiarities, many other facts supported Lombroso's belief in the existence of the "born criminal." The frequency of tattooing, the blinding, violent passions insisting on vengeance, the wild courage that stands on lack of foresight, and the special argot of the underworld, were psychological anomalies coinciding with physical peculiarities. The criminal's conscious avoidance of everything civilized man held dear proved to Lombroso the atavistic nature of the criminal man.

"They talk like savages because they are veritable savages in the midst of this brilliant European civilization," Lombroso wrote. In epilepsy, Lombroso saw a condition that proved the bond between the physical defective and the criminal. The "morbid causes" of criminality were fundamentally those of epilepsy. Thus he spoke of the "epileptoid criminal constitution," the basic defect of the born criminal.

Beneath Lombroso's scientific compilations of stigmata of degeneration lay concealed the kernel of distrust and hatred for an abnormal person which was so characteristic of the thinking of earlier centuries. From our present position in a psychological era, we can recognize in the theory of the criminal man the same sadistic impatience toward the anomalous human which witchcraft encompassed. The connecting link between the "degenerate theory" and the demonology was embodied in the connotation of immorality associated with bodily deformity. This idea, though medieval in its derivation, is still not too deeply buried in our feelings. It is a human tendency to accept the concept of a "born" criminal and thus to comprehend in one figure set off from the rest of humanity all the characteristics which man fears in himself. Bodily or mental deformities in others evoke unconscious anxieties in ourselves, and scientists, like others, are not immune to this universal psychological influence.

With the development of the theory of a structural basis for evil-doing came the basic notion of human degeneracy. Thus Morel, as the result of his long research, published, in 1857, proof that the process of human degeneration was represented in physical, intellectual and moral changes of the

criminal and the mentally sick. As physical evidences he found head mal-
formations, poor dentition, deformities of extremities, goiters and improper
growth of the body (infantilism); as mental and moral evidences, absence
or disorder of intellectual or emotional faculties and the development of
moral depravity. All these defects were considered to be unmodifiable varieties of degeneracy afflicting the dejecta of the human race.

Quantitative measurements of anthropologists like Lombroso or clinicians
like Morel were clearly scientific in their method, but their conclusions
were unconsciously directed by the prevailing religio-moralistic philosophy. The theory of degeneracy was accepted by various social philosophers.
Nordau pointed to the overwhelming degeneration with which every branch
of life was infiltrated. Even literary historians (Jean Carrère) wrote of the
"Degeneration in the Great French Master," tracing the unhealthy germ of
thought from Rousseau, the father of morbid Romanticism, through Cha-
teaubriand with his melancholy, to Flaubert, the incurable nihilist, Verlaine
with his moral decadence, and Zola, the pessimist. The notion of degeneration of the human stock, which filled the European atmosphere for a quarter
of a century, undoubtedly made an impression on scientific research.

Scientists, putting Lombroso's theories to the test, intensively studied the
skull and brain of the convict. Studies made on notorious criminals were
the chief sources of criminal anthropologic findings. Alienists then referred
to these "signs of degeneration" in court to prove the inescapable criminality
of men on trial. Varied assertions that criminals were structurally degenerate, destined to "a short life span," had small, "uneasy" eyes, congestion of
the eyelids, etc., were obviously related to artifacts, such as the living
conditions within prisons where the subjects were examined. In time, these
methodologic difficulties were recognized. Lydston (1890) epitomized
scientific opinion when he wrote: "In my humble opinion, there has been
much of rubbish in the alleged development of modern criminal anthropology. . . . It has perhaps added something to the gaiety of nations, but has
done more to prejudice logical thinkers."

The first decade of the twentieth century found less credulity in the belief
that degeneracy was a natural physical concomitant of criminality. The doctrine that a criminal possessed a different kind of nerve tissue was abandoned. As Munsterberg of Harvard pithily remarked: "No one is predes-
tined by his brain to the penitentiary." * A critical attack on Lombrosian
anthropology was attempted, in 1904, by an English commission headed by
Charles Goring. His report, following eight years of work and examination
of over 3,000 English criminals, was published in 1913. It unequivocally

* Münsterberg, Hugo: On the Witness Stand; Essays on Psychology and Crime, New York,
(Clark Boardman) Doubleday, 1923, p. 245.

denied the significance of the findings of criminal anthropologists. Various types of criminals were compared with each other and with noncriminals, including Oxford and Cambridge graduates. "Our results nowhere confirm the evidence, nor justify the allegation of criminal anthropologists." * Goring concluded from his statistically accurate work that what distinguished the criminal from the noncriminal was a shorter stature and a mental inferiority.

The contribution of the Lombrosian school, like the work of many pioneers, was more valuable in the breach than in the observance. Measurements were carefully made, but the minutiae of the structural detail effectively hid the object of their research—the offender himself.

Scientific findings in the field of genetics also exerted an influence on social attitudes toward the criminal in the latter half of the nineteenth century. The laws of heredity, evolved from experimental studies on plants, had become scientifically established, and the eugenics movement sought to apply the principles of hereditary transmission of unit characters to human beings. Experience with many criminal and socially dependent individuals who demonstrated the apparent transmission of structural and mental inferiorities led eugenists to hope for improvement in the human race by weeding out defective stock.

This line of thought, readily supported by the tendency to consider crime a unit hereditary character, was aided by the work of Dugdale, who, in 1877, published a genealogy (dating from Colonial times) of a subnormal couple. Dugdale's study of the Jukes family strikingly proved the inheritance over several generations of undesirable characteristics present in the large number of criminal, immoral and mentally defective descendants of two simpleminded progenitors. Many hailed the investigation of the Jukes family lineage as final proof of the menace which degenerate stock presented to society.

It was inevitable that the concepts of hereditary transmission and degeneracy should unite in the minds of students of criminology. The linkage of criminal behavior and the hereditary nature of mental and bodily stigmata contributed an ominous tone and a moral connotation to criminologic thought. Starting with the false assumption that criminal behavior was capable of hereditary transmission, early thinkers utilized such social-genetic studies as that of the Jukes family to justify the theory that the presence of stigmata of degeneracy was sufficient to identify individuals destined for criminal careers. The fields of criminal anthropology and heredity were tragically interlocked in the minds of many who were more inspired than scientifically critical. Jurists, ministers and figures in social life united in pointing to hereditary degeneracy as a precursor to a social catastrophe

* Goring, C. B.: The English Convict, London, His Majesty's Stat. Off., 1913, p. 173.

which could only be prevented by sterilization of feeble-minded or antisocial progenitors. The movement for sterilization of criminals and mental defectives gained support to the degree that by 1915, thirteen states in the Union enacted laws providing for compulsory sterilization of major criminals.

Besides believing that poor heredity was a subtle factor predisposing individuals to a criminal life, socially minded persons decried the degeneration that was caused by the abuse of alcohol and drugs. Medical writers on hygiene taught that alcoholism bequeathed permanent physical and mental abnormalities to succeeding generations, determining moral depravity in these individuals. Alcoholism was thought to cause actual changes in nerve tissue, conceivably transmitted as constitutional defects, directly translatable into criminal behavior under appropriate social conditions. In the early years of this century, it was widely believed that crime, inebriety and insanity were due to a basic degeneration of the nervous system.

An expression of this attitude is seen in the classic formula of the period: "Alcoholism in the parents equals crime and pauperism in the offspring." The eugenics program added uncritical preachments based on beliefs that passed beyond the bounds of scientific knowledge to an awareness of growing social problems. The acme of moralism was reached in writings of criminologists like Boies, who set down (1901) as a criminologic law: "The cause of crime is the moral depravity of the criminal. . . . The restriction of criminality depends mainly upon prevention of the disease of moral depravity." *

Nineteenth-century biologic studies colored social attitudes toward the criminal in a way to stress moralistic values. Examples of criminologic thought demonstrate that intrinsic moralistic feeling toward evil-doing usurped critical judgment. The constant pressure of a bias for righteousness can be traced in the growth of individual and group attitudes toward criminals. Analysis of this preoccupation with morality in social issues proves it to be related to the constant struggle in all individuals with the ambivalent tendencies of good and evil. The socially adjusted person resolves this conflict through repression of his antisocial feelings until the good impulses eventually emerge dominant. In this happy result an aura of righteousness remains to cloud any sympathetic perception of the conflict between good and evil in others. Thinly disguised irritation with the criminal betrays the underlying intolerance of the average person with his own repressed aggressive impulses. Even objective reactions to so understandable a human failing as that of evil-doing are seldom free from residues of disguised or unconscious anger.

Opposing emotional forces, called ambivalent tendencies, rarely have

* Boies, H. M.: The Science of Penology, New York, Putnam, 1901.

representations in consciousness at the same time. When one of the modalities of thinking and feeling is on the surface the other is repressed, although active in influencing attitudes and ideas unconsciously. The presence of a "good" impulse presupposes the complete repression of a "bad" one. This mental mechanism accounts for the subtle perfusion of hostile feelings which is visible in the socially adjusted individual's reaction toward the criminal. The resultant reaction or attitude is undeniably righteous; the criminal thus receives added condemnation from repressed unconscious feelings within the law-abiding citizen. Those who are socially adjusted can easily consider the person who is antisocial as being irretrievably so.

The normal individual expels his own hostile tendencies from consciousness, transforms them into community mores and heaps them on a scapegoat—the criminal. Thus the antisocial person is evil, ungodly, unrealistic, unadjusted and hated. Attitudes toward the criminal bear the indelible stamp of hatred mediated through the mechanism of repression and subsequent projection of "evil" impulses.

Duality of thinking and feeling has been manifested in many fields of social study besides criminology. Philosophy has understood the fundamental human tendency to dichotomize emotions and ideas. This action of the mind is reflected in the ethical concepts of good and bad, the philosophical opposites of nominalism and realism, the demonologic doctrine of God and the Devil, the orthodox antagonists of heaven and hell and the psychological concept of ambivalence, the simultaneous presence of love and hate. The demonstration of the action of ambivalent tendencies in human beings in cases of nervous disorders, in normal human traits and in social institutions, has been a major accomplishment of modern psychological science.

The important role which projection of repressed antisocial impulses plays in the final judgment of criminality necessarily requires consideration when one views the legal and social environment of the criminal. Emotional overtones which rise from our cultural and psychological heritage seriously influence present-day criminologic attitudes. Unconscious feelings still dominate attitudes toward criminals, and it is a prime task of psychiatric criminology to expose the resulting reaction formations which have interfered with successful management of antisocial elements in our society.

ANTISOCIAL IMPULSES IN SOCIETY

It appears paradoxical that impulses which could result in criminal acts if allowed expression exist freely in law-abiding members of society. Yet reflection will show that antisocial impulses which are completely buried slumber deep in the minds of everyone. It will be recognized that the desire to do away with a human being who obstructs our wishes is an extremely common unconscious impulse. For although killing is a final solution for the frustration facing an individual who has reached an emotional impasse with another, it is the most impractical solution of human tensions. It is the first to spring into the imagination and the last to become an act of reality. Contained in the daily speech of the most law-abiding people, the notion of death and murder occurs in the form of jokes or allusions with surprising frequency. On every hand can be heard expressions such as, "He gets away with murder," or "You'll get killed by so-and-so" (for a minor transgression) or "He slays me," referring to a comedian, or "I nearly died," at an embarrassing situation. Anyone who has seen children kill their imaginary enemies in play with little compunction or who has listened to dreams involving injury, death and destruction, appreciates how frequently human beings entertain fantasies of the death of others.

Powerful forces within us—the conscience, and equally powerful institutions within our social structure: morality, religion, law and attitudes like that of "common decency"—restrain us from carrying out or seriously entertaining murderous impulses. The very strength of these inhibitory forces allows us to read of murder and death without damaging emotional tension. A murder mystery story both horrifies and intrigues us but does not lead to action. Reading of aggressive crimes permits repressed assaultive urges within the reader to be satisfied in fantasy but simultaneously allows him to heed the limitations of reality. Moreover, the sense of guilt aroused in the reader by his own unconscious aggressive impulses is quieted by the circumstance that the criminal character in a novel or a play meets a just reward for the crime committed. The reader's pleasure is hence unmarred by his conscience.

The appeal of criminal offenses or crime stories does not only pander to those instincts in us which are acted out by the criminal. Also involved is a curiosity regarding the criminal mind and the criminal way of life. The allegedly adventuresome life of the criminal offender stimulates our fantasy. Literature and the theater have, in innumerable instances, glorified the romance of the brigand's camp, the glamour of the highwayman and, in our own day, the color and excitement of the gangster. Some of our literary masterpieces depend for their appeal on the unconscious identification of the law-abiding population with criminal instincts portrayed in the characters, e.g., *Dr. Jekyll and Mr. Hyde, Les Misérables, Native Son* and a host of modern novels. This identification undergoes a sudden modification after the apprehension and conviction of the criminal occur. The glamour of the offender fades when the chase is over. The hunted robber, colorful when at large, becomes an evil creature in jail. In stories of crime there is always a turning point when antisocial impulses are defeated and the forces of good (law) triumph. Commonly in books or plays, public vengeance, embodied in the law, finally vanquishes the criminal, or the latter may reform at the hands of a good man (such as a clergyman) or woman. Sometimes the author seeks a way out of total condemnation of antisocial impulses in his character by saying that the criminal is "psychopathic" or has some other-wise redeeming feature; he is not "all bad." It may be noted in this con-nection that in actual court cases someone can always be found who, in idle conversation, sees a reason for siding with the criminal or a plausible excuse for his actions.

In literature the murderer always meets his punishment. Behind this tour de force can be seen the operation of the conscience of the author and of his public. It is these ethical currents in the thinking of the public which influence the author himself in his treatment of his subject. The balance between wild, antisocial impulses and the prohibitions of society must be maintained. Society operates on the principle of the exercise of free will, but for a successful society the "good" impulses must outweigh the "bad." In spite of the identification of some aspects of the public's unconscious with that of the real or portrayed criminal, there can be only one attitude toward the offender: that of vanquishing him by punishment or extermination, and destruction, thwarting or cure of the evil intentions he supports.

The vast majority of people never commit crime because their sense of reality and their life experience join with promptings of conscience. Control of antisocial impulses by the conscience, initiated in childhood and fixed into a habitual pattern in later life by early training, is the obvious explanation for the preponderance of law-abiding individuals in society. Nevertheless, there are many ways consistent with lawful living by which normal persons demonstrate the presence of suppressed or, more accurately stated, unconscious antisocial feelings. Under special circumstances where large groups are involved, otherwise controlled urges express themselves in unlawful acts. Mass looting in war or at times when authority is unable to cope with the situation, is the occasion for the emergence, in otherwise law-abiding people, of impulses identical to those experienced by criminals. No better example can be seen of this phenomenon than in the behavior of soldiers of an invading army in relation to enemy property. Aside from the consideration that to the victor belongs the spoils, there is discernible a momentary rush of predatory feeling which replaces otherwise controlling ethical standards.

Another example, not necessarily influenced by mass emotions, is observed in the practice of "hotel stripping." Managers of large private or public institutions, such as hotels, steamships, national parks, etc., tell of large yearly losses from thefts of small articles taken as souvenirs. There are two psychological requirements for this casual larceny by normal individuals. The first is that the institution from which they steal is large and impersonal and, by implication, limitless in its resources. The second factor is the insignificance of the articles taken. To the average person, a small article stolen as a souvenir appears to have the psychological meaning of a not unexpected gift from an all-powerful institution. In a similar category belongs a common attitude toward government agencies. Few will deny the presence of an urge to decrease taxes destined for governmental bureaus, to modify rationing or outwit customs officials. The psychological basis for these impulses is the attitude that the one from whom articles are taken is a symbol of a limitlessly endowed, fabulously wealthy, beneficent figure. It is not difficult to see the replica of the child's view of the parent-figure in this fantasy. That the opulent parent-figure is a projection of individual unconscious wishes onto a large institution can be readily confirmed by study of cases of burglars and robbers convicted of criminal acts. In its wider group expression, the infantile emotional attitude of each individual toward parent-figures is coalesced and comes to expression in behavior when authority is absent or has apparently relaxed.

It is obvious from these examples that situations arise in which larcenous impulses among normal individuals are openly tolerated. Their presence in law-abiding persons is known to every confidence man. Not infrequently successful confidence men freely aver that their victims clearly belie their larcenous wishes by eagerness to join an apparently profitable enterprise. That larcenous impulses do not lie too deeply repressed in the average citizen is indicated by the continuation over the centuries of swindling practices. Again, experience with large numbers of complaints of larceny brought against those convicted of the crime leaves no doubt of the presence of a larcenous impulse in the average person.

Larcenous impulses spring from basic needs of the human organism. The infant automatically "behaves" in reaction to needs in its initial relation to the environment, i.e., the mother. Its first act is to reach out with lips or fingers to grasp something. As the infant grows, this hunger impulse finds expression in other areas through the cry: "I want; give me." Later the processes of education exert their influence and the generalized acquisitive feeling gradually comes under the direction of controlled activity. During its developmental period the child learns that it must give allegiance to certain ideals of honesty and must control its acquisitiveness in order

convicted on evidence. The offender objects especially to the delineation of the impulse and its designation as criminal and less to the fact of law-breaking. By pleading guilty, the offender tacitly acknowledges that society has a reason to prosecute him but does not allow the specific psychological impulse to be paraded. To put it another way, no prisoner or criminal will allow his unconscious motives to be plumbed but he will permit the outward expression of his crime to be mentioned. This strong tendency to avoid looking directly at one's unconscious impulses is natural. Normal people will explain how a murder story "thrilled" them but will not be induced to believe that a heinous murder coincided with buried aggressive tendencies in themselves. If resistance is strong in normal individuals, how much more powerful are the defensive forces in the criminal, whose urges have come to fruition in a prohibited act.

The conflict, then, is an intrapsychic one within the offender. As a member of society, he had been influenced at some time in his life by ethical concepts. Whereas the law-abiding citizen chose a course of action early in life designed to control varied antisocial impulses, the criminal never solved the problem of control of such impulses. His predicament is that the forces of control have never been under his domination, either because unconscious urges were too strong or his conscience (super-ego) was too weak. The practical importance in emphasizing emotional conflicts in the criminal resides in their influence on his behavior with society or its legal agents.

The denial or evasion of the impulse behind a crime is a practical problem which every criminologic psychiatrist meets in his daily work. It is a blanket reaction which springs up as an automatic bulwark against both the reality of the law and an inner perception of the offender's own conflicts. The most frequent defensive maneuver is that of lying. Lying is a self-protective tendency based on the wish to escape punishment. It is common observation that lying occurs mainly when the facts are known to those who are empowered to administer punishment or injury, i.e., those in authority. Lying is not only restricted to criminal offenders. Children lie to their parents and adults lie to their acquaintances or friends when the situation seems to involve the possibility of punishment, either real or mirrored in feelings of guilt. From fear of punishment some children develop the habit of lying when no threat of injury is imminent. When this tendency becomes ingrained in children and arises automatically, psychiatry has called it "pathologic lying," a characteristic also of some types of personality deviates. Lying is so frequent a phenomenon in daily social intercourse that it is dismissed ordinarily as being unworthy of psychological study. Protection against real or anticipated injury has become so much a part of our social armor that it is discounted beforehand in the listener. We are constantly on guard for misinterpretations, half-truths, or hidden lies in any given statement, as is evidenced by the common statement: "I don't believe half of what I hear." Casual view of human beings in conversation out of earshot will demonstrate to the observer characteristic facial expressions indicating slight or marked incredulity. It is vital to this discussion, then, to realize that into our whole framework of social intercourse are interwoven proper safeguards for the perception and evaluation of lying. In delinquency and criminology this complicated social interrelationship centering around lying is close to the surface.

Among criminal offenders, lying occurs in two distinct ways: one through words and the other through direct behavior. Lying through words is so routine that methods of police apprehension, indictment and criminal prosecution have at their base a technic for the evaluation of possible lies. In the questioning or "third degree" of police officials, the wily efforts of prosecuting attorneys or the calm judicial weighing of the facts by the trial judge, it is obvious that the procedure is oriented around the basic premise that offenders lie. Lying through behavior assumes more complicated forms. Behavior reactions in criminals extend from simple denial of criminal acts to actual mental conditions requiring psychiatric attention, such as rage reactions, reactive psychosis, malingering, prison psychosis, etc.

When the depth of the ego participation in lying extends to the point of controlling behavior, the resulting state is considered to be true mental disease. Psychiatrists have long noted how the shock of imprisonment brought about an acute excited state developing into a condition where the prisoner was blocked in his emotions, mute, silly, rigid (catatonic) or hallucinating, apprehensive and noisy. These reactions were considered to occur only in "degenerative" (mental) soil. However, study of offenders who were otherwise mentally sound showed that intense emotional shock at the anticipation of punishment or the effect of actual imprisonment accounted for sudden bizarre changes in behavior. Careful study of these cases demonstrated that they were not insanities in the common sense but "psychogenetic psychoses" (Bernard Glueck) in which the ego of the prisoner collapsed under the terrible threat of legal punishment. These reactive psychoses arise from the inability of the ego of some criminals to withstand the emotional shocks attendant upon incarceration.

In each reactive state the underlying mechanism of flight from unpleasant or intolerable reality is visible. The frustrating element varies from humiliation before the eyes of society following apprehension in a crime, through fear of retaliation and punishment by society to the actual deprivation of liberties in prison. Viewed in this dynamic way, reactive states represent varying degrees of ego disintegration. They start with simple denial or lying about a crime. From denial the reactions become deeper as they involve repression of larger ego areas, so that the resulting picture shows more of the earlier infantile mental function. Thus, anger and lying is the rudimentary reaction; amnesia, perhaps aided by alcohol, constitutes a deeper inhibition of mental function, while malingering, hysterical states, reactive depression, prison psychosis and catatonic stupors indicate more complete involvement of the ego.

Although the majority of offenders deny their offense, there are a few chronic offenders, usually professionally successful, who do not fall into the denial patterns. This group of offenders readily acquiesce to their crimes when apprehended. Their behavior, so much at variance with that described in this section, is due to a feeling of overwhelming superiority to the police which allows the offender to admit his guilt directly. Successful chronic criminals hold their own self-esteem so high that there is no loss of face involved in an admission of their crime to society. These are individuals who actually make crime pay both literally in money returns and figuratively in terms of ego-satisfaction. Since they are completely identified with an antisocial way of life, no psychological gratification is obtained from defensive maneuvers which are practically universal in the average criminal.

The varying grades of denial of crime in speech and behavior involve technical problems in psychiatric diagnosis. A fuller discussion of the subject will be given in the chapter on psychopathic personality. At this point a case illustrating the spectrum of denial reactions will demonstrate the clinical appearance of the more severe types. A few years two brothers, heavily armed, perpetrated a brazen robbery at midday in a crowded section of New York City. When approached by the police they ran amuck. Several citizens were wounded and two men killed, including a policeman, during the melee. The public was incensed and the press dubbed the slayers the "Mad Dog Killers." The personal history of both men was characterized by vicious criminalism. The offenders came of a family which had a long history of social difficulties; both men had long criminal records and their family was known to welfare and probation agencies as being particularly antisocial.

At their arraignment on a first-degree murder charge the brothers began to act peculiarly, showing increasing dullness and confusion. Where they had been noted by many to be alert, street-wise gangsters before the murder and during the street battle, they became dull, stupid and unresponsive. At the hospital the younger, Louie, aged twenty-nine, said, in response to the examiner's questions, "I don't feel so good; come around another time." When asked what his occupation was, he responded, "Make dolls." When questioned as to how he made them, he said, "Cut them out of anything" (pointing to bed linen). Asked for his father's name, his answer was, "Which father?" In response to a question as to why he did not answer questions, he wrote as follows: "Don't talk in the enemy camp." When asked his name, he wrote, "Sir John Garibaldi." He seized a piece of paper on which he had been writing, tore it into bits, pushed it into his mouth, made chewing movements and then spit out the paper. Asked what he had been eating, he wrote, "Chicken." He went through similar performances at other times. The behavior of Harry, his thirty-five-year-old brother, pursued a similar course under custody. During the first month after the offense, he showed signs of mental confusion. For example, after the Wassermann test was made, he said to the nurse, spontaneously, "What are they trying to do with me? What did I say? I like you; you have been very good to me." In response to an examiner's questions, he disclaimed any knowledge of past events and began to act in a manner which was considered obvious malingery by the examining physician. For instance, he would take a hard-boiled egg which he had for breakfast, place it on the floor and, on his hands and knees, push it around with his nose. On another occasion, while taking a showerbath, he put the soap in his mouth.

During the trial of the brothers, three months after the offense, their behavior became progressively worse. Louie assumed a fixed posture; his head was bent, his expression was at times reflective, then depressed, apathetic and bewildered. Harry's behavior was characterized by gargoylelike grimacing, by periods of tremendous preoccupation with pieces of paper in his hands, by restless movements and episodes of excitement. There were periods of weeping and childish tantrums when he struck his head against the table. Neither brother showed the slightest interest in the prosecution of the trial. Their behavior persisted throughout the presentation of evidence, the prolonged testimony of expert psychiatrists, deliberations of the jury and their verdict, and the pronouncement of death sentence by the presiding judge.

Because of the presence of a strong element of malingery, a commission appointed to decide on their sanity considered the reactive psychosis to be comparatively superficial. The brothers were declared legally sane and hence responsible for their acts. En route to prison a sudden flurry of fighting, shouting and wild resistance occurred, but in prison they returned to a torpid, mute state, refused to eat or to wear clothes, tore up the bedding and had to be kept in isolation. They remained in a condition of complete dejection, bewilderment and absolute lack of co-operation for simple excremental functions of life for eight months preceding their execution.

The various conditions of prison psychosis were represented in the clinical picture outlined. Essentially, the mental state started with malingery upon which was engrafted a hysterical neurotic reaction deepening in the direction of the personality bent of the individuals. Under the pressure of fear of execution the reaction regressed to a vegetative state in one and mute, depressive apathy in the other. In attempting to understand the mixed picture which these two men presented, it was less important to place them in the correct categories of psychiatric conditions than to understand the emotional dynamics of their reactions. In each individual who develops a mental reaction, the resulting picture is colored according to his personality make-up. In the case of Harry, the history of his psychosis showed an exaggeration of a tendency toward brutishness, which was evident throughout his life. When he slipped into a mental state, even a simulated one, the picture assumed the characteristics of aggression and animality in consonance with his personality. Similarly, Louie developed a mental state in the direction of his personality pattern, characterized in his case by bewilderment and apathy, reflecting confusion in the face of a situation where he could not gain his ends aggressively.

The defensive reactions which have been illustrated have the same emotional basis as is observed in the characteristic attitude of the criminal individual towards society. The professional criminal seems to acknowledge his pariahlike position to himself and to his colleagues, though not to society. He refers to the law-abiding population as "citizens" in contradistinction to his own group. He seeks and obtains ego-support for his unconscious acceptance of an inferior position by rationalizing that "citizens" and the police are against him. The criminal goes even further in search of emotional ease and relief of his deeper anxieties by forming a bond with other antisocial persons, thus creating a criminal group. His struggles continue, however, as his defensive lying, denials and regressive psychotic behavior demonstrate.

The gang demonstrates vividly the defensive meaning of the antisocial attitude. The gang spirit reverses ordinary standards. If society regards chivalry toward women and courtesy to his fellows as desirable characteristics in a young man, the gang calls him soft. If society applauds the youth who studies, the gang calls him a sissy. If an adolescent is unwilling to be unnecessarily injured or has no interest in inflicting punishment on others, he is a weakling. If he wishes to uphold standards of idealism or even ordinary consideration for others, he is worthless. All the elements that constitute the correct equipment for living a civilized life are decried by the gang. A special set of world attitudes is set up, at the base of which is antagonism to authority and the society which upholds it. The antisocial attitude is a coalesced defensiveness shared by members of a gang or those criminally inclined against the ethical standards of society.

3

Psychiatry in the Law Courts

Psychiatry made its earliest appearance in criminology during court trials on the issue of individual responsibility for criminal acts. Medical men were requested to assist the Crown in deciding whether a person unable to understand the meaning of his criminal acts because of insanity should be punished. In the common law of England, individuals called natural fools (idiots) or madmen (of unsound mind) were not punishable for criminal acts, inasmuch as they were bereft of reasoning power. The basic theory stated that understanding of wrongdoing was an essential aspect of criminal intent. It was in the interpretation of the terms "natural fool" or "unsound mind" that medical experience and judgment were of value to the Crown's advocates. Standards of mental competence first developed by medieval judges were of a simple type, couched in general social, rather than medical terms. Interpretation of mental conditions became complicated as concepts like "non compos mentis" were introduced. The earliest records indicate that the specific definition of acts of madmen were far from exact. In the thirteenth century, Bracton, chief justificiary of England, stated the fundamental definition of insanity with respect to legal responsibility: "An insane person is one who does not know what he is doing, is lacking in mind and reason, and is not far removed from brutes." The "wild beast test" of Bracton, promulgated in 1265, was amended about 1535 by Fitz-Herbert, who defined an idiot as "such a person who cannot account or number 20 pence, nor tell who was his father or mother, nor how old he is." A century later an even more practical test of mental deficiency was elaborated by Sir Matthew Hale, the so-called "fourteen-year-old-child" test. This stated that "such a person as laboring under melancholy distempers hath yet ordinarily as great understanding as ordinarily a child of fourteen years hath, is such a person as may be guilty of treason or felony."

As the complexity of the subject demanded, sporadic attempts were made during the next four centuries to define more clearly what constituted an idiot or a madman. Medieval "psychiatry" of the criminal courts rested on the medical concepts of the day. The prevailing theory stressed the fact that madness was tempered by "lucid intervals" and that when such individuals were distraught and under the influence of their "distemper" they should not be held criminally responsible. The basic legal test of responsibility depended on the notion of the lunar influence on the diseased brain. The moon was thought to exert an effect on all diseases of the brain in such a way that "in the full change of the moon (such persons) . . . are usually in the height of their distemper." During the intervening phases of lunar activity, a lucid interval supervened and madmen were temporarily sane. The doctrine of lucid intervals played a role in the judgment of criminal responsibility. In Sir Matthew's words (1671): "Such persons as have their lucid intervals (which ordinarily happen between the full and change of the moon) . . . have usually at least a competent use of reason, and crimes committed by them in these intervals are of the same nature, and subject to the same punishment, as if they had no such deficiency. . . ." Experience with old rule of thumb methods of judging mental disease finally narrowed the test for excusability on the grounds of madness to those signs of insanity which would be recognizable as such to a judge and jury.

Early in the nineteenth century the courts in England agreed that both the presence of a delusion and presence of sufficient insanity to prevent a person from knowing right from wrong was an adequate basis for excuse from criminal responsibility. The legal concept known now as the "knowledge of right and wrong test," adduced from eighteenth-century legal and medical opinion, is firmly established in modern English and American law as a test for insanity.

Two legal cases in England aided in establishing the precedents upon which the "knowledge of right and wrong test" for responsibility was fixed in our present-day law. One was the famous trial, for murder, of the Earl of Ferrers, who, while under trial by his peers in the House of Lords, defended himself by proving the presence of insanity in himself and his family. In the Ferrers' case, not insanity per se but its effect on reason was considered to be the legal test.

The second case was that of an Englishman who attempted to kill King George III in a Drury Lane theatre and whose solicitor tried to prove that the knowledge of right and wrong was not as important a mark of insanity as the presence of delusion. The discussion surrounding these points modified the "knowledge of right and wrong test" for responsibility to the point where the presence of a specific delusion was regarded as an essential aspect of madness.

An event of national interest in England in this period focused attention on the medical specialty of psychiatry in a manner which emphasized its growing importance in legal and social matters. The special circumstance was the madness of King George III, who suffered from intervals of excitement and mental aberration which seriously obstructed the guidance of affairs of government. The prime minister, parliament and the public were anxious to know from the attending doctors the possibilities of King George's remaining on the throne. The vagaries of his mental illness and its effect on the regal judgment received countrywide publicity and was later made a subject for inquiry by parliament. Several eminent physicians who were acquainted with the special problems of lunatics, including Dr. Willis and Dr. Munro, the latter physician to Bethlehem Hospital, popularly called "Bedlam," were interrogated on His Majesty's condition. The subject of the treatment and behavior of madmen was aired at great length. General comment on King George's madness and the discussion following investigation into affairs at Bedlam contributed toward a better understanding of the legal function of psychiatry in eighteenth-century England.

Public recognition of the significance of the social importance of mental disease, in addition to the growth of interest by physicians in the problems of the insane, marked the emergence of psychiatry in the nineteenth century. Knowledge of the human mind, hitherto locked in the provinces of philosophy, psychology and natural science, was restudied and developed by psychiatrists. Two areas which reflected the importance of this new branch of medicine were the treatment of the insane and the management of insane criminals before the law.

The evolution of medicolegal principles sketched above came to a head at the trial of the murderer of Edward Drummond, Sir Robert Peel's secretary. The prisoner's defense, that at the time of the killing he was insane, became the basis for the famous M'Naghten decision of 1843. M'Naghten, under the delusion that Sir Robert Peel was his mortal enemy, shot the latter's secretary, thinking he was avenging himself justly. M'Naghten was acquitted of the charge on the ground of insanity. Because of public criticism of the verdict, the House of Lords addressed a group of eminent judges, requesting once and for all a statement of the decisive factors which would relieve a man suffering from madness or delusion of responsibility for a crime. Her Majesty's justices, after careful study, reported the majority opinion that established the tests for relief of criminal responsibility.

The test involved two essential questions: (a) whether the accused party did not know "at the time of such a crime, that he was acting contrary to law," and (b) whether "the party accused was laboring under such a defect of reason, from disease of the mind, as not to know the nature and quality of the act he was doing, or, if he did know it, that he did not know he was doing what was wrong." The justices also decided another question of great significance from the standpoint of psychiatry. The judges decided in their answer that once the facts of a case are admitted, medical science then becomes the sole arbiter of the relationship between alleged mental illness and responsibility for an illegal act. In the words of Lord Chief Justice Tindal: "The question becomes substantially one of science alone . . . it may be convenient to allow the question to be put in that general form to the medical man."

This portion of the chief justice's opinion was of particular significance in that it established the function of the alienist in trial procedure involving mentally affected criminals. General acceptance of this formulation subsequently led to the use of medical experts who gave opinions on behavior to which they were not witness. This device allows a medical expert to furnish the court, through the hypothetical question, with an opinion based on assumptions of fact about a given case. With the establishment of this precedent the psychiatrist assumed the place that his training in the intricate field of mental disturbances allowed. In this sense the use of the hypothetical question requires the psychiatrist as well as other experts to act as an arm of the court. But the courts limit the opinion of the psychiatrist to the specific question of criminal responsibility of the accused. The physician is not asked for an explanation of the mental state presumed to be involved but only of its effect upon the issue of responsibility. Within the framework of legal criteria, medical knowledge is permitted to touch upon the biologic and psychological problems of the criminal. The narrow limits within which the justices proscribed psychiatric assistance to the courts, considered to be appropriate under the law, have in effect restrained the modern psychiatrist from substantially influencing judgments about the criminal.

The "knowledge of right and wrong" test and the "knowledge of the act" test soon came to underlie the law regarding sanity and criminal responsibility in England and this country. Notwithstanding this ready acceptance by the judiciary, criticism of the M'Naghten "rule" arose from legal quarters. Legal experts felt that the M'Naghten decision was too generalized and of "doubtful authority." Psychiatrists also objected because they felt that the "knowledge of right and wrong" test involved a question of a moral "faculty," a discarded nineteenth-century psychological concept. They held that the mind as a totally functioning unit cannot be divided into units which are concerned with knowledge apart from emotions. Mental disorder is a concept that cannot easily be interpreted in terms of its influence on ethical knowledge. The legal test of insanity is described by psychiatrists as an anachronism which leads to an impasse between the demands of legal criteria and an explanation of mental illness as the reaction of a total personality.

There are good reasons for dissatisfaction with the present use of psychiatry in criminal trials. One is that all-important differentiations of many shades of mental reaction are not describable by "yes" or "no" answers addressed to the question of knowledge of right and wrong. Another is that in the prevailing judicial system alienists are not appointed to examine and return an impartial diagnosis; they are hired, rather, to support one side or the other. Their use is in the service of expediency rather than in the interests of a true scientific determination. When presented on the witness stand, psychiatric information may be manipulated by lawyers. Should a psychiatrist be naïve in the ways of legal tactics and testify with the intention of explaining all that he has discovered about the prisoner's mental aberrations and their relation to the crime, he will soon discover the court's disinterest. He is expected to do only one thing—unequivocally pronounce the prisoner responsible or irresponsible.

In spite of complaints that it is impossible to crowd the complicated phenomena of disorderly human personality into a legalistic strait jacket, legal authorities contend that no better formula has been devised to meet the problem before the court. The words of Judge Charles Knott * present the judicial viewpoint: "The law has laid down what may be termed a working rule . . . and, while medical men may criticize that rule . . . yet when you see . . . its extreme simplicity, the ease with which it can be applied . . . I am not aware of any better working rule than these medical men or anyone else has ever put forward." The judicial viewpoint preserves the age-old function of the court of protecting society. The court, in consequence, cannot allow preoccupation with the underlying psychology of crime to supersede its original function. Uppermost in the philosophy of law in its dealings with criminals is the maintenance of these attitudes and principles to which the reasonable man, unequipped with special knowledge of human beings, can subscribe. It is for this reason that knowledge and technics growing out of psychological understanding of the criminal are most effectively utilized in treatment and management of the offender rather than in pleas before the bar of justice.

The gradual introduction of psychiatrists as technical advisers to the court resulted in a widening of the field of psychiatric interest to include cases of borderline mental disturbances. This perplexing group of emotionally unstable individuals required psychiatric analysis to adequately interpret their behavior in legal and social terms. These borderline cases were not insane nor yet mentally normal. Knowledge of the psychological background and cause of such conditions as moral insanity, kleptomania, pyromania, epilepsy and irresistible impulses was and still is comparatively fragmentary. Trans-

* Peo. vs. Purcell, New York, 741.

lation into legal terms of the behavior and underlying disorder in these cases by medical experts with a still sketchy knowledge of the vagaries of the human mind, was even more difficult. Since these perverted individuals satisfied the criteria of knowledge of right and wrong, they were not actually insane; nevertheless, their apparently uncontrollable emotional impulsiveness resulted in antisocial acts. Just where the dividing line lay between distortion of the mental processes which rendered an individual unable to know what is right and an impulsive act which the individual knew was wrong but could not control, was a puzzling question for the court. As the courts gave more careful attention to the problem of insane criminals, the impulsive, unstable, eccentric and wayward individuals who bordered on mental diseases came into more prominent view. For the past century and a half, both psychiatry and the law have given unstable psychopathic personalities their most serious attention.

THE PSYCHOPATHIC PERSONALITY BEFORE THE LAW

Investigation of the group of individuals whose antisocial impulses did not appear to influence their intellectual capacity brought the attention of psychiatrists to the peculiar disturbance of the moral aspect of the psychopath's nature. Their asocial behavior pointed to a derangement in the "moral faculty." In the first part of the nineteenth century the designation "morally insane" was considered an adequate description of the group. Individuals in this group are now classified as psychopathic personalities or morbid personalities. Although their acts betray a pattern within the personality which is distinctly abnormal, they do not demonstrate the signs or symptoms of insane individuals. The psychopathic personality is neither insane from the standpoint of legal criteria nor sane in the medical sense.

The present concept of psychopathic personality has a history which is virtually a recapitulation of the evolution of psychiatric thinking during the past century and a half. At the time when psychiatry assumed the form of an independent mental discipline, the prevailing idea stemmed from the belief of the English philosopher John Locke that insanity essentially comprised a disturbance in reasoning power. Locke's definition of an insane person as a delusional one differentiated the latter from idiots. Insane persons, unlike idiots, reasoned correctly from false premises. As Locke wrote: "They err, as men do that argue right from wrong principles." Until emotional rather than intellectual components of mental disturbances were fully appreciated, the basic psychology of maladjusted personalities could not be understood.

The initial step in the elucidation of the psychopathic reaction came with the publication in 1806 by Phillippe Pinel of a classification of mental diseases. The significance of his classification was that Pinel included a type of emotional disturbance without perceptible impairment of the intellect among the groups of recognized insanities. This new class of mental disease was considered to be due to a type of moral perversion of the "affections and moral feelings." Pinel's innovation was eagerly discussed by physicians in England and on the continent. Many individuals who did not show delusions or other signs of impairment of reasoning power were recognized by psychiatrists as fitting into Pinel's newly described group.

The term by which personalities whose "passions acted involuntarily . . . without any disease in the understanding" came to be known was contributed by James Prichard, an English physician, in 1835. Prichard enlarged Pinel's original concept by including cases who showed willful perverseness and immoral behavior. He was the first to accentuate the antisocial and eccentric character of this group of maladjusted persons and gave them the name of "morally insane." The division between insane persons and the morally perverted individuals became clearer in the pronouncements of psychiatrists as their knowledge increased. The term "moral insanity," so readily usable as a diagnostic concept, became generally accepted. At that time the word "moral" had a connotation at variance from its present conventional meaning of "virtuous." It denoted what is now called "affective" or "emotional."

In medical jurisprudence, where the concept of moral mania had its greatest use, it became apparent soon that various antisocial acts could be excused on the grounds that this affective disturbance motivated perpetrators of the acts. An influence in this medical judgment was the view of Esquirol, a student of Pinel, that many cases of murderous assault were due to unrecognized moral insanity and hence could be excused from punishment for crime on the grounds of irresponsibility. This accepted view led to controversy in medicolegal circles about the applicability of the diagnosis of moral insanity to the legal tests of criminal irresponsibility. Conflict between the two schools of thought regarding the existence of a moral mania in which rages and homicide resulted from impairment of the moral faculty reveals itself in the contradictory views of American psychiatrists in the nineteenth century. Thus Isaac Ray (1860), then spokesman for American psychiatry, affirmed the existence of a "propensity to destroy" in certain criminals, a "horrid phenomenon which argued for a primary disease of the moral side of man's nature." On the other hand, the views of the opposing group were expressed in an editorial in the American

Journal of Insanity for April, 1853, which cautioned against the diagnosis of moral insanity in crimes involving murderous assaults. American psychiatry, which became an organized specialty just prior to the Civil War, finally assumed the view that moral insanity did exist and was a potent factor in many heinous crimes. The concept that a disturbance of moral function constituted a form of insanity remained active in American psychiatry for half a century. Many court decisions were influenced by the acceptance of moral insanity as a diagnosis where the issue of irresistible impulse was raised.

At this writing the irresistible impulse theory has been largely abandoned; only fifteen states in the Union allow the plea as defense against criminal responsibility. In the remaining states, frenzy of passion, jealousy, emotional excitement and the like, even though uncontrollable, do not result in exemption from responsibility in a homicide *unless* the offender does not know the nature and quality of his acts and otherwise conforms to the legal concept of insanity. In New York the law goes even further and states that "psychopathic inferiority" or, in the language of the Penal Code, "any morbid propensity to commit prohibited acts," in the absence of an incapacity to know right from wrong, is not a legal defense for criminal responsibility. *

The circumstances which, in part, reversed the medical opinion of illness of the moral functions was one that arose in the courtroom in the trial of Guiteau, the assassin of President Garfield. Guiteau's trial in Washington, D.C., brought the country's foremost alienists together and focused their attention on the relation of moral insanity to criminal responsibility. In this celebrated case † the medical concept of moral illness received its crucial legal test.

On July 2, 1881, Charles J. Guiteau, a self-confessed Redeemer and disappointed office-seeker, shot the President in Washington. President Garfield died some two and a half months later from the effects of the wound. The nation was stirred by this outrageous act.

The history of Charles Guiteau was that of an abnormal individual. His father was eccentric, a paternal uncle died insane, two paternal cousins were insane, and a sister had epilepsy. The prisoner's childhood was spent under the influence of his father's ideas in the Utopian Oneida Community. The father espoused religious ideas, among which was the theory of a personal union with the Redeemer which would prolong human life into an "earthly immortality." Guiteau was shown to have developed an inordinate vanity which rendered him sensitive to criticism and averse to manual labor and

* N.Y. Penal Code, Flanagan vs. Peo. 52 N.Y. 467.
† U.S. vs. Guiteau, 1 Mackey, 498, 47 Am. Rep. 247.

which also imbued him with a burning desire to become the leader of the Oneida Community. In letters he wrote: ". . . I say boldly that I claim inspiration. I am in the employ of Jesus Christ & Company. . . ." Four years before the assassination, Guiteau began to show signs of mental unsoundness. For months he turned his attention toward securing an ambassadorial post to France, which was repeatedly refused him. The idea of removing the President came into his mind when the conviction had settled on him that "the President's removal was a political necessity because he had proved a traitor to the men who made him and thereby imperiled the life of the Republic. I shot the President as I would a rebel, if I saw him pulling down the American flag. . . ."

The chief issue in the trial was that of criminal irresponsibility because of insanity at the time of commission of the act. The defense attorneys attempted to establish the position that the criminal act of the accused was the result of an "insane, deranged" mind. The prosecution battled to prove the defendant a willful murderer. Both sides had a formidable array of specialists ready to support their respective views. Neurologists and psychiatrists of prominence testified during the lengthy trial. One group emphasized the prisoner's hereditary background, fanatic religious beliefs, his chaotic life and the physical stigma of degeneration which were found in the asymmetry of head and eyes. The opposing group of specialists decried the physical abnormalities and pointed to Guiteau's ability to direct and control his inspirations and alter his lunacy at will. The defense alienists stressed his delusions of grandeur, his deficient reasoning power and inability to know right from wrong. The prosecution experts denied the hereditary nature of Guiteau's moral disease. Indeed, they denied the existence of moral insanity. The case quickly became a battleground for opposing schools of psychiatric thought, as attention passed from the unhappy prisoner to the issue of moral insanity.

The jury verdict that the prisoner was guilty and responsible for his acts was generally favorably received. Since the verdict was brought after a complete hearing of the pros and cons of moral illness, it contained a message which modified the moral insanity issue. The public, represented by the jury of laymen, applied the criteria of reasonable judgment to the welter of scientific information they had heard and found the position of an insanity of the moral faculty untenable. Approximately from this time onward, the concept of a "moral monstrosity" as a psychiatric entity allied to the insanities gradually fell into disuse before the courts.

The expansion of the clinical mental sciences, psychiatry and its companion field neurology, in the last half of the nineteenth century extended interest to the understanding of impulses demonstrable in socially and legally significant acts. At the turn of the century, a new concept was gaining prominence among those working with criminal material. The older viewpoint of "moral disease" was replaced by the concept of "psychopathic inferiority," which considered the criminal, the vagabond and the misfit as individuals with ill-formed constitutions. Whether heredity, environment or some physical factor was the cause of this constitutional variation could not be answered. Findings among these antisocial or peculiar individuals indicated that they had been marked with mental and physical inferiority. The constitutional aspect of the deviant was accepted when Koch, in 1888, introduced the term "psychopathic inferiority." Later, Adolph Meyer (1905) clarified the whole concept with the term "constitutional psychopathic inferiority." It was reasoned that the criminal was no longer an individual whose ethical and moral sense was tainted but that the body and mind of such a person were so constituted that education and training could not produce the expected normal effect. As intensive study of this group proceeded, numerous classifications were developed in an effort to fit the varied pictures of eccentric, antisocial individuals into the diagnostic schemes compatible with what was known of mentally ill individuals.

Emil Kraepelin, the German psychiatrist who is known as the founder of modern clinical psychiatry, about 1900 brought the constitutionally impoverished individuals into his modern classification under the term "morbid personality." The German school of psychiatry which grew out of Kraepelin's descriptive orientation stressed the distortion of the emotional component at the root of the psychopath's misbehavior and divided these cases into subgroups according to their emotional disturbance. For example, the depressive, insecure, fanatic, self-seeking, emotionally unstable and weak-willed types of psychopaths were differentiated. British psychiatrists continued to utilize the diagnostic idea of distortion of the moral sense in their classifications. The American group emphasized the difficulty in social adjustment because of emotional instability or some lack of personality balance. Some students of criminal psychopaths shed light on the unconscious forces involved in the development of the "psychopathic" personality. They pointed to early emotional stresses in the life of the psychopath which emerged as distorted attitudes and behavior toward the self and society.

It is evident from the outline presented of the various approaches leading to an understanding of the psychopath that the problem is extremely complicated. The intricacy of the human personality does not lend itself to ready description with a term or phrase. The morbid personality presents even greater difficulty when the manifold facets of a maladjusted personality are scrutinized for common elements which would facilitate a descriptive term. It is significant of the fascination which this psychological puzzle exerts on those who deal with personality abnormalities that literally hundreds of workers have contributed phrases aimed at a final delineation of the term psychopath. Diagnostic terms have been developed in the attempt to capture in a word or phrase an impalpable yet clearly defined spirit guiding the behavior of certain individuals. Diagnoses have been urged which employed the words constitution, psychopathic, inferiority, instability, delinquency, deficiency, abnormality, inadequacy, personality disorder, emotional perversity and antisociality in a score of permutations and combinations. Today, what D. K. Henderson of Edinburgh calls the "psychopathic state" is a clearly delimited concept which, though described in various ways, is readily apprehended by all who deal with difficult personalities and the troubles they create.

Universal acceptance of the psychopathic concept demonstrates that psychiatrists are agreed in maintaining the viewpoint that the chronically maladjusted person is endowed with a different, albeit mental, "constitution" from that of the normal individual. The consistently inexplicable, almost uncivilized, behavior of morbid personalities readily lends itself to thinking in structural terms. A psychopath's behavioral dissimilarity to the normal was formerly believed to exist in the delicate fibers and tissues of the brain and nervous system or in their physiologic substrate. Present-day studies by means of the electro-encephalograph, which appear to demonstrate variations in brain wave patterns, lend support to this hypothesis. The baffling question of the probable nature of underlying psychological disturbances in the psychopath will be treated more comprehensively in the next chapter.

The problem of psychopathic behavior is an urgent one. It is apparent that the dissidents and the maladjusted cannot be neglected or disregarded. The cost to society in human misery, avoidable accidents or catastrophes, in wrangling and nervous tension due to the emergence of impulses that have no place in harmonious social systems, is great enough to demand all the research and thinking that is being done. Psychopathic behavior has been described as a major social problem of today. It is a problem that particularly confronts those dealing with crime and is dealt with daily in courts, juvenile delinquency bureaus, clinics, schools and in the military services and industry—in short, in any area where one abnormal human being interreacts with others.

PRESENT-DAY USE OF CRIMINOLOGIC PSYCHIATRY— JUVENILE DELINQUENCY

The main instruments through which psychiatry and psychology materially aid social and judicial agencies today are welfare agencies, foster home placement bureaus, juvenile courts, county (criminal) courts and their probation departments, reformatories, state schools and prisons. Juvenile courts were chronologically the first to employ psychologists and psychiatrists with their charges. A preliminary step in this evolution was the separation of child delinquents from adult criminals in detention jails and reformatories during the last century. The present system of treating juvenile delinquency as a special problem in criminology started in 1899 with the establishment of the Juvenile Court in Chicago. The segregation of children with a view to correcting their antisocial tendencies rather than solely to punish them has received world-wide acceptance as a sound principle. One of the significant original efforts in this field was that of William Healy, director of the Juvenile Psychopathic Institute in Chicago from 1909. Similar activities were carried out in England and on the continent following the pioneer work. In Vienna, Aichorn's technic of handling wayward youth further refined the principle behind the analysis of the emotional background of juvenile delinquency.

The study of psychological backgrounds of child delinquency by Healy demonstrated that emotional conflict within the offenders themselves was responsible for specific offenses. Innumerable instances of delinquent behavior, such as petty thievery, car stealing and running away, were found to stem from distorted or mistaken sexual knowledge, from guilt arising from masturbation and from other emotional traumata to which children are especially subject in environments featured by ignorance or neglect. Acts which had been regarded as fortuitous or the result of bad environment proved to be reactions to emotional stresses or to the effect of repressed instinctive urges. Communication of these findings to the court led to revised attitudes toward punishment. Boys were sent to placement bureaus where social workers studied their needs, placed them in foster homes and treated the underlying emotional stresses according to the individual problem.

As a result of the introduction of the psychiatric viewpoint into the juvenile court, a new attitude toward detention and criminal court procedure is being adopted. The atmosphere surrounding criminal punishment, which is obviously harmful to the child, is discarded. In the juvenile court the delinquent is presented by the social worker or probation officer as a problem which has come to his attention rather than as an indicted criminal. This practice remains an important feature of the newer court procedure; it removes the sting of criminal prosecution and presents the delinquent in his true light—that of an individual unable to adjust to his environment. It emphasizes to the delinquent himself that he is handled as one whose disturbing behavior in the community is regarded as a symptom of emotional and social disease. This attitude, which has been observed in children's and juvenile courts for several decades, has been adopted also in adult courts where the probation system is operative. Although a part of the legal procedure, the report of the probation officer, with a psychiatric evaluation, gives the offender an opportunity to perceive that he is a social problem in a sense other than that of a wrongdoer whom the state wishes to punish. The probation worker and the psychiatrist are two forces in the legal environment with a nonemotional, objective interest in the offender. The judge, society's spokesman, is aided by the probation worker and the psychiatrist to maintain the objective attitude with which society strives to neutralize its punitive impulses. The reorientation involved in viewing the offender as a "case" represents a vast practical step forward, the significance of which is not often known and certainly not appreciated by that section of the public not professionally dealing with crime.

More recently the youthful or late adolescent group also began to be separated from hardened offenders in jails and prisons, and the lessons learned from experience with juvenile cases were extended to adolescents. Adolescent courts, beginning in 1935, developed along lines similar to juvenile courts and now emphasize rehabilitation, using both psychiatric and social means. The movement is now being considered in many parts of this country under the stimulus of the Youth Correction Authority Act. The American Law Institute, organized in 1923 for the purpose of promoting "clarification and simplification of the law and its better adaptation to social needs," headed by William Draper Lewis, has in the enunciation of the Youth Correction Act presaged a veritable revolution in the treatment and handling of youthful offenders. The principles underlying this act, briefly stated, are that (a) the objective of criminal justice should be the protection of society, (b) the treatment of condemned youth should take into account his characteristics and other casual factors and (c) that treatment should be directed primarily to the correction of antisocial tendencies and the offender controlled until it is reasonably certain that he is cured of these tendencies. The act, which is a proposed model to be adopted by each state, sets up an authority in the state consisting of three persons chosen from the professions of education, probation (social work), penology and psychology to whom the sentencing judge shall refer the convicted offender, except in capital offense cases, where the judge has statutory power to impose death, life imprisonment or a fine. All power to treat the referred offender then resides in the hands of the authority, one of whom must be a psychiatrist. Since the Youth Correction Authority Act is so radical in its implication, taking actual sentencing out of the control of judges, considerable discussion has developed and will develop before it is adopted by most of the states. Thus far the states of California, Wisconsin and Minnesota have adopted the Youth Correction Act (1947). Twenty-three other states have the plan under study at this writing.

PROBATION AND PSYCHIATRY

The coincident rise of the mental hygiene movement and child guidance clinics and the spread of juvenile courts stimulated general recognition of the fact that social case work involved special knowledge of applied psychology. Psychiatric social case work, in the form of probation in adult or adolescent courts and in juvenile courts, contains the essence of the contribution of psychology to criminology under the existing legal structure. Probation started a century ago with the experiment of a Boston cobbler, John Augustus, who bailed out offenders who could not pay their fines and gave moral support and guidance to the unfortunates who had nowhere to turn on release from custody. The work of a few pioneers was placed on a firm footing by the first probation law in 1878 (Massachusetts). By the turn of the century, six states had enacted probation statutes. At present almost every state has a probation law or its equivalent.

Probation is the technic of supervising and treating convicted offenders outside of penal institutions. Offenders who have been convicted may have sentence suspended on them when, in the judgment of the court, they have sufficient potentialities to be rehabilitated while in the community. Such an offender is under the supervision of a competent probation officer who endeavors to change the offender's habits, attitudes and associates in order to give him the maximum opportunity to become rehabilitated. If the probationer violates the trust which the judge has placed in him, he is returned to court for possible imprisonment. Probation, since it is invoked when a suspended sentence is meted out, is not leniency but is a trial at living under control. This system can be utilized with all but the most vicious criminals, who may be a public menace when at large.

To determine the offender's possibilities for probation, a pre-sentence investigation is prepared for the sentencing judge. The probation investigator visits the areas of contact of the convicted offender, studies his environment, family group, associates, habits, work record and behavior pattern, as well as the background of the offense itself. Through skilled interviewing, the probation worker can judge the emotional and environmental factors operating in the offender's life and the possibilities for future adjustment under guidance. The offender is then brought before a psychologist, who estimates his intellectual capacity, schooling achievement and special mental defects or assets. The psychiatric examination which follows attempts to determine the presence of mental disease and to assay the structure of the personality of the offender in relation to his offense and behavior in society. Particular attention is paid to the elasticity of the personality and whether it will allow successful rehabilitation. Frequently the psychiatrist will consult with the social worker at various stages of the investigation to help the worker interpret the psychological meaning of his client's behavior. The presentence report is then presented to the judge, who decides whether probation or incarceration is in order, on the basis of the intensive investigation of the offender and the statutory regulations governing the crime.

The second task of the probation officer involves treatment of his client. In this program, the worker utilizes all environmental resources, including employment of recreational facilities, family rearrangement and other social agencies. What is most important is that a helpful person-to-person relationship is developed with the offender. The treatment of offenders on a probationary status involves the gigantic task of building up personality assets in the individual and refashioning his behavior patterns. In this attempt the probation officer can offer the probationer a healthful relationship enriched with professional knowledge and standards of adjusted social conduct. This new direction in the legal environment is of tremendous psychological significance to the offender. Up to that time the experience of the offender in court has impressed him with the power of the law as an impersonal force. Contact with probation officers entails quite different psychological elements. The personal acceptance by the officer of the offender as a human being brings a new light to the criminal. Persuasion, suggestion, guidance and the interpretation of the offender's behavior to himself add to the emotional security which the probationer enjoys in the new world to which the skilled, professionally trained social worker has introduced him.

It is obvious then that the probation officer's activities are an important part of the therapeutic effort which is carried out in the original environment in which the crime has been committed. Psychiatrists play a vital role in giving direction to the probation worker's efforts to ameliorate the emotional stresses, the personality inadequacies and the tensions of the individual case. Usually offenders under probation treatment are first seen in the doctor's office and then in consultation with the social worker who carries out the treatment program. Not only the probation worker but the judge also takes a hand in planning treatment for the offender. Offenders obviously vary in the amount of psychotherapy required. Sometimes a judicial warning or suggestion suffices. Most often, however, the efforts of all three therapeutic agents are needed to effect rehabilitation. An example will demonstrate how a psychiatric viewpoint on the part of the court allowed a felony offender to rehabilitate himself while on probation.

Theodore M., a young clergyman, was convicted of first-degree grand larceny. At the age of twenty-nine, a father of two children, an unusually successful clergyman, active in religious and social movements, a leader in his community and an orator of brilliance, Theodore had had a quixotic crime career of several years duration. At the time of his marriage, six years prior to the offense, he had accumulated debts due to loose financial management which were covered by his father-in-law. During the years of his marriage, when he was successful in the pulpit, he continued his misbehavior. During summer vacations, he would hire an automobile and chauffeur and, giving the impression he was a physician, drive to various hospitals throughout the city. On other occasions, he hired impressive automobiles from dealers without paying for them, drove them at high rates of speed into the country to see his family and abandoned the cars wherever he chose. In the last offense, he evaded the chauffeur and drove to the Canadian border, where he abandoned the car. At other times during these years, Theodore took expensive diamond rings on consignment and pawned them to pay debts. This misdemeanor involved his wealthy parishioners, who covered the loss under the pressure of a public scandal. He forged two large checks on a Canadian bank in which he had no funds. His financial peculations amounted to about $10,000 during his years of pyramided trouble. Some debts were covered and some were unpaid at the time of his conviction.

The probation report established the offender's situation and behavior as recorded. Psychologic examination showed him to have between high average and superior intelligence. His verbal intelligence was his outstanding asset. Psychiatric examination found the offender to be a psychopathic personality. During the interviews he spoke fluently, even floridly, talking in abstract terms most of the time. He displayed less knowledge than one would expect, especially on current events and current political history. At the beginning he had a sanctimonious, professional air which gave the impression of sincerity. His speech, though fluent, was not particularly well controlled, and his expressions were not precise or well thought out. Theodore's verbal type of intelligence was suited to his vocation, especially since he was known to be an outstanding pulpit orator. His wordiness helped him in the direction of social prestige also. An example of the sacrifice of thought for words was seen when he talked fluently about having been "purged" by his arrest and in the next breath blamed his wife and the attitude of his in-laws for his present predicament. He professed at one time to have insight into all his larcenies and other thefts and in the next moment he brushed it aside and said he wanted to "rehabilitate" himself. The brilliance and promise which impressed everyone had, it is true, some partial basis in fact; but it was sustained on rationalizations and fluency of speech rather than on any fundamental quality of thought. Careful study showed that underlying his verbal ability was the magic wish to rule by the Word, a type of submerged megalomania which fitted well into a religious atmosphere. It is obvious that the immaturity evidenced by his behavior, his drive to keep up his ego-stature, was an expression of deeper conflicts which could probably be treated.

It was concluded that although he was technically a psychopathic personality of the emotionally immature type, his impulses and immature acts were the result of deeper drives based upon an inner feeling of inadequacy unconscious to him. The full report was submitted to the presiding judge, who considered the extent of the felony, the statutory requirement for this crime and the possibility of reclamation of the offender. The court agreed to a trial period of a year under treatment at a private institution where the type of observation and psychotherapy initiated at the court clinic was continued.

Treatments * proceeded for the first few months with the therapist assuming a passive role. At first, Theodore absorbed his anxieties, which arose from his being removed from the area of activity, the pulpit, through social activities with the patients at the hospital. His grandiosity continued as he swept into a position of big brother, spiritual guide and religious leader to the other patients. The next development was that of projection onto his wife and in-laws of his own inadequacy; he accused them of being selfish, restricting, aggressive. At the same time he related that his father was the "Saint" and a great biblical scholar. Gradually it became clear to the patient, through the treatment, that his verbal pressure was in compensation for a dreaded inferiority feeling. Numerous anxieties arose in reaction to the realization of this idea, but he responded to these emotional movements by redoubling his

* This case was treated by Dr. Louis Wender, Katonah, N. Y., and the author.

literary activity, writing book reviews for publication and conducting a hospital journal.

As therapeutic contacts continued, the anxieties quieted. The emotional support furnished by the physician allowed Theodore to see that the car stealing and the forgeries, the oratory and literary effulgence in the hospital were compensations for his inferiorities. No attempt was made to search deeply into the unconscious basis for the immaturity, for it was considered sufficient that insight was given into his previous behavior and his offense. This, combined with the general discussions about his marital situation, improved him to the point that he was paroled after a year from the hospital and embarked upon a business career, giving up all interest in the clergy. His traits were sublimated in an acceptable way by writing advertising copy and broadcasting for a radio station. After a year of real economic tribulations, Theodore was able to make a living in advertising and radio broadcasting. The year of convalescence brought back again and again reactions against the "crass" business world, yearning for the old spiritual values, impatience and anger projected on his wife's relatives. Through all this emotional stress a gradual solidification of his assets occurred as he turned them to the reality of the commercial world. He was discharged from probationary supervision.

Almost ten years after the offense, Theodore has had no further legal difficulties and has attained a level of success consonant with his actual assets. Through a difficult net of circumstances, he has managed, with the aid of therapy, to develop insight and to start a new life adjustment.

PSYCHIATRY IN THE PRISON

Institutional psychiatrists whose task is treatment of convicted offenders utilize different technics in a totally different environment. Early in the history of work houses, jails and penitentiaries, physicians were concerned predominantly with medical problems such as tuberculosis and malnutrition. In the earlier days many insane persons were thrown into county jails, and, as a consequence, mental cases were maltreated as common criminals. Until there was a clear understanding of what constituted insanity, mental deficiency, psychopathic personality and other mental disorders, little work of scientific value resulted from the attendance of physicians in penal institutions. It was not until early in the twentieth century that psychologic and psychiatric classification of prisoners was developed to its present state. At the present time, every prison has a classification clinic which aids in sorting out prisoners in various groups to the end that proper rehabilitative methods may be employed on responsive subjects. The system of classification adopted in prisons throughout the country has, as its first task, selection of the prisoners for the purposes of security. The usual divisions of institutions are into those of maximum, medium or minimal security, for custodial care, vocational training and re-education, respectively. There is also the need to sort out the insane and mentally defective prisoners for segregation to special departments or separate institutions. The classification staff of a prison usually comprises psychologists who test the mental capacity and literacy of the prisoners, psychiatrists who examine their personality structure and the possibility of developing emotional reactions, and an educational expert who plans the training program. In addition, a chaplain and an industrial officer estimate the needs of the prisoner in each of these fields, while the social worker reassesses the home environment and surveys the social environment, if there is a possibility of a return to the community. Usually the classification board meets with the warden or administrative assistant. Prisoners who regress and become disciplinary problems or, on the other hand, show marked improvement, are re-evaluated from time to time by the clinical team. The social and recreational program is developed according to the board's findings. An important aspect is the teaching given in literate, technical and trade subjects to facilitate later civilian adjustment.

Attempts at scientific classification of prisoners were initiated about 1913. Early work by psychologists was concerned mainly with estimating mental levels of prisoners. By 1916, two psychiatrists, at the Bedford Hills Reformatory for Women and Sing Sing Prison, in New York State, had begun to analyze the emotional status of prisoners. The work of Dr. Edith Spaulding and Dr. Bernard Glueck in the two institutions was epoch-making because it led to the discovery of the types of mental abnormalities among inmates which, until then, had been assumed to be due solely to feeble-mindedness. Since the pioneer work of Dr. Glueck, many state prisons and penitentiaries, including the Federal Prison system, have adopted the practice of routine psychological and psychiatric examinations of all incoming prisoners.

Prison life constitutes a complex situation wherein special, and at times staggering, stresses are exerted on the inmates. Discipline in the prison community looms as an almost overwhelming force in the lives of inexperienced or unstable prisoners. An individual passing from civil life to confinement experiences a sudden change in living routine which inevitably causes emotional upheavals before he is able to adjust to the unnatural environment with emotional tolerance. Only an understanding of the meaning of emotional trauma on normal or abnormal personalities permits intelligent management of convicted prisoners and prepares the way for future rehabilitation. Those trained in psychiatry appreciate immediate and late reactions to frustration and are able to distinguish between problems arising from the effects of prison and those purely personal in origin.

The offender, upon conviction and sentence, leaves the law court, where he enjoyed the rights of a citizen and was entitled to defend himself within legal limits, and enters prison, where deprivation of rights is the outstanding feature. This aspect of punishment is supplemented by other deprivations, such as loss of opportunity for sexual activity and loss of personal initiative through detailed regulation of daily living. Monotony and regularity of work, unceasing supervision and complete dependence on established routine sooner or later cause reactions of frustration and resentment in all prisoners. In time most of them are able to perceive the social reason for enforced control of their lives. There are others, however, less elastic emotionally, less able to understand the restraining goals of discipline and routine, who develop emotional crises and reactions that cannot be managed so easily.

Disciplinary violators constitute the larger of two main groups most troublesome to prison authorities. The rebellious type of inmate develops reactions to the frustration and monotony of prison life. These extend from transitory rages to psychotic conditions of long duration and include various manifestations of emotional excitement, such as stimulation of riots, prolonged anger, constant complaining and suicidal attempts. They require medical treatment as well as physical control. Frequently, prolonged emotional reactions necessitate removal to a sick ward or to a hospital for the criminally insane. The lesser degrees of such reactions are dealt with by the psychiatric staff in conjunction with the administrative officers. It is not generally realized that every prison or penitentiary has within its walls the problem of disciplining inmates who are antisocial members of the prison environment itself. The psychiatrist is active in these problems because he appreciates the fact that, without an intelligent understanding of psychological currents in these refractory individuals, no measures for control or modification of their behavior can be effective for more than brief periods of time. The psychological mechanisms underlying rebellious behavior in the prison will be discussed in detail as an aspect of treatment. It should be noted at this point, however, that the importance of psychological knowledge of the meaning of rebelliousness lies in the fact that punishment tends only to increase the problem of intolerance to authority.

The second group of difficulties which presents problems to the prison authorities is that of homosexuality. The initial screening by the psychiatric staff allows the segregation of known homosexuals from the main body of prisoners. The more pressing concern of the prison administration however, is with those men, apparently normal sexually in civilian life, who yield to perverse impulses in reaction to enforced deprivation of normal sexual satisfaction while in confinement. The frustration of emotional gratification, inherent in prison life, is difficult for all inmates to withstand. In neurotic and immature prisoners the summation of emotional tension forces an outlet through one specific area of emotional expression, namely, sexuality. The sexual area, which has already been sensitized by absence of normal sexual objects, becomes the pathway for release of tension through masturbation or homosexual activity. Although this psychophysiologic process occurs in many men, analysis reveals that those individuals who succumb to homosexual impulses have a strong, though unrecognized, homosexual component in their make-up. In addition to the personality factor, the social organization of a prison tends to stimulate homosexual expression. Thus prisoners serving long sentences prevail upon the younger inmates to act as sexual objects by conferring special privileges and favors or through coercion. Further, the development of friendships between men may be increased through constant and close association to the point where homosexual impulses, otherwise latent, rise to the surface. At times the eruption of these hidden impulses may cause feelings of anxiety and nervousness in the inmate which take the form of homosexual panics. The handling of transitory panic reactions of this type in men who do not have a perception of their homosexual impulses until they find themselves in a perverse sexual relationship, becomes an administrative problem in which the psychiatrist is an active participant.

The emergence in the prison environment of homosexual impulses, sometimes unrecognized by the inmate himself, is illustrated in the case of R., a man of 23, who was convicted of fraud. Several years prior to the current offense R. had been dishonorably discharged from a branch of the military service for a similar offense, issuing worthless checks. He claimed that the first offense occurred because his wife had depleted their joint bank account (following which she applied for an annulment of the marriage) and that the second embezzlement was the result of "unfortunate circumstances." Psychological tests showed the prisoner to be of superior intelligence. His manner, evasiveness, lack of self-critique and irresponsibility pointed toward a diagnosis of psychopathic personality of the swindler type. During the psychiatric examination, suspicion was aroused of the presence of a sexual disturbance, but nothing conclusive was elicited beyond evidence indicating decreased sexual libido.

About four months after admission to the prison, during R.'s apparent adjustment to the institution routine, the offender was caught in the lavatory in a homosexual act with another inmate. It was discovered that R. had made many overtures over a period of weeks to induce a younger prisoner to permit R. to perform fellatio. Reviewing the sexual history of the offender in the light of his perverse desires and acts, it was revealed that his marriage annulment, which R. described as due to "sterility," was in reality due to his diminished heterosexual drive. There had been no sexual relations during seven months of married life. Further examination revealed that, although there had been no earlier homosexual activities, there had been partial sexual impotence with women and a great deal of immature sexual fantasies. In prison R.'s sexual psychopathy, which had hitherto been submerged, had come to the fore, and his latent homosexuality was openly expressed in perverse sexual acts. Constant association with young inmates at a time when he was otherwise deprived was a stimulus to the expression of R.'s perverse feelings.

The many questions which the management of disciplinary violators and homosexuals in prison brings to the foreground demonstrate the need for psychiatric research in this field. Prisons provide a fruitful field for research into the personality structure of the criminal recidivist within the limits of a special environment. Studies of this nature, which can be the only rational basis for effective punishment and rehabilitation, are being exploited to an increasing degree at the present time.

There are other areas than prisons where psychiatry is clarifying the intricacies of criminal behavior. Traffic violators have recently been studied in metropolitan traffic courts (Detroit Recorder's Court) with the finding that a high percentage of traffic violators have mental and physical disorders which make it impossible for them to be relied on in situations demanding quick reactions and good judgment. Individuals who are of borderline intelligence or feeble-minded individuals, and those with specific visual, auditory or neurologic handicaps not obvious to the casual examiner, have been discovered by neuropsychiatrists and psychologists in traffic courts. Similarly, the alcoholic driver has been found to require a neuropsychiatric examination to evaluate the effect of the alcohol on his reflexes and judgment, the impairment of which results in accidents and fatalities.

Since the beginning of World War II, military authorities have been faced with the problem of large numbers of military and naval offenders. It was found necessary to staff the Army and Navy brigs and prisons with military psychiatrists who examined each incoming prisoner routinely to determine the direction of retraining and the intensity of discipline required.

The technic of handling prisoners, the classification and day-to-day routine were modeled after the basic system developed by the Federal Bureau of Prisons. Attempts to study and treat prisoners with psychologically oriented methods reached their apex in the military prisons and brigs during the war.

There are other areas of human misbehavior claiming judicial attention into which psychiatric methods are beginning to penetrate. These areas involve minor crimes or misdemeanors or social disturbances which do not merit imprisonment. For example, recent interest taken in neighborhood quarrels by psychiatrists at the Municipal Court in Chicago revealed that many an incipient psychosis which might result in a fatality or an assault is uncovered by a neighborhood quarrel. Such querulous and litigious individuals, when uncovered in the lesser courts, can be treated before a major crime occurs and thus save a great amount of distress to the public and expense to the state.

The social and legal environment of the criminal is permeated with prejudices and biases imbedded in tradition. While some of the attitudes developed toward the wrongdoer were built on the prime practical consideration of protecting society, elements of moral castigation and righteousness have remained in active force. The understanding which the psychological sciences seek to gain of the phenomenon of antisocial conduct includes a thorough appreciation of the psychological crosscurrents surrounding the criminal and his society. An objective view of these emotional currents and their representations in social behavior is a preliminary step in the program for rehabilitation of offenders and prevention of crime.

PART TWO

The Individual Criminal

4

The Psychopathic Personality

The psychological matrix of crime is complex, involving the emotional interreactions, attitudes and traditions existing between criminals and society. Previous chapters have dealt with prejudices and unconscious impulses common to each member of society as they actively influence attitudes toward the criminal. But the personality of the offender is a prominent aspect of this psychological relationship. The criminal's personality, which mediates expression of his antisocial impulses, also requires examination. The objective view of social and psychological phenomena, evolved through psychiatry's constant scrutiny of the human personality, has proved the personality to be the effective agent in social adjustment or maladjustment. The second part of this book, then, will deal with the personality distortions of various types of criminal offenders in the commission of major criminal offenses.

The viewpoint espoused here considers the offender in his dynamic relation to law, i.e., the criminal is considered to be in a state of active antagonism to society. At the moment of a given offense, criminal behavior obviously represents reactions of abnormality. Such reactions have been traditionally the material of criminologic interest. But beyond this recognizable behavior lies a great expanse of personality elements involving the emotional and impulse life which are of greater importance to the understanding of the criminal than is the surface picture supplied by his behavior. An adequate understanding of crime necessarily includes knowledge of the offender's total personality resources, which entered into and, more importantly, preceded a criminal act.

The emphasis on individuality in personality description brings to the fore inherent difficulties in presenting a composite picture of a group of markedly diverse individuals. Although many criminals fall into a given personality diagnosis, the individual picture of each is blurred by inevitable

53

generalities concerning the group and distorted by the absence, in the individual case, of characteristics common to the group. Nevertheless, exposition of the meaning of personality structure in the individual who commits crime requires a systematic presentation such as is indicated in the following classification: the *psychopathic, neurotic, immature,* and *occasional* offender.

The group that supplies the most comprehensive and unmistakable illustration of maladjustment to social life comprises those persons referred to as psychopathic personalities. Although this is not the only personality abnormality represented in major crime, it accounts for much of the antisocial activity therein. Moreover, the study of psychopaths illustrates in unmistakable form the particular conflict between human impulses and the restrictions of society. Whereas other types of personality abnormalities, such as neurotic disorders, manifest themselves in the inner reactions and complaints of the individual, the psychopathic personality expresses his conflict in behavior which is readily recognized as social maladjustment or crime. The psychopath tends to "act out" whatever disharmony and conflicts exist in his make-up; in contrast to the neurotic, who himself suffers from symptoms, the psychopath causes the environment to suffer. When the psychopath, for example, is frustrated on a job, he "acts out" by fighting with his fellow workers, ruining the material with which he works or by sudden resignation. In a similar situation the neurotic will become depressed, develop inferiority feelings or become physically (i.e., neurotically) ill. The psychopath insists upon gratification of his impulses without thought of the appropriateness of time or place; he has no consideration for others and will not understand the need for, or obey, social conventions. As a consequence he is involved in constant turmoil and conflict and is never in complete adjustment with society.

The psychopath can also be described in terms of his internal characteristics. One of the basic characteristics of the psychopath is the inability to achieve a goal. There is a disinclination to seek anything but immediate gain from his visibly sustained efforts. Other basic psychological characteristics in the psychopath are his outstanding egotism, impulsiveness, resistance to discipline and training and an appalling lack of sentiment and gratitude. The psychopath takes things for granted and thinks only in terms of personal advantage. Whether intellectually brilliant or dull, he feels himself to be always right. He lives in an egocentric world and gives the impression of being calloused to the feelings of others. He is unable to stand adversity; his goals are in terms of short-lived values, while his judgments are unreliable. As his judgments shift rapidly, so do his emotions vary quickly, and for any practical purpose he is <u>untrustworthy</u>. Added to this is a lack of insight into his own difficulties and a strong tendency to project blame for his troubles to others.

The psychopath can be a criminal, a ne'er-do-well or an eccentric, depending upon the social field with which he is in conflict. An extremely significant point is that <u>the pattern of misbehavior can often be traced from childhood</u>. A careful history shows this type to have been always unmanageable, untrainable, even cruel, and unscrupulous with playmates or siblings. As a child, he fought with his brothers and sisters, could not accept teaching in school, became a truant and later became involved in minor delinquencies, such as burglary, or in precocious sexual activity. Often these repeated acts led to his being sent to a reform school or a foster home. As a result, his schooling was interrupted and his character lost the balance which schooling and contact with fellow-students help to provide. As the psychopath grows older, he often <u>has trouble holding a job</u>, fights with <u>his superiors</u>, tries to get what he wishes by <u>stealth or trickery</u>, becomes unemployable and a malcontent and ultimately finds his way into relief agencies or the criminal courts. His aggressions are turned against the society which gave him a "poor" start.

The following case is representative of the psychopathic personality and demonstrates the instability, impulsiveness and egocentricity which eventuate in difficulties in many areas of social contact. Thomas, 26, was received at a naval prison after conviction because of a period of desertion in time of war. During his several years in the service he had been convicted five times for similar offenses. The instant offense occurred because the prisoner became intoxicated while under orders and, feeling unduly restricted by the regulations of the service, deserted his duty. In previous offenses, bouts of drinking played a prominent part in his desertion. During these periods he would live a roustabout life for several days. His school life early showed the pattern of his behavior. The offender was a truant frequently and stopped school at the age of 16 because he did not "care for" further education. He worked sporadically in a tire shop and a shoe factory. Prior to entering the Navy he spent five months in the peacetime Army and was dishonorably discharged for being A.W.O.L. During his postschool years he had been arrested almost weekly for drunkenness and disorderly conduct in his native state. At one time he was confined in the county jail for six months for carrying a pistol without a permit. He wrecked two motor cars, the cost of which was met by his father. The father was a railroad engineer and the family situation was comfortable. At the age of 23 Thomas entered into a common law relationship with a girl and married her seven days after their baby was born. He contracted gonorrhea on five occasions up to the time of imprisonment.

Psychologically, the offender was of average intelligence. He was blustering in his attitude, independent and self-centered in his viewpoint. He complained of headache and dizziness because of an early head injury, but there was no indication of brain disease. His attitude of emotional indifference was exemplified in his relationsihp to his wife, whom he married because she was pregnant. Thomas stated, "I decided she was no good to me now because I could not support her while in prison." He added as an afterthought, "Besides, she is not my nationality." Thomas explained that his family had lived in the South for four generations and were "full-blooded Irish," whereas his wife was of Italian descent. His impatience with ordinary ethical ideals, his preoccupation with events of the moment, his complete and crass realism, the absence of any life goal or sentiment or ideals was visible in his speech and manner as well as in discussion of his life situation. The prisoner described a moral code of his own. He fought anyone who called him a name, and would brook no reference to himself. His social relationships were built around the viewpoint that insults, even in jest, called for vengeance. If his revenge resulted in serious injury or death to someone, it evoked no particular emotional reaction in him. Alcoholism was excessive and periodic. When Thomas drank he became even more ruthless than otherwise. He had little respect for naval regulations and felt that his current difficulty in the service was due to the "hounding" he received at the hands of the authorities.

Unable to adjust to industrial life, some psychopaths, in place of becoming criminals, develop in other directions—they become swindlers, "philosophical tramps," or racketeers, malcontents or agitators. Another group seek release in an adventuresome life, join the peacetime Army or Navy, where they conflict with military authority, and come to official attention as guardhouse inmates or are dishonorably discharged from the service. Still another group develop paranoid attitudes and find their way into the courts because of their litigious tendencies. Some rise high in the social and economic scale before their difficulties become apparent; they become involved in national scandals as entrepreneurs or create mischief as promoters of international intrigue. They try in some cases to solve their personality inadequacies by multiple or spectacular marriages or notorious liaisons, so that numerous divorces and scandals bring them to civil courts or into the newpapers.

The wider our experience and knowledge of various difficulties subsumed under the phrase "psychopathic behavior," the clearer it appears that no one psychological or behavior pattern represents the full clinical picture. Yet through this maze of variegated behavior, which partakes of many of the excesses of normal behavior, there shines enough of a constant distortion of *total* personality performance to warrant the diagnostic classification of psychopathic personality and its clinical subdivisions.

THE PARANOID PSYCHOPATH

Abnormal personalities are extremely varied in their manifestations, but the conventional clinical groupings into which they fall have some specificity for types of crime. For example, the paranoid type of psychopath is frequently involved in assault and murder cases. Paranoid individuals are characterized by the persistent feeling of being constantly discriminated against by everyone. Such persons tend to misinterpret the actions of others and to misconstrue simple coincidence in a way which seems to place them at a disadvantage. Paranoid individuals are tense in their manner and continually on the alert for adverse reactions toward themselves, and much of their energy is aimed at righting fancied wrongs or improving the unhappy situation in which they constantly imagine themselves. As a consequence of this attitude, the paranoid person is frequently in court either defending himself or seeking to restrain someone whom he feels might injure him. A distinction must be made between the psychotic individual whose judgment is so distorted by the delusions of persecutions as to be mentally ill and the psychopath whose feeling of being prevailed upon does not pass beyond a paranoid attitude. In both cases the criminal acts in which they become involved are usually of an assaultive nature. However, the paranoid psychopath in whom persecutory attitudes are not crystallized into delusions often becomes involved in crimes such as blackmail and extortion which entail verbal rather than physical aggression.

The psychology of the paranoid individual is marked primarily by a feeling of grandiosity and secondly by a tendency to react aggressively toward others. The crimes of blackmail and extortion provide a nice illustration of the operation of these two mental mechanisms and show, moreover, that unconscious factors direct the actual technic of the crime. The usual blackmailer arms himself preliminarily with knowledge of his victim's character defects, e.g., sexual irregularities or other indiscretions not generally known by the victim's circle of friends. The blackmailer wields this knowledge as a threat against the victim, since the subject wishes to keep his earlier difficulties from public attention. The power held over the fate and fortunes of another person, which results from the acquisition of such intimate knowledge, coincides with the feeling of grandiosity (omnipotence fantasy) in the criminal himself. The ability to see through a victim by awareness of the obscure aspects of his personal history allows the blackmailer a symbolic gratification of his unconscious wishes for power in the position of an all-knowing one. The fact that the blackmailer usually hides behind a pseudonym or anonymity adds to his mastery of the situation and thus increases his Messianic grandiosity. By rendering the victim vulnerable to injury at his hands, the extortionist enjoys an aggressive advantage and a deeper sadistic gratification.

The paranoid psychopath, the litigious type, who demonstrates the psychological features outlined, is more prone to be involved in civil than in criminal court actions. Charlotte G., a writer who was charged with libel and attempted extortion by a United States senator, is a case in point. Sensitive, tense and querulous, Charlotte had demanded $50,000.00 from the senator on the threat of publishing a slanderous book revealing alleged amorous liaisons which she unearthed from his past. Behind her libelous attacks was the persecutory idea that the senator had attempted to drive her from the journalistic profession. For weeks Charlotte believed that references in a column of a daily newspaper contained veiled allusions to her and were inspired by the senator. She insisted on defending her own case in court, trusting neither her attorney nor her witnesses.

The criminal offender who engages in blackmailing through an organized extortion ring demonstrates predominantly the aggressive component of the paranoid reaction. The technic in group extortions practiced on persons of social standing and wealth is to select an individual who is a clandestine homosexual and have him approached by a young confederate for sexual purposes. The other members of the ring, one posing as an outraged father of the youth and the other as an officer of the law, apprehend the couple and, with the use of a spurious police officer's badge, demand payment of money on threat of exposure to the police. The victim, aware of the deleterious effect which exposure of his sexual irregularity would have on his life, readily assents to the extortion. In this variety of offense the extortion group usurp the authority of the police, and the frightened victim is unable to detect the impersonation. The effective psychological maneuver in the extortionists is that of borrowing the authority of a governmental agency. The extortionist identifies himself with the law, by which psychological device he serves his unconscious wish for omnipotence and his impulses toward aggression. The mode of operation of the extortionist betrays deeper relationships in his own psychology to that existing in the victim. It is sufficient to note at this point that play on the victim's sexual irregularities indicates the presence of a corresponding psychosexual difficulty in the criminal. This reflection of the personality problem of the blackmailer in his crime will be considered in detail in the section on the swindler.

In another variety of blackmail, a factor already encountered in the case of Charlotte comes into play. It is the utilization of the magic power of the written word in the service of omnipotence feelings. The control over another person through the agency of the written word is again a symbolic representation of the grandiosity found at the core of every paranoid individual. The meaning of this ramification of one aspect of the omnipotence fantasy can be seen in the following case of an immature, unstable youth whose blackmail technic is almost a caricature of subtler methods used by more practiced extortionists.

The case was brought to the attention of the authorities by the president of a large department store, who received several threatening letters, written crudely in pencil and demanding $6,000.00. The first letter demanded the money to be paid immediately on pain of having the store "blown up." The second letter, written a few days later, stated, "We felt sorry for you so we didn't blow up the store yet but your time will come. This time you have to pay $1,000.00 more. If you inform the police, inform your undertaker." Elaborate instructions were added for paying the money. The letter was flamboyant and full of semihumorous quips. Using a ruse, the extortionist, who proved to be a sixteen-year-old boy, was easily apprehended.

The youth proved to be one of seven children whose father, an alcoholic, died when the children were very small. The family was known to many social agencies. When Anton was four years old, he and four other siblings were sent to an orphanage. At fourteen, Anton was caught by the police after he had entered a building from the skylight. At that time he had made extravagant statements about his ambitions. He fancied himself in all sorts of roles; sometimes he was a trainer of horses in the West, an expert "yegg man or just an all-around crook." He stated definitely that he was exactly what he wanted to be and had no intention of changing, indicating that he was prepared to live an embittered, self-willed life of antisociality. Some time later Anton was busy writing letters to the department store head. When he was brought before the judge on the blackmail charge, Anton requested ten days to prepare his own defense. The youth declared that he knew he talked "crazy" but insisted that everything which happened to him was part of his own plan. He spoke of blowing up public buildings by means of explosives which he could extract from ordinary substances such as matches or by telephone by secret processes known only to himself. At one point he burst out to the examiner, "I know more about chemistry than anybody in the world. . . . If you knew the secret you could be as powerful as I am. I can give it to any of the boys in any of the institutions where I have been, no matter how dumb they are; if I told them how, they could be the biggest criminals in the world." His bizarre statements and his emotional superficiality were striking. He was jocular in an exaggerated, aggressive manner and later tense, with marked push of speech and flight of ideas, bordering on a psychosis. With the cessation of the period of excitement, the picture of infantility became clearer. Anton's frustration at the apparent pusillanimity of his omnipotence wishes as they crashed against reality gave rise to transitory psychotic reactions.

The psychological force behind this youth's efforts at extortion was that of aggression toward the victim vented through the mediation of the written word. The crime represented a vehicle for the expression of inner tensions agitating the offender. The youthful extortionist utilized the magic of his fantasy to deny his inner perception of a deprived childhood. The object he took for blackmail, the department store, was clearly a symbol of magnitude and plenty which served his unconscious need for a magical denial of early deprivation. His oral aggression, extravagant speech and flamboyant boasts were also evidences of the offender's striving to overcome overwhelming inferiority feelings. The crime for Anton was a living replica of his psychological problem and an attempt at its solution through the magical power borrowed from words.

The delineation of finer psychological movements within the paranoid psychopath who engages in extortion indicates how emotional problems fixated in a character structure compel the individual to engage in a specific crime. On the other hand, the frankly paranoid individual who attacks a presumed enemy is reacting to his delusions directly, and his offense does not partake of the complex train of psychological interreactions discussed in the psychopath. In assaults or murders resulting from persecutory delusions, the emergence of a psychosis on the occasion of a criminal act in an individual not generally suspected of being mentally ill is not an uncommon occurrence. It is a technical question whether or not the severely paranoid personality is really constantly delusional. A similar situation exists in the schizoid psychopath whose personality distortions, otherwise unnoticed, come to light only after the commission of a crime. The schizoid personality, like the paranoid psychopath, whose criminal offense is an external expression of a long-standing personality dissociation, may have been in reality a mentally ill person at the time of his crime. The study of both these groups of abnormal individuals when they become involved in criminal offenses reveals the thin shell of emotional rapport on which apparent conformance to the social world was based up to the time of the crime.

THE SCHIZOID PSYCHOPATH

The schizoid personality has been conventionally included in the psychopathic group. Most observers agree, however, that the emotional disturbances in these individuals are so specifically characteristic as to warrant consideration as a separate diagnostic entity. From a descriptive point of view, the schizoid psychopath, as has been indicated, falls into one bracket with the paranoid psychopath in relation to the criminal expression of existing mental pathology. The diagnosis of schizoid personality encompasses many levels of psychopathology, varying from frank insanity (schizophrenia) to attitudes of aloofness and introversion. Although the schizoid personality constitutes an important problem to psychiatrists dealing with maladjusted individuals in clinical practice, it is comparatively rarely a primary concern of the criminologic psychiatrist. The very nature of the schizoid make-up indicates the reason for this. Such persons tend toward introspection rather than action, living in their dereistic thinking and fantasy rather than within the world of reality. The schizoid element, often a precursor of the mental disease schizophrenia, is likely to be expressed in daydreaming and inactivity rather than in active behavior. Nevertheless, schizoid personalities do commit aggressive crimes. In contradistinction to other types of psychopathic offenders, schizoid personalities who commit crime are likely to be more seriously affected in terms of disintegration of their intellectual and emotional life.

In an exposition of the mental mechanisms of schizoid personalities which lead to crime, cases of murder appear most valuable for demonstrating the interreaction between the impulses of the individual and their eventuation in a criminal act. The mental dynamics can be traced in such cases when the inner conflicts in the offender, which give rise to the delusion, become externalized on the victim. Those who have studied murderers with the wish to understand the psychologic meaning of the murder agree that the victim may be a symbolic representative of the murderer's self. The conflict within the schizoid person becomes so intolerable that suicide looms as the only possible solution. Impulses arising from emotional conflicts which point toward self-destruction become distorted in their aim. The original suicidal impulses suddenly change to assaultiveness or actual murder when tendencies toward self-injury are projected onto the victim. Psychologically considered, the resultant killing can be regarded as an attempt at the solution of a conflict within the offender which is unfortunately projected to the object of the persecutory delusions—the victim. A deeper study of the basic psychological conflicts indicates that they are often related to unconscious fear of injury because of sexual guilt. The conscious entertainment of sexual thoughts or feelings stirs up anxieties regarding the individual's right to exercise his physical prerogatives. Anxiety is directly related to fear of injury to the sexual organs, technically castration fear, which arises in response to strong unconscious guilt feelings. The psychopathic or psychotic individual with this sexual conflict projects his castration fears and guilt-directed punishment tendencies to someone in his environment who has, in the offender's mind, come to symbolically represent himself.

The mechanisms which operate in the schizoid personality to cause aggressive crime unfortunately are not apparent until after the crime is committed. However, the mental abnormality of these individuals usually has been previously noted in areas of social maladjustment such as the school, at work, in the lower courts, in social groups or in military organizations. Experience shows that apparently inexplicable brutal crimes which are perpetrated by psychopathic individuals emerge from a matrix of emotional stress produced over a long period of conflict. The following dramatic history provides an example of the psychological movements lying behind the crime of murder perpetrated by an individual in an advanced state of schizoid psychopathy.

The life story of Irwin, age 29, was replete with personal and social maladjustment. He came from a family with a history of physical, mental and social pathology. His maternal genealogy was notable for crime, emotional instability and mental disease. The mother was a deeply religious adherent of a revivalist sect whose fanatical forcing of religion on her son produced strong antagonism. He insisted he was an agnostic. Two brothers had served long penitentiary sentences. The mother and these two sons had been found to be congenitally syphilitic when examined at the time of the offender's first delinquency, when he was twelve. For several years in his youth Irwin worked as a sculptor and was considered to be a "talented" artist. He taught art for several years with considerable success. During this time he complained of insomnia and the inability to concentrate and became a patient in a psychopathic hospital, where he was sometimes depressed and suicidal, more frequently quarrelsome and assaultive. On one occasion he spoke of planning to kill someone so he "would be hung." The patient was diagnosed as a psychopathic personality and released after considerable improvement. Within a few months he was readmitted to the hospital with a self-inflicted laceration at the base of his penis. He explained that castration was part of his plan for sublimating sexual energy into creative channels. "I wanted to be a great sculptor," he explained, "I didn't want anything to do with women. I got my idea from reading Schopenhauer."

For two years the patient was in and out of mental hospitals, where he was notably productive in modeling heads in clay. He spoke of making psychologic experiments to develop his art to full capacity. The central idea was to cure his inferiority feelings through "visualization"; by practicing his technic of visualization daily he would influence his "unconscious" mind and become a great sculptor. As his ideas developed he became more restless and finally evolved a plan of action—suicide through murder. He had become obsessed with the idea of a "universal mind"; he felt he could become a part of it if he could get up enough internal pressure to liberate himself. Self-sacrifice was required to gain sufficient internal pressure to liberate himself from human bonds. Easter Sunday, the day of resurrection, was the day. No one dies in the stage of universal mind; the murderer was immortal. Even if sent to the electric chair, nothing would befall him. Irwin went to the apartment of his chosen victim. He gained entrance and awaited the arrival of the woman he planned to murder. She was the mother of an artist's model of his acquaintance.

On Easter Sunday, a fifty-four-year-old woman, her beautiful twenty-five-year-old daughter and a male boarder were found murdered. The boarder had been killed by an ice pick plunged into his brain, apparently while he slept; each of the women had been strangled on her separate entrance into the apartment. There was no evidence of struggle in the apartment, and from the circumstances it was apparent that the murderer, having gained easy access to a home with which he was familiar, strangled them with ease. The police quickly established that the sculptor, known to be a former boarder in the home of his victims, was the assailant. He eluded the police for two months and was finally recognized by a fellow worker while employed in an Ohio city. He was charged with first-degree murder.

The history of Irwin is that of a slowly progressive schizophrenia. At the age of twelve the patient gave evidence of emotional disturbances and by eighteen he was already elaborating his theory of the development of sexual feeling. His idea of "visualization" was fastened to recognized art forms. Thus the onset of the delusional system was covered by his art activities which received recognition and support. As the self-assurance behind his hopes for an art career began to wane, the prisoner was forced to face his deep feelings of inferiority. Irwin's early attempt at psychologic defense against the recognition of inner inadequacy took the form of faulty rationalization that he could develop artistic visualization beyond that of any other artist. It was at this point that the impulse to destroy himself by mutilation arose. The problem of masturbation with guilt feelings and ensuing ideas of unworthiness had always troubled the patient. The solution that appeared to Irwin was actual castration, destruction of the part of the body which sexual tension utilizes and which he imagined obstructed his artistic achievement. At the same time, renunciation of "fleshly" drives stimulated the construction of an intellectual compensation, which took the form of theories of "visualization." Under the title, "The Art Theory of Robert Irwin," the prisoner wrote:

> Before anything can take form it must first have a mental prototype. Before a sculptor can make a statue he must first get the mental statue in his head: then out of matter—clay, marble or bronze: but we must first understand our own minds and our relation to the Universal Mind. . . . The only way we can ever hope to rise to that higher plain is to develop these fundamental senses for use in that rarified atmosphere. . . . To develop this mental eye . . . you simply sit down every day and practice *visualizing.* . . . The result of such an accomplishment is almost beyond our comprehension . . . everything that ever happened to a man from birth to death is indelibly recorded in the "unconscious" mind that is the "Universal Mind."

But intellectualization was not sufficient to absorb the emotional tension beneath. If he castrated himself, he would appear as a woman, shorn of power, and this weakness he also abhorred. The duality of maleness and femaleness which was struggling in the offender has been noted by others in criminal offenders (Alexander, etc.) as the struggle between basic passive (feminine) impulses and aggressive (masculine) compensations. In Irwin, the rejection by his ego of these weak "female" attributes influenced him to turn his self-destructive impulses to women. The beautiful artist victim was an unconscious symbol for the criminal himself. In the resolution of his conflict, the unconscious wishes for passivity were gratified by the substitution of murder for suicide, while aggressive impulses were openly expressed.

THE AGGRESSIVE PSYCHOPATH

Crimes such as murder and serious assaults attributable to clearly delimited psychological reactions suggest a consideration of aggressive crimes which are not based on the symbolic expression of strong emotional drives. Offenders involved in such nonsymbolic crimes fall into the class of Aggressive Psychopaths. This group of individuals appears to be endowed with neuromuscular bodily organizations of a nature which impels them spontaneously toward physical violence on inadequate provocation. Coincidentally, their emotional equipment is insensitive, and their ethical standards are blunted to a degree which justifies their being included under the diagnosis of psychopathic personality. Conventionally these individuals are classed as Emotionally Unstable Psychopaths, Explosively Aggressive Psychopaths or, more dramatically, as "enemies of society." Known also at one time as Criminal Psychopaths, these individuals display an attitude of social aggression beyond what is considered normal in our competitive world. It is an attitude that functions continuously and hence can be regarded as a primary type of aggression. Professional assassins, gangsters and racketeers belong in this category.

The attempt to analyze the internal emotional life of the aggressive psychopath meets with little success. Their attitudes are fixed; the law, they feel, will exact its toll from them as they have exacted theirs from society. Any discussion aimed at an understanding of the psychological processes in such an individual, in the face of the state's punishment by death or long imprisonment, is regarded as naive. Psychological analysis is met as an intrusion upon a closed circuit accepted by both law and lawbreakers. One meets the accepted attitude among professional killers that the supreme crime among men is answered by death. Paid killers waive their guilt feelings toward their victims before the offense is completed. Their attitude toward the law and their crime is fixed in a balance between accepted guilt and murderous impulses. It is noteworthy that the earliest attempts to understand the aggressive psychopath tacitly considered feeble-mindedness to be a common denominator. Since Dr. Glueck's study of the Sing Sing prisoners, the factors of temperament, emotional and personality organizations were regarded equally as important as mental defects in the cause of violent crime. Although there are aggressive defectives who have all the emotional coldness of the professional murderer, their social immaturity proves to be a more important factor than their mental deficiency.

Benny V., a twenty-year-old hoodlum with a record of four previous arrests and several convictions, was convicted of first-degree murder after he and two other criminals strangled a prosperous citizen while stealing sixteen dollars in currency and personal jewelry. The defendant's responses to test questions were vague; his I.Q. was 68, indicating a mental level of high-grade moron. He was emotionally excitable, aggressive and ruthless in attitude, immature in his emotional and social concepts and completely egocentric without the capacity for mature social judgment.

Discussion of the aggressive psychopath leads to a consideration of individuals such as professional thieves, racketeers and labor union racketeers, whose aggressive acts are not perpetrated through personal use of physical violence but by organized bands under their control. The racketeer is basically an aggressive psychopath, influenced by the sociologic atmosphere which nurtured racketeering in the third and fourth decade of the present century. Racketeering is a form of extortion, and its special character arises from the similarity between the organization and methods of rackets and the form and method of governmental control of commercial enterprise. In providing "protection" or organizational service to various industries for huge sums of money, racketeers encroach upon the function of government, which alone has the right to regulate and tax industrial enterprises.

The organization of a racketeering gang parallels that of a governmental agency. At the head of the group is a leader chosen for his resourcefulness, political connections and organizing ability. Each member of the group is delegated to a specific task, while strategy and planning are left to the leader. Records are kept, territories delimited and the payments collected regularly. Apart from the practical value of the organization with its division of labor, a psychological reaction which perpetuates self-deception arises in racketeers from the assumption of this form of organization. The racketeer cannot perceive that he has only seemingly forced his primary aggression into a socially acceptable mold; he is aware merely of the external similarity between approved methods of conducting business and his organizational technic. The leader of such organized groups offers the specious argument for racket control by pointing, as an example, to the confusion surrounding the liquor industry during the Prohibition era. The racketeer explains his activities on the grounds that he organizes industry for the betterment of the consumer and the worker in that industry. The fact of usurpation of the governmental function of taxation for protection is veiled by the implication of service rendered. Labor union racketeers likewise righteously maintain that their exertions served large numbers of inarticulate individuals who would otherwise be victimized.

Examination of this group of men shows them to be flatly realistic persons, without visibly unsatisfied drives and without psychological conflicts. The case of Tucker, sentenced to thirty years in a state prison for operating a compulsory prostitution ring, illustrates this aspect of racketeering. Tucker developed the business of supplying prostitutes to brothels in eastern metropolitan cities in a scheme to allow him to extort enormous sums of money. His organization improved methods of supply and distribution of women, provided regular medical inspections for venereal disease, arranged for legal counsel and bail-bonding services for those arrested by the police. The men on Tucker's payroll included agents for booking business, lawyers, gunmen for the elimination of complaints and henchmen covering any services required. Prior to his conviction for compulsory prostitution, Tucker had a long police record involving various types of felony offenses. The examination of the prisoner disclosed a well-poised individual, concerned only with gratification of his own wishes. Apparent shrewdness and enterprise were combined with a complete identification with an asocial viewpoint. Neither emotional instability nor impetuousness was observed in his personality pattern.

The labor union racketeer presents a less obvious criminal identification. He demonstrates a sanctimonious, moral attitude toward his union members which coexists with opportunism and the wish for personal gain. It is an interesting commentary that many union "czars" who utilize their position for personal gain are voted complete confidence by their constituency. Underneath the professed devotion to the ideals of betterment for workers is a thinly disguised contempt for the masses whose economic destinies he controls. The union racketeer, in his own defense, stresses the right to fight for economic and social advantages which he considers consonant with the philosophy of American individualism. But while he performs lip service to commonly held ideals of democracy, he gives rein to his contempt for people by using his position of trust to extract payment from those he is championing. The reality considerations surrounding the fight for economic independence become a rationalization for the racketeer's own primary interest in depredation. The confusion of issues between the American privilege, the tradition of struggle for economic security, and the disregard of legal restrictions to personal gain can be plainly seen in racketeers who invade trade union activities from a lifelong association with the underworld. Such a one was Lepke Buchalter, who was in constant association with criminals until he gained ascendancy over a union membership. Lepke seized leadership of the crucial teamsters' union and hence controlled the immense activities of the fur and garment industries in New York City. He brought gorilla tactics to his task of levying tribute from the workers and employers. The technic, borrowed from gangsterdom, involved supplying strikebreakers for the employers at the same time that he extracted payment for "protection" from the union members. Extortions by Lepke and his criminal associates constituted the introduction of a blatantly larcenous spirit into trade unions where an element of idealism had always been implied. Criminal practice on the part of the racketeer rests on the psychological basis of contempt for other individuals. This is a controlling factor, whether industry-wide extortion was accompanied by the introduction of underworld tactics or by quasi-political control of the union constituency. In the case of the thug who infiltrated labor union fields, his contempt was scarcely hidden. With the labor union leader who utilized his position of trust to extract payments, contempt was buried beneath a hypocritical attitude of idealism.

The political implications of union racketeering lead to a consideration of politically active individuals who acted as go-betweens for organized rackets and judicial or other governmental officials. Such persons exploited legitimate pressure groups or political clubs in order to facilitate illegal enterprises or to soften the restrictions of the law on racketeers. These individuals accepted the philosophy and practice of spoils and patronage and utilized pressure tactics and political power on elected officials to gain advantages for a special group. The impulse which moves political racketeers to try to modify laws and regulations in favor of illegal groups is allied to the impulse to steal from a powerful, impersonal government, a tendency observed also among normal individuals. For that reason the political go-betweens are not psychopathic in the sense which has been described in this chapter. The psychology of politically affiliated racketeers is the psychology of bad government. For obscured in the traditional use of political favoritism is the same element of contempt for the people and the same disregard of idealism that exists among the more blatant union racketeers. These tendencies are so heavily veiled in the individual as to appear, on casual view, to be part of a balanced personality. The conviction of sincerity observed in these individuals, a defensive mechanism erected against an inner perception of the social meaning of their beliefs, gives plausibility to this view. The basic asocial psychological orientation of political racketeers will be evident in the following case.

A mature, intelligent man of sixty-two, for many years a political leader and member of a nationally known political organization, was convicted of extortion and bribery of certain judges, coercion of police and conspiracy in aiding an illegal lottery. Y. had been a prominent and respected citizen for many years. He was a leading figure in his community and a power behind its political life. Y.'s generosity was unquestioned, and many of his political activities resulted in more gain for those who supported him than for himself. The ability to help others through the use of political friendships and pressure provided deep satisfaction to his ego. The social setting and the political tradition in which Y. grew up provided rationalization for a feeling of righteousness that arose when his influence helped friends. The fact that it impeded good government did not appear to be a consideration sufficiently strong to oppose traditional political thinking. The environment in which the offender received his cultural nourishment accepted as praiseworthy the tacit usurpation of the position of public benefactor by a leader or by a political party in the name of the spoils system.

Although the dishonest politician can be distinctly differentiated from the racketeer and extortionist, there are elements suggestive of the aggressive psychopath in all three groups. The significance of this extension of a psychopathic attitude is apparent in the relation between the personality of the political boss and his political philosophy. The philosophy behind the spoils system allows the politician to control to some degree the processes of government by arranging appointments of officials or influencing their decisions. The aggressive tendencies of the politician, which demand ever greater and greater power, are likewise nourished by this system. The corollary attitude of contempt for the masses, uncovered in our discussion of the psychology of racketeers, is also gratified by the practice of the spoils system. Because political patronage implies contempt for those members of the public who implicitly accept the processes of government and place their trust in democratic forms, the system coincides with the particular personality distortion in the political boss. By the same token, illegitimate pressure exerted on government officials for special advantage implies an inner derision at the efforts for good government that are constantly being exerted by law-abiding citizens. The unconscious derision of social ideals, characteristic of the aggressive psychopathic personality, infiltrates into government through the activities of corrupt political bossism to effect a slow process of deterioration. It is at this point that psychopathic behavior constitutes another danger to social institutions.

ALCOHOL, DRUGS AND THE AGGRESSIVE PSYCHOPATH

Alcoholism generally has been considered to be the immediate cause of much violent crime. The sum total of present-day clinical experience indicates clearly that alcoholism in crime is more directly related to the repressed aggressive tendencies of the user's personality than to any other factor. A study of the mechanism by which alcoholism stimulates aggression in nonpsychopathic individuals sheds light on the psychological currents in the aggressive psychopath who more frequently expresses his violence without the use of alcohol.

Alcoholism influences aggressive impulses through narcotization of conscious control in the individual. A vital factor in the release of inhibitions is related to the social value placed on aggression. It is a matter of common observation that drinking stimulates an individual's need for prestige to the point where open boasting is commonplace in social gatherings. Normally the egocentric position of the alcohol imbiber is dismissed as a harmless social by-product, but, among men where drinking occurs in a male environment, the spirit of bravado may be a potent factor in assault cases. In the social code of culturally limited groups, boasting of physical power is a measure of masculinity and has a distinct social prestige value. The more intoxicated the boasting individual, who is reacting to his own feeling of inferiority, the stronger is the social value he places on his claims to physical prowess. This inverted attitude, however, seems quite natural to the drinker and those in his environment. Hence, the emergence of motor patterns which may result in physical assault is not an uncommon concomitant of drinking. Alcoholism alters the social environment for the drinker so that a new and otherwise suppressed attitude toward aggressive violence rises to the surface. The new attitude is the effective force in releasing aggressive impulses or rendering them invulnerable to the critical and inhibitory action of the ego. This is the significant aspect of the accepted statement that alcohol releases inhibitions and the control of aggressive impulses.

Alcoholism itself has no specific affinity for aggressive impulses but does exert an influence on inferiority reactions in the individual by means of compensatory attitudes of aggression. In addition to the altered social values placed upon aggression by a person who is under the influence of alcohol, one further element in the total reaction can be observed. Alcohol allows the emergence of whatever latent homosexual impulses exist in an individual. The stimulation of deep homosexual impulses by alcohol causes a reaction characterized by the struggle of the ego to keep the homosexual component from view. This reaction takes the form of anger which becomes outwardly expressed by an assault on a drinking companion. The individual cannot tolerate awareness of his own unconscious homosexual impulses, made manifest by drinking. The automatic repression of such impulses results in their exploding in an immediately aggressive act against the individual who may be the homosexual love object. Many cases of assault or murder committed under the influence of alcohol are based upon this mechanism.

Analysis of an actual situation revealed the operation of these trends in a man whose common practice was to berate his drinking companions with epithets of a homosexual nature. On one occasion a recipient of these epithets, who ordinarily did not resent the offender, protested the insult. The argument led to blows and the fight resulted in death for the victim who had protested. Examination showed that the homosexual epithets delivered in jest by the offender were in reaction to his perception of homosexual inclinations toward his fellow tippler. The offender, unable to tolerate the threatened exposure of his socially condemned impulses, assaulted the victim, who, he imagined, perceived the true nature of his sexual feelings. Support for this explanation is provided by numerous instances where alcoholic belligerency, including that which ends in assault or manslaughter, was preceded by an affectionate attitude toward the victim on the part of the offender.

It has been generally held that addiction to narcotic drugs, opium, morphine and cocaine plays a definite role in aggressive crime. Recently marihuana has been considered to belong to this category of drugs which stimulate violent crime in confirmed users. These drugs have a popular, if not scientific, reputation for causing the emergence of the most reprehensible impulses in calloused, criminalistic individuals. However, as studies of of personalities of criminals accumulated, authorities agreed on the basic principle that narcotic drugs and alcohol act to remove inhibitions or to deaden the ethical sense of individuals already predisposed to antisocial acts by virtue of their psychopathic make-up. Experience with many hundreds of major criminals has corroborated the fact that a basic psychopathic make-up is of overwhelmingly greater importance in the causation of violent crime than is the narcotic drug itself. For example, a study by Rodgers and the author of 8,280 major naval offenders during the war years showed only 0.0048 per cent of the total unselected group to be users of marihuana. It further demonstrated no significant causal relationship between the use of marihuana and aggressive crime, either in the offenders' previous civilian convictions or in their present naval offenses. Drug addiction and crime can be shown to have almost no cause and effect relationship when compared with the influence of the criminal's personality and his antisocial impulses. An example of the significance of the underlying personality in a vicious crime is illustrated in the case of a drug addict of thirty-five who hacked his roommate, also a drug user, to death and stuffed the body into a trunk. The offender claimed in his defense that he had been seduced into marihuana addiction by the deceased and hence claimed the drug to be the cause of his crime. Careful study, however, demonstrated clear evidences of homosexual jealousy in the relationship between the victim and offender which proved to have been the motive force behind the murder.

Another explanation for uncontrolled explosive aggression among psychopaths has involved epilepsy. From time immemorial epilepsy, because of its spectacular symptoms, has been naturally looked upon as a disease likely to be associated with unpredictable behavior. In antiquity, epilepsy was called the *sacre morbus* (sacred disease), the implication being that the sufferer had some tie with the supernatural. The psychological effect on the observer of the epileptic convulsion, and the inexplicable nature of other epileptic phenomena such as the epileptic trance (fugue) states, during which a few brutal offenses were known to have occured, impressed physicians with the possible connection between violent crime and this disease. It was a clinical axiom for neuropsychiatrists of the nineteenth century to search for hidden forms of epilepsy as causes of heinous assault. In recent years this tendency has decreased, since with the aid of modern neurologic diagnosis and the electro-encephalograph, a more certain diagnosis of epilepsy or epileptic predisposition can be made. The imputation that hidden epilepsy, manifested in fugue states, or postepileptic automatic furor, is the cause of otherwise inexplicable violence, carries less validity at the present time.

The results of a survey of the frequency of clinically diagnosed epilepsy among criminals tend to deny the importance of this disease in violent criminal acts. Of 35,648 unselected felony offenders observed * over a period of nine years, no more than 0.66 per cent were diagnosed as epileptics, epileptic psychoses or epileptoid personalities. The cases studied comprised all types of major crimes, including assaults and murder, and represented the total number of persons convicted of major crimes in New York County for the years from 1932 to 1940, inclusive. The findings suggest, therefore, that epilepsy is not a numerically vital factor in major crime nor a basic factor in those convicted of aggressive offenses.

At the present state of our knowledge, the genesis of the aggressive, explosive type of psychopath is obscure. The possibility exists that this primarily aggressive individual has some sort of specific predisposition to assaultiveness in his neural organization, the nature of which is unknown, in addition to the social and psychological factors already discussed. One suggestive analogy is in the similarity between the aggressive psychopath and the hyperactive child in whom hyperkinesis seems organically determined as the result of inflammation of the brain (chronic encephalitis). Further evidence about the physiologic factor in aggressive individuals is being discovered through the use of the electro-encephalograph. Although this work is as yet incomplete, some investigators have found evidence of abnormal cerebral electroactivity in a majority of a group of delinquent boys whose brain waves were studied. Similarly, in a group of behavior problem children, a majority showed cortical rhythm irregularity in the electro-encephalogram recordings.

THE PSYCHOPATHIC SWINDLER

The term swindling is loosely used to denote crimes of fraud. The distinctive character of fraud involving swindling depends on the victim's unawareness of the loss he faces until the crime has become an accomplished fact. In a strict sense, swindling is not a statutory crime. It is a technic

* Bellevue Psychiatric Hospital and the Psychiatric Clinic of the Court of General Sessions, New York.

employed in certain kinds of larceny which may range from swindling schemes in stock market manipulations to bigamous marriages contracted with the hidden purpose of gaining control of money or property. The means by which the fraud is accomplished involves deception on the part of the swindler to the extent of giving an impression of legitimacy to the enterprises with which the victim becomes involved. The deception permits the victim to become associated unwittingly with an enterprise the legitimacy of which is accepted without question. Technical perfection in swindling requires the complete mastery of trickery and lying as elements of the criminal's personality make-up. The psychopathic swindler has developed the habit of prevarication and deception to the point where these psychopathic features are an integral part and a constant feature of his behavior pattern. His use of fabrications is so skillful that the listener cannot distinguish the statements presented from truth or the undertaking proposed from honest business. The degree to which pathologic lying tendencies are integrated into the swindler's character determines his success in his fraudulent activities. Thus the loose use of the term swindling by the layman includes the prominent characteristics of the swindler's personality. Swindling, as a commonly understood term, correctly divines the essential basic abnormality of the pathologic swindler's make-up. Although the swindler easily deceives his unsuspecting victim, he readily reveals his psychopathic character upon psychiatric examination.

The swindler's bearing is marked by unctuousness of manner and his speech by fluency and facility. This impression is contributed in part by his persistent pattern of pathologic lying and in part by his passive make-up. In considering the psychological background of the swindler, an analogy between the pathologic liar of childhood and the adult swindler suggests itself. In the child, tendencies to fabricate are recognized as normal components of the active fantasy of childhood. Where they are exaggerated to the degree that every question is answered automatically by a lie, the child is regarded as a pathologic liar. However, the analogy between the child's development of pathologic lying and that which is a part of the technic of the adult swindler cannot be consistently maintained. Many swindlers prove on examination to have no history of pathologic lying in their early development. Further, pathologic liars among children do not necessarily evolve into swindlers in their adult years. Case histories of child pathologic liars show that the trait is present as a carry-over in unstable adult psychopaths who never adopt criminal practices in any way akin to swindling. Nevertheless, the emotional needs and dissatisfactions which drive children into pathologic lying have a similar psychological basis, although expressed in different clinical forms, to that uncovered by analysis of the adult swindler psychopath. In the adult psychopathic liar, his tendency to fabricate is dovetailed with unconscious elements of his personality. As shall be seen in the case material, these unconscious tendencies are of sadomasochistic character and represent a serious distortion of personality structure.

Within the group of swindlers a psychological differentiation can be made between those whose lies and misrepresentations are for self-aggrandizements (as in the offense of impersonating an officer) and those who are primarily interested in money (as in the confidence game). For the former, social position, gaudy uniforms, high-sounding titles and the like represent the chief source of gratification. The psychological mechanisms here are not particularly difficult to follow. Karl Abraham found, in analyzing the case of an impostor in the German army, that grandiosity developed from deprivation of love in childhood. He termed the mechanism a narcissistic libidinal regression, indicating that the impostor was forced by his emotionally starved childhood to seek gratification in an imposing military title. Such persons lie habitually and fabricate their background, education and family connections in order to convince themselves and others of the reality of their fantasies. They are extremely self-protective, even becoming paranoid under examination. For these men, being known as a physician or a nobleman is sufficient recompense; their gratification resides in living the part which they portray. An illustrative case may be cited.

M. S., a Swiss of forty-seven, was brought before the court on a charge of forgery of a check. Although S. had a desultory education, he managed to hold many medical positions of trust in various parts of this country. His record included several convictions for fraud in Germany, three convictions in this country for practicing medicine without a license (one while he was employed as a physician in a large city health department), an unwarranted position as psychologist in a governmental project and several penitentiary sentences for minor larcenies. He was a man of superior intelligence, with a considerable smattering of psychiatric knowledge, glib in speech and suave in manner. Careful check of his activities indicated that almost all his activities for most of his adult life were guided by his inveterate lying. M. S. invented stories about his education at leading universities in Germany, his nationality, his war experiences, including several miraculous escapes, court martial for treason, etc., and his medical education. On the claim of being a psychiatrist he once mixed freely at a psychiatric congress. All through the period of examination and observation he showed marked instability, excitement and distinct paranoid tendencies when his record and accomplishments were questioned. After a time he admitted that all his claims to having been a physician were fraudulent and that the diplomas and papers he presented were forged. The object of a lifetime of pathologic lying and deception in this individual was the achievement of high position and the inner gratification derived from this spurious achievement.

Self-elevating tendencies, disregard of the thinness of deception and feelings of invincibility and infallibility characterize the swindler psychologically. No victim, he feels, can see through his machinations. This is traditionally conceded to be due to the overwhelming egotism of the swindler, but there is another factor often overlooked which constitutes the pivotal point in the swindle relationship, namely, the emotional state of the victim. The emotional relationship brought into existence between victim and operator, with its psychological effect on the victim, is the source of the swindler's success. The feeling of infallibility in the swindler feeds upon his ability to understand and influence the victim's psychology. For example, in many cases involving wildcat schemes promising high returns, the very audacity of the swindler and his implied invincibility are sufficient to remove incredulity in the avaricious victim.

The swindler utilizes several tricks in his technic which have the function of impressing his apparent invincibility on the victim. The feeling of infallibility, which grows out of the swindler's inner emotional needs and has become an integral part of his personality, is accepted by the victim. At the same time, the study of the swindler's victims reveals the presence of similar unconscious tendencies within themselves, namely, the wish for unlimited bounty and, second, the feeling of personal infallibility. The swindler is aware of these deeper psychologic currents in his victim and utilizes them in his approach. The technic of swindling features elements of secrecy, mystery or intricacy which befuddle the victim by blinding his judgment and allowing his unconscious wishes to emerge. It is for this reason that the various types of larceny by trick require glib conversation on the part of the offender or depend upon the detailed explanation of an intricate industrial transaction. A nice example of the use of mystery to subdue the victim's judgment is provided in the common switch-game swindles executed by gypsies. In such instances, the gypsy fortuneteller gives back a package which allegedly contains double the amount of money originally entrusted to the gypsy but which was "switched" for a package containing worthless paper. Why do people still succumb to such blatant trickery? It is because magic and the occult power to perform miracles are projected to the gypsy by the victim's unconscious wishes. The aura of romance with which the world invests the gypsy eases the way for indulgence of deeply buried fantasies by the victim.

There is another series of emotional tendencies brought into play by the swindling technic. Sexual feelings, particularly of perverse or homosexual order, are often stimulated in order to blind the victim's judgment prior to being defrauded. On the pretext of witnessing or becoming a party to some sexual irregularity, the victim may be lured to a hotel room where a card game in which he is eventually cheated is in progress. The swindler who builds up sexual tension in his victim astutely detects in his victim an interest in homosexuality or other sexual perversion. Further, the swindler is aware of the social meaning of sexual deviation. Abnormal sexuality is commonly interpreted as a species of moral inferiority, and society maintains an attitude of disdain for one who professes interest in homosexuality. The clever swindler is cognizant of this general attitude and utilizes that portion of it which calls forth a feeling of mastery in the victim, who will presumably encounter some variety of sexual perversion. The accent on sexual perversion in this variety of confidence game represents psychological bait held out to the prospective victim. The opportunity provided the victim to build up feelings of social mastery allows the swindler to bring his deceptive tactics skillfully into play.

This stress of sexuality in certain varieties of swindle games is not accidental. It is part of the complex unconscious relationship brought into being by the swindle. The criminal, with his knowledge of victim psychology, expects to maintain his hold on the victim by apparently socially debasing himself. At the same time, unconscious elements in the offender's personality force him to adopt the submissive position, which he regards only as a maneuver in his skillful handling of the swindle. While the offender consciously perceives the weakness in the victim's emotions, unconscious masochistic elements in his own personality play a role of which he is not aware. The strategy of the total swindle relationship is that of a shrewd use of victim psychology by the criminal and is combined with the interplay of the unconscious elements in both parties to the fraud. In every swindle this intricate interreaction can be demonstrated in the victim as well as in the swindler. The latter, however, shows the psychological disturbances to a degree which makes this demonstration clearly perceptible.

Swindlers and pathologic liars show deviations in their sexual life. In routine examination of criminal psychopaths it was found that more than half of the swindlers recorded dimunition of heterosexual impulses. Sexual impotence, diminished libido accompanied by little psychosexual satisfaction, marriages for convenience or for money and frequent change of sexual partners were common findings. Some swindlers had feminine or homosexual tendencies in their dress and manner. The passivity of the swindler serves his emotional needs as well as his criminal projects. The question may be put: What is the crime value of a disturbed psychosexuality among swindlers? Is there a dynamic significance in the common technic of the swindler in which he assumes the masochistic or submissive role in the swindler-victim relationship? The indications are that the adoption of a passive role toward the victim enables the swindler to overcome the former. Thus it may be said that the strength of the swindler lies in his weakness. Analysis of a case of a swindler suggests that taking something from the victim is an unconscious re-enactment of an older pattern of taking something from the parent. This particular reaction to the earlier struggle against parental dominance takes the form of retaliation in the unexpected form of submissiveness and trickery.

The case of Francis P., convicted of grand larceny on six counts, illustrates the psychodynamic elements in the swindler. At the age of twenty-six, a successful statistician and securities salesman, Francis joined a group who operated an international money-pool subscribed to by German-Americans and calculated to effect a devaluation of the French franc. The appeal to the patriotic bias of the subscribers received impetus from the rising tide of National Socialism in Germany at that time. Writing to influential German-Americans all over the country, the operators of the pool promised a high rate of interest to subscribers. Within a short time funds for the purchase of French francs poured in. People literally begged the backers of the pool to take their money. Over a period of two years the syndicate widened its lure from the promise of a monthly rate of interest of eight per cent to plans for marketing a machine which would transmute base metals into gold. During this time Francis P. directed the fraud from a key position. Of the money which flooded in, Francis spent some on lavish living; the rest he paid back in interest to other subscibers. Finally the offender was indicted for misappropriation of a large sum of money on the complaints of six of his victims.

On examination the offender proved to be a man of superior intelligence, suave in address and forceful in speech. His mood was often elated during interviews. He was fastidious in dress, his clothes stylish and carefully cared for. His personal problems were in the foreground in his conversation. Early in adult life marital difficulties had made their appearance. A few years before the offense for which he was being examined he was arrested for bigamy, having married a radio singer, A., without legally terminating a marriage of ten years. He had neglected his first wife since he became engaged in the stock swindle. After he had promised marriage to A., he produced spurious divorce papers, which were sufficient to erase her doubts.

During the period preparatory to their marriage he caused her considerable inconvenience, ordering house furnishing for which he paid with worthless checks. Following the marriage, a charge of bigamy was brought. He was given a sentence of five years but was placed on probation. During his probationary period he made a poor adjustment, continued to get into difficulties, neglected his family, passed bad checks and finally was brought to court on the larceny charge. He had been born in a small town in the Midwest, and his parents were rigid church people, the father being a Fundamentalist minister. The parents were frequently involved in church work, and he was relatively neglected. He attended a small denominational college where he was valedictorian for his class, and later took sporadic courses at a university. Francis' parents insisted that he become a minister, but he rebelled against adherence to the Fundamentalist tenets. The restrictive religious atmosphere at home irked him. Although he achieved no degree at the university, his intellectual interests were wide: history, philosophy, law, art and music. Within a few years he had become a free-lance lecturer, an authority on Wagnerian operas, made a great deal of his interest in philosophy and spent much time in libraries and lecturing, often without pay. For several years he held teaching positions in high schools and once in a small college in the Midwest where he was forced to resign because of affairs with female students. He lost two positions where he taught sociology and psychology because of his "utter financial irresponsibility." He frequently passed bad checks, many of which his father covered.

The sexual life of the offender was clearly pathologic. At eight or nine years of age he practised manual masturbation with boys and girls. With one of these boys he continued this activity into adult life. Heterosexual life began after college. In it he demanded that his partner take the lead in all aspects of the sexual act. Otherwise he only cared to manipulate his partner manually. It was particularly exciting for him if his partner writhed in pain. He had a homosexual affair with a man during the period from his fifteenth to seventeenth years and with the same man from twenty-two to twenty-six years of age. Later, when he was making money from stock schemes, he spent a great deal of money in night clubs with women who did his bidding. Francis looked upon manual manipulation as a more esthetic and less primitive form of sex activity than normal intercourse. He often rationalized this weakness by saying that his intellectual pursuits destroyed his sexual libido. He left his first wife because he stated he was unsatisfied sexually. Both wives of the offender concurred that he did not care for the usual sexual relationship. When the first wife became pregnant, he flew into a rage, claiming the pregnancy was impossible.

Because of the depth of the sexual psychopathology, a psychoanalytically orientated study * was undertaken. The patient was free in his productions. He regarded his father as a cruel, stern, harsh man. Most deeply he resented his father's callous treatment of mendicants. The patient felt that his mother was against him. He could not use his mother as a confidante since any confession to her was invariably repeated to his father and led to subsequent punishment. He was ashamed to walk with his mother in the street as a child because she had a goiter and he fantasied that the goiter was full of some kind of poison and would burst and spray people around her with poison. An important source of his resentment was the fact that both parents neglected him during his boyhood because of their church activities. This meant many lonesome afternoons and evenings for him. Toward his mother Francis maintained a special relationship. He was never friendly with her because she resented his kissing or hugging her. Later in life, when she became ill, he found it difficult to be solicitous about the illness. He was not entirely sure he wanted her to get well. There had always been a feeling of strangeness between his mother and himself. He frequently thought of and dreamed of her as dead. She would often punish him as a child by keeping him without food. Despite his aggressive feelings toward his mother, it was toward his father that his hostility was openly expressed. As a child he entertained many fantasies of an aggressive and sexual nature. His play as a child frequently involved a boy who was about to be executed. He was always the executioner. Another of his childhood pleasures was to pay another boy to beat an "enemy" and to watch from some vantage point. He had "blacklists" of people on whom he would someday take revenge. While fantasying executions, he experienced sexual excitement. Once he recalled getting sexually excited as a boy when he saw a moving picture in which a man was being hanged.

These aggressive fantasies continued throughout his adulthood. He would often picture himself about to be killed by hanging or leaping in front of a train, when he would actually feel his arms or legs being severed from his body. While walking on the street, he would picture the sexual organ of some man being cut off, with blood running down. At the same time he would feel his own genitals shrinking or being cut off. He would also visualize cutting off the breasts of women, cutting off their heads or ripping open their abdomens with a hooked instrument. These fantasies were vivid and accompanied by anxiety. Often they would terminate as he saw himself about to be executed for the murder, making a final speech from

* In conjunction with Dr. Sylvan Keiser, New York, N. Y.

the execution platform. His dreams were full of castration fears and guilt feeling for attempted sexual contacts.

The alternation between masochistic and sadistic attitudes was obvious. The patient's ambivalent attitude was expressed toward women predominantly, as the following dream indicates: "I am master of a terrible land of ferocious men. I direct the torture of women captives. Women are tied to a pole and javelins are thrown at their stomachs, heads and breasts." The sadistic attitude toward women, frequently observed in his sexual relations with his wives as well as in his dreams, represented an unconscious wish to destroy them. At the same time Francis' dream life showed a strong fear that women would destroy his virility by enveloping him: he would be crushed, mutilated, emasculated. In the dream he is the omnipotent infant, paying them back by being "master of a land of ferocious men." Sexuality meant punishment and not pleasure to him. Early Oedipus trends apparently lay behind this material, but direct proof was not uncovered in the associations. The offender's castration anxieties were probably the basis for his desultory and ungratified sexuality. Francis' attitude of distrust and hostility to the father and his feeling of emotional coldness toward the mother were direct, conscious expressions of his ambivalent tendencies toward both parents.

The psychological analysis of this case showed a neurotic individual whose emotional conflicts and repressed aggression were expressed in terms of swindling behavior and perverse sexual practices. His strong fear of bodily injury, a derivative of castration anxiety, was projected upon women. Thus he wished to injure and belittle them through denial of sexual gratification, by perversion and by bigamous marriage. At the same time there was a strong desire to excel the father, whose domination he felt as a child. His oratory and teaching, intellectual strivings and effusive manner were probably manifestations of unconscious aggression against the parent. A large number of the victims of his swindling activities were older persons who were countrymen of his father and associated with him in social organizations. The swindling technic for this offender served both unconscious purposes: retaliation against the parents through the utilization of trickery and gratification of his passive, masochistic tendencies.

The case detailed above demonstrates the powerful influence on total behavior exerted by the operation of unresolved sadomasochistic components in the swindler's personality. In seducing his victims in order to belittle them, the swindler reflexly reassures himself with further proof of his own omnipotence. The need for bolstering his ego by entertaining omnipotence feelings represents a carry-over from the infantile period of life, when masochistic fantasies toward the father were actively operative. Perverse sexual impulses which followed in the wake of active sadomasochism predominate in the resulting personality organization of the adult psychopathic swindler and subtly direct his criminal activity.

SEXUAL PSYCHOPATHY

Study of the swindler psychopath has demonstrated that the profound disturbance of his psychosexual organization is represented in nonsexual misbehavior. On the other hand, in the sexual psychopath, who also suffers from serious distortion of his sexual impulses, the abnormality is expressed directly in the form of sexual crime. The swindler has amalgamated his psychological problems into a socially presentable address: the sexual psychopath gratifies his impulses in a socially abhorrent manner. The highly developed ego-organization of the swindler allows a more successful repression of abnormal impulses. But in the sexual psychopath, the need exists for immediate gratification of perverse impulses. The latter, struggling with the restrictions of social convention, finally discards his inhibitions and succumbs to his urges. The outward result of this conflict is the gratification of abnormal erotic impulses in sexual practices which are contrary to law and mores.

In contrasting the swindler and the sexual psychopath, the tremendous variation in the social significance of their characteristic crimes becomes evident. From the point of view of society, direct sexual gratification is more onerous than substitutive gratification, as practiced by the swindler. Because perversions of the erotic life are frowned on by society, the sexual psychopath is under greater social pressure than is the swindler. The former's guilt reactions are stronger, he suffers more from the pressure of his conscience (super-ego) and from society's contempt. The abnormal expression of the sexual impulses has always been looked upon with disgust and horror by our civilization. Condemnation and fear are the constant public attitudes toward sexual offenders.

Reflections of the universal feeling of abhorrence toward sexual perverts can be observed in the criminal law also. There is an observable impatience toward sexual offenses written into the law, as if the abnormal sexual impulse was too repulsive to be objectively delineated. Legal and medical descriptions of the phenomenology of sex crime do not coincide. In the crime of assault, for example, law and medicine can agree that aggressive behavior and assault have in fact the same impulse and the same result. In sex cases, no such unanimity occurs; the impulse does not always coincide with the offense as denominated by the law. There is a conflict between delineation of sexual offenses in the Penal Code and the sexologic or psychological descriptions thereof employed by the psychiatrist. Thus, incest in most states is not treated as a special problem; such offenders are indicted for rape or assault. Clearly, incest, which breaks down century-old taboos, has a deeper psychological significance as far as the offender is concerned that has either statutory or forceful rape. Again, under the indictment of Impairing the Morals of a Minor, several widely differing psychological motives are included under one* statutory crime: anal intercourse with girls under ten, voyeurism, dice-playing, sex play with boys through masturbation, etc.

Sexual psychopaths, as a composite group in society, react to this implied disdain in the law and contempt among the public. The first barrier met in attempting to study or examine sexual criminals is the defensive attitude of the sexual offender. Fear of public censure is more deeply rooted in this type of offender than in any other. They regard the psychiatrist, no less than the judge, as part of the disapproving environment which pursues the sexual pervert wherever he turns. Hence, defense through denial is characteristic of the sexual offender. Sometimes denial of the offense assumes paranoid proportions, as in the case of one defendant who insisted that an enemy of his sent small children to him for the purpose of enticing him into sex play with them. Frequently such individuals assume a sanctimonious, pretentious air, decrying any but heterosexual intercourse as proper. Few look upon their offenses as an outgrowth of their own maladjustment. Rather, they see in victims aggressive, offensive persons who force them into abnormal acts. Only occasionally can prisoners be found who readily admit the offense and demonstrate some degree of insight regarding their perverse sexuality. More often the reactions against their sexual urges take the form of moral preachment. A man of sixty-six, arrested for sexual play with children, complained, "They ought to have separate beaches for men and women. Wearing shorts for girls is like advertising. They (girls) are worse than any criminal for the public. You can't help blushing when you are in their presence."

This group of criminals demonstrates the strength of ego defenses of offenders toward their own psychological abnormality. Criminals convicted of assault, murder or larceny will discuss their inner reactions with relative emotional calm, but the sexual criminal meets any investigation of his feelings with unassailable defensiveness. The taboos ingrained in public attitudes toward perverse sexual impulses influence the individual sex offender to the point of making the subject anathema for him. Actually

* Penal Code, New York.

the feelings against sexual perversion are almost impregnable in the minds of court and prison officials, and the sex criminal has the experience of bitter reality to support him in his defensive attitude.

Society's attitude of repugnance toward perverse sexual impulses, as contrasted with heterosexual ones, apparently has always been reflected in the law. Two examples may be given in illustration, selected because in their historical perspective they graphically embody the attitudes under discussion. Compare the account of a projected rape in early Colonial days taken from the first criminal records extant in the United States in Eastville, Virginia, on Cape Charles (1634), with the court record of a case of sexual impropriety by a schoolmaster in New York in 1807. The Virginia account, which relates of a heterosexual offense, retains the bawdy quality of an Elizabethan comedy: the New York case, detailing a crime of sexual perversion, exemplifies a severe view of the aberrant sexual impulse.

On the eighth of September, 1634, on Cape Charles, one John Littell, a common laborer, was arrested for attempted rape. The indictment reads:

Upon the complaynt of Phillipp Taylor agst John Littell for abusinge his house going to bed to the mayd of syd Taylor's. . . .

The court took certain human tendencies into account, however, for the court record continues:

The next day the sy^d Littell . . . boasted that the cock was up, and the steale down and reddy to gove fire, but as the sy^d Littell confesseth he was disturbed . . . And for as much as the sy^d Littell Confesseth himself to be drunke that tyme . . . It is ordered that . . . he shall pay 5^s.

In the New York case* it appeared that a schoolmaster, forty-five years of age, was indicted for "gross indecency toward certain young females" who were his students. The court was unwilling to stain "the purity of the page" with description of the offender's actions. The evidence at the trial indicated that the master sat at his table while his young charges were reciting in such a way that he could put his hand under the clothes of the girl closest to him, palpating her buttocks and genitals without being observed by the other students. During the recitations he would often change the order of the pupils so that new children would be placed in line closest to his desk, screened from the other students. As the prosecuting attorney proceeded to develop his case, the court directed him to stop because "sufficient evidence had been proved to support the indictment; and the court

* City Hall Recorder for 1816. Vol. I, Peo. vs. W. W. Jenner, Court of General Sessions of the Peace.

would not hear details so disgusting." On the day of sentence, the judge said:

> On this occasion public expectation is excited, and a punishment commensurate with the atrocity of your offense is looked for with anxiety. The court regrets that it is not in their power to inflict a punishment which your offense merits; but we deem it proper to apprize you that we shall make a public example of you; we will not, on this occasion, enter into a detail of the circumstances of your case. They are grossly indecent, disgusting and scandalous. . . . The world knows your conduct. . . .

Before any intelligent treatment can be planned for the sex offender, much must be known of the motives, conflicts and drives that lie behind acts which are "contrary to nature." Objectivity can be the only satisfactory attitude on the part of those who study phenomena so universally abhorred in our civilization.

TYPES OF SEXUAL CRIME

Sexual offenses can be grouped in accordance with the particular abnormality of the sexual impulse which is manifested in the crime. For example, the group of rape cases commonly called statutory rape, which includes intercourse performed without the use of force with females under the age of consent, involves the least degree of sexual abnormality in the offender. Attempts at sex relations under threat, duress or with violence, or where the victim is mentally unable to comprehend the intent, embraces a greater degree of abnormality. Rape under unusual conditions, such as incest or when accompanied by sadistic excesses, encompasses a wide departure from gratification of the heterosexual impulse. An even more morbid manifestation of the sexual drive occurs in pedophilia, in which any type of perverse sexual activity is perpetrated on male or female children. Homosexuality constitutes another group of sex crimes based on obvious distortion of the goal of the sexual impulse. In this group, the criminal action varies from relations between adults who openly avow their inclination, to homosexual activity with young boys or adolescents under threat or through the use of trickery. In the main, homosexuality between acknowledged inverts has a slightly less pathologic significance than have crimes where perverse sexual impulses in the offender are submerged from public view. Conventionally, bigamy is included among the sex crimes, but here the sexual disturbance in the offender is less prominent than are other factors in his make-up. An understanding of the psychological background of sexual offenders will be facilitated by grouping sexual offenders according to variations in the intensity of their inherent sexual abnormality.

Sexual offenders prove on examination to be highly individual problems, and generalization about them may prove to be somewhat hazardous because of the artifacts attendant upon their appearance before a psychiatric examiner in court or in prison. Some offenders are examined upon conviction of their first offense, and it is not always possible to be certain that the pedophiliac of today will not become a child murderer next year or that he will not give up his perverseness in time. Other offenders are apprehended and convicted after a lifetime of sexual perversion of a type differing from that of the instant offense. A third group of sexual offenders have been guilty of robbery, larceny or other crimes in the past. In spite of this difficulty, to which all social data are subject, a composite picture of the convicted sex offender can be obtained.

A statistically composite picture of the sex offender indicates that he is numerically a less frequent offender than larcenists, robbers, burglars or forgers. The appended table provides a comparative view of crime frequencies.

Comparative frequency of major crime
groups, Court of General Sessions, New
York, from 1932 to 1938, inclusive:

Larceny	4108
Burglary	3698
Robbery	3004
Assault	2139
Forgery	889
Sexual Crime	709
Carrying Concealed Weapon	665
Homicide	513
Criminally Receiving Stolen Property	167
Extortion	154

The sex offender is more frequently white than Negro, native-born and a professed member of a religious denomination. He is not apt to be a recidivist, but, if he is, he has a distinctly psychopathic make-up. The sex crimes which necessitate the use of violence fall among the younger offenders, whereas the homosexual or pedophile is more apt to be a man about forty years old with serious social and psychological maladjustment. The older age group have a history of sexual deviation throughout adult life. The sex criminal is not predominantly a mental defective nor is he insane; he is of average intelligence and not a serious user of alcohol. From the standpoint of his total personality and social adjustment in other areas, he is likely to be without serious personality disturbance, aside from his abnormal sexual impulses.

AGGRESSIVE SEXUAL CRIME

It is apparent from the composite picture presented of the sexual criminal that his disturbance lies within the psychosexual area of his personality. Analysis of the emotional forces which influence sexual function in these individuals points toward the operation of neurotic mechanisms. Even in crimes where normal heterosexual urges are involved, obvious psychological conflicts are discerned. In forceful rape or sexual assault, the sadistic impulses which emerge are compensatory reactions for feelings of sexual inadequacy within the offender. Closely associated with these compensatory feelings in the rapist is a sharp decrease of the romantic and idyllic aspects of relations between the sexes. From the occurrence of these two tendencies, a deduction can be made that will serve in the over-all view of the offender involved in aggressive sex crime: namely, the greater the age of the criminal, the greater the likelihood that force or perversion will occur in the rape. This axiom is in sharp contrast to the finding that frequency of violence in all other crime categories is more regularly encountered among youthful offenders.

The neurotic mechanism operative in rapists is based on an underlying inferiority feeling which is reflected in sexual attitudes. The form taken by such feelings is a concealed fear of the usual masculine sentiments and attitudes surrounding sexual contact with women. Ruthless, egocentric attitudes toward women as sexual objects mask the disinclination to accept social standards of masculinity because of a fear of sexual inadequacy. Aggressive sexual psychopaths are driven to repeated sexual conquests in pursuit of the emotional security that successful masculine sexual dominance brings. The frequent clinical finding of unconscious feminine tendencies in criminals convicted of forceful rape can be understood on this basis.

The factor of aggressive sexual reaction to inner fear plays a greater part in directing the actions of rape-murderers than has been realized. The rapist who murders the object of his sexual impulse is motivated by fear of the social consequences of his act and, to an even greater degree, by fear of the strength of his own sexual aggression. The murder is the response to the pressure of guilty feelings and is not a true lust murder since the killing is not a sadistic aspect of the sexual act. Such crimes occur among individuals who are schizoid in their personality organization or are neurotically inhibited in their search for an acceptable sexual object. In schizoid individuals, the romantic coloring surrounding relations between men and women is compartmentalized in the mind and remains unrelated to sexual impulses. This situation was exemplified in a mild, aloof young man who was experiencing an ideal, adolescent romance with a girl in his community. During this period he impulsively raped and then strangled a woman whom he met casually in the course of his daily occupation. In this youth the schizoid personality precluded an appropriate merging of emotion, impulse and volition in his behavior.

The ultimate degree of pathologic disturbance of the sexual instinct is found among cases of true lust-murderers. Studies recorded in the literature point to the frequency of mental disease among these criminals. The paucity of lust-murderers in modern criminologic experience makes an analysis of the basic psychopathology difficult. There has been much speculation but little precise knowledge of the psychological factors in the depredations of Jack-the-Ripper or other legendary sex fiends. The few actual cases encountered have yielded little information of dynamic value. One example is the lust-murderer Hans Schmidt,* who was convicted in the New York courts in 1913 for a crime involving dismembering and subsequent violation of the corpse of his mistress. An even more repulsive variant of this group is the necrophiliac. Though such cases are uncommon in modern experience, A. A. Brill has recently reported two such sexual psychopaths, who, upon study, showed distinctly neurotic problems in connection with their necrophiliac fantasies. The sexual psychopath is characterized by disturbances in the appropriate fusion of the sexual impulse into his emotional life. Crimes of forceful rape and sadistic attack indicate that several forms of personality disturbance may be responsible. These can be either compensatory behavior for neurotic inhibition, schizoid withdrawal into fantasy life or, less commonly, intellectual dissociation due to insanity.

Psychological understanding of rape and other sexual crimes is enhanced by analysis of the meaning of the victim in terms of the offender's ego. Study shows that the victim is a source of unconscious gratification for the aggressive sex offender quite apart from her value as a sexual object. By placing the sexual object in an inferior, degrading role through rape or sadistic and perverse acts, the offender satisfies his need for a position of sexual dominance. This sense of dominance, implied in rape or any form of sexual crime, has the corollary effect of belittling the sexual object. To the sexual pervert, belittlement of the sexual partner is a source of unconscious gratification because it satisfies hostile impulses directed toward women. In actuality, rapists show strong elements of misogyny and distrust toward

---

* Peo. vs. Hans Schmidt, 216 New York.

the women they place in the position of sexual objects. Sexual inverts likewise are impelled toward an attitude of misogyny by feelings of inadequacy regarding their own sexual vigor. Aggressive sexual crime, on analysis, proves to have the meaning of a symbolic statement of the inferiority feelings of the criminal and an expression of hostility toward the objects of his lusts. These tendencies are integrated in the personality of the sexual psychopath as the result of long-standing emotional conflicts and stresses.

PEDOPHILIAC CRIMES

The neurotic and schizoid mechanisms described in offenders guilty of rape or sadistic sexual crime also are found in varying degrees in pedophiliacs who make sexual advances to children. Pedophiliacs are particularly afflicted with anxiety regarding their sexual potency. Like the rapist, the pedophiliac is not a hypersexed individual, but one whose sexual impulses are distorted by crippling anxiety. A large number give histories of impotence or partial impotence. It is evident that the pedophiliac's inferiority feelings lead him to search for younger and less formidable love objects whose ignorance would prevent his deficiency from becoming obvious. The child sexual object saves the offender's ego from blows which might prove destructive to his mental equilibrium. The female child replaces an adult sexual object, which appears unattainable to the inhibited pedophile. The boy upon whom preversions are visited is a substitute for unacknowledged adult homosexual interests. The fact that pedophilia develops out of a background of neurosis is partly demonstrated by its occurrence as an "occasional" crime in an apparently adjusted individual. Such an offender may have a satisfactory relationship with his wife and live with a family to whom he is devoted. When the wife is pregnant or ill, ungratified infantile tendencies may appear, often as a startling phenomenon to the criminal himself, in the form of sexual play with a child. The mainspring of this abnormal sex drive proves to be the wish to be a child again, a regression to an earlier period when the sexual instinct was expressed in partial impulses of playing, seeing, touching, and so on. Disappointment with the spouse for one reason or another stimulates infantile yearnings, for the spouse represents both mother-figure and wife in the fantasy of the neurotic husband. Sexual satisfaction is never achieved with the wife because the yearning is for the loving mother of old who allowed the boy-child full play for his sexual fantasies. An added factor is the unconscious hostility of emotionally immature men for their wives which is based on old patterns of sibling rivalry. Regression to infantile sexual levels, which is portrayed in sexual crime and is unknown to the criminal himself, is at the core of this type of sexual psychopathy.

Pedophilia, when scrutinized, is less an abhorrent sexual lust than a sign of serious neurotic conflict in the offender. The study of a case may provide a clear picture of the genesis and development of this not uncommon personality distortion. Egan was fifty-two years old at the time of his charge of indulging in various acts of sexual perversion with several girls ranging in age from twelve to fourteen. He worked as a journeyman printer in a government printing office. His first marriage at the age of twenty culminated in the death of his wife two years later. He remarried at the age of twenty-six and had six children with his second wife. This marriage was marked by bickering and resulted in a separation prior to the present offense. Egan never had a close emotional bond with his children or with his wife. The rationalization he offered for the final break in the home was that his wife had a job and wanted no more sex relations.

Egan's early life was significant. He had no recollection of his father, who was said to have been an alcoholic. His mother's people were Romany Gypsies; they lived in poverty and squalor. His earliest recollection was that at the age of three, when walking with his mother, "A man who came out of the saloon grabbed me." At four years of age he recalled wearing kilts and long curls. He said, "I feel so bad about my mother I can't talk. She drank a great deal and my stepfather beat her all the time, then left her."

At eight years of age he was placed in an orphan home, where he remained until he was sixteen. He visited his mother only once more, at the age of eighteen. "Seeing her in the same condition disgusted me." When he was eight years old he recalled that his grandmother had a cancer on her nose which was "eaten up." She used to have him urinate on a rag and then she would place the rag on her face to relieve the pain, in conformance with an old gypsy tradition. He suffered from enuresis until ten years of age.

At the orphan home he recalled that when he was about nine years old, a brother "picked me off the ground, whipped me with a cat-o'-nine-tails, and while I was hanging in the air squealing, I wet myself."

Egan's sexual life was early featured by neurotic practices. From the age of twenty-one he had practiced cunnilingus, to which he was introduced by a prostitute. Masturbation began at the age of twelve. As a boy he was guilt-laden and considered masturbation a mortal sin. At thirty years of age he was relieved to find that the practice had no effect on him, that he had not become insane, as he thought he might. Even during the second marriage, he would sit alone and masturbate in the dark when the family was out. At the age of forty-three, he had an episode of bed-wetting, which surprised him. The offender had always had difficulty with micturition; he felt that he could not urinate before another man. "I feel as though someone is looking at me. I can urinate before a woman and not be embarrassed."

He maintained contact with prostitutes all his life and had relations once or twice a week with them. He complained that for twenty years he was trying to cure an excessive sex desire. Egan's urinary perversion was outstanding. During sexual activity, he wanted his partner to urinate on him. It stimulated him to masturbation, also. The offender regarded with pride his excessive sexual drive and sexual competence and considered them an indication of unusual endowment, but his dreams illustrated the tremendous anxiety evoked by examination of his sexual impulses. Dreams involving death, mutilation of the teeth, nose and face, mirrored the fear which lay beneath the surface of his satyriasis. The manifold sexual drive, which passed from wife to prostitutes to children, was never-ending and was psychologically unsatisfactory. It represented the neurotic acting-out of a constant search for a loving, protective mother on whom he could vent his retaliatory infantile fury while invoking her love. The severe conflict which developed, based on reality experiences of emotional deprivation, raged between hostile impulses toward his mother and dependency on her. This conflict had become associated with his psychosexual function, so that he could not love or experience sexual satisfaction without perversion. The urinary perversion became attached to the sexual impulse to a degree that made sexual gratification dependent upon it. The urinary perversion was an expression of infantile hostility, originating in early feelings toward mother and grandmother and spreading to other females in adult life.

INCEST

The preoccupation of certain adult males with children as sexual objects brings the crime of incest into the foreground. Sexual relations between adult men and young but mature girls is a relatively common sexual offense, a fact which can be attested by social workers dealing with families of low cultural level. Unquestionably, more cases occur than are brought to court. Incest between father and daughter is the most frequent type. Even more common relatively are relations between father and stepdaughter. The influences behind incest are chiefly cultural and sociologic and are identified with primitive family organization. In the large family, in which incest is frequently encountered, the father comes to occupy the position of patriarch and is somewhat emotionally removed from the members of the family as an integral part of the family unit. He becomes the titular head of the tribe and, as such, all his children are subjects of his rule. Disagreement between husband and wife or beginning evidence of sexual incompatibility may stimulate the father to extend his sexual sovereignty to his daughters.

The psychological atmosphere in which incest is perpetrated differs from that surrounding pedophilia. Nor do the personalities of incest offenders contain the neurotic reflections observed in other sexual criminals. It is not uncommon to note that the responses of incest prisoners are much less clouded by evasion and by complete denial than are the responses of offenders involved in perversions. Offenders appear to have caught the connotation that incest, being essentially a normal type of sex relationship, is not as reprehensible from the standpoint of public morals as is perverted sexuality. Although the guilt of incestuous relationships is strong, there is still a forthrightness which is utterly different from the half-hearted admission by sexual offenders of perverse relationships with female children. This difference in attitude has a direct bearing on the psychology of the two groups of offenders. Whereas incest, although taboo, is a mature form of heterosexuality, pedophilia is akin to repressed infantile sexual experience.

Homosexual Offenses

Homosexuality, a variant of sexual psychopathy, has been long an arresting problem from psychological and social points of view. The professed homosexual, though he suffers from public obloquy and lives a life of social ostracism, has few contacts with the law, under ordinary circumstances. Even the homosexual who exhibits his passive trends openly through wearing feminine clothes, i.e., the transvestite, is a minor figure in crime. Such individuals belong to communities that remain aloof and are blatantly feminine in attire and manner, often outdoing women in their femininity. But not all active homosexuals are so readily detectable by their manner, clothes or cosmetic adornment. The active homosexualist who preserves his peaceful status has recently been the subject of careful study by Dr. George Henry and his associates. Henry found that active homosexuals were either constitutionally deficient in glandular function or subject to a specific family pattern in which abnormal psychosexuality developed easily or lacked social opportunities for the development of normal heterosexuality. Other observers have been impressed by the emotional disturbances in the early life histories of homosexuals. Whatever the basic cause of homosexuality may prove to be, the invert who is convicted of a sex crime demonstrates more than one causative feature in his make-up. Since interest in this book is limited to the psychopath whose misdeeds bring him before the criminal courts, the homosexuals who do not reach legal agencies will not be dealt with further here.

It is evident that every homosexual psychopath has a specific history of his own perversion which is related to his offense. The homosexual who becomes involved in cases of sodomy or impairing the morals of a minor has a strong neurotic conflict revolving about his perversion which impels him to expose himself to possible injury in quest of sex objects. The less neurotic homosexual, on the other hand, voluntarily remains in the company of those similarly afflicted. The presence of neurotic admixtures provides the stimuli which change a private vice into a sexual crime. The effective factor in cases of overt homosexualists who become involved in sexual crime, then, seems to be the influence of neurotic guilt on their actions. These offenders are uncomfortable with their homosexual impulses yet they are subject to the unconscious need of exhibiting their sexual problem. Feelings of inferiority and guilt are the stimulating forces causing these individuals to seek sexual contact with minors rather than with available adult homosexual objects. Displacement of the goal of intercourse with adult homosexuals in favor of minors marks the fear of public censure and indicates a simultaneous exhibitionism aimed at the exposure of their guilty feelings. These opposing wishes lie behind the conflict that is evident in those homosexuals who become sex offenders.

While it is difficult to generalize about the homosexual with neurotic elements, every studied case of sex criminality involving perverse acts proves to be the acting-out of a neurosis. The following detailed study of a sodomist, whose one offense at the age of forty-nine was the only antisocial or perverse outcropping in his entire life, will illustrate the dynamics which are uncovered when the individual sex offender is carefully examined.

A sales representative, forty-nine years old, unmarried, a man of short stature, born in the north of Ireland but reared in this country from infancy, was convicted of third-degree assault for perpetrating sodomy on two Western Union messenger boys. Of splendid reputation and successful in business, Jones' employment history extended back continuously to his fourteenth year, when he left school. In the main, his life had been comfortable. He was the eighth of nine children. He resided with a single brother and sister, with whom he went to live after his mother's death, a year before the offense. Jones became involved in the present offense about three and one-half years after the appearance of homosexual impulses, first noted in connection with high school boys whom he saw in public places; he complained that he felt impelled to look at their genitals instead of their faces. For several months he had talked about sex with messenger boys, masturbated one boy on several occasions and then committed the present offense.

The offender's heterosexual experiences, starting at nineteen, were uncomfortable for him because of the jibes of sexual partners concerning his small genital organ. Sexual contacts with prostitutes occurred about once or twice a month, but were less frequent for five years preceding the offense. A marked genital anomaly, phimosis, was a further impediment to his heterosexual adjustment. At twenty-five he had a platonic relationship with the daughter of a minister which was broken off by the girl's mother. Beyond this there were no love affairs. The offender drank moderately, especially during the last twenty years.

The offender was given a suspended sentence on condition that he receive psychotherapy. Under treatment, the patient responded by pouring out his life history. He seemed to experience great relief from discussing his sexual problems with the doctor. His feeling of inferiority was obvious, but more striking was his guilt, encouraged by the habit of secrecy, which haunted him because of years of concealment of homosexual desires. Upon being told at the first visit that he might be helped, he said it was the "best thing he had ever heard." The offender's free associations showed a relation between childhood insecurities and current anxieties. His earliest recollections were of his father's appearance in his bedroom, when the patient was three, to announce that he was going to America alone. Another affect-laden experience occurred at the age of sixteen, when he stated he was struck in the abdomen by lightning which passed out through his legs. Later in life he frequently dreamed of playing competitive games with friends but was always unsuccessful. "I never got anywhere in my dreams."

Early in the treatment, he complained that if he dreamed of rats, trouble was to be expected. Anxiety arising from the pressure of his homosexual drives was extreme and was accompanied by strong feelings about the punishment and humiliation Jones received from the authorities at the time of his arrest. As this experience moved away in point of time, he became a little more confident, and deeper masturbation anxieties came to the fore. His attitude alternated between sensitivity toward the outside world because of the humiliation occasioned by his offense, and an appreciation of the therapist's interest and nonpunitive attitude.

With his guilt somewhat mitigated, the homosexual impulses reappeared. He dreamed of resisting the advances of messenger boys. In compensation, he spoke of the good he had done in church work, where he was especially interested in a gymnasium for boys. Numerous dreams reflecting masturbation anxiety were reported. Following the circumcision operation for phimosis, Jones developed many castration dreams accompanied by the constant fear of being rearrested. At one time a roundup of sex offenders was announced by the police, and Jones was terribly frightened that he might be rearrested on sight as a recorded invert. He related his difficulties in business, which was at a low ebb at that time, and also his anxieties concerning his sexual inadequacy. At this time he began to berate the Western Union messengers as being commercially interested in homosexuals. Numerous dreams occurred of deluges and storms in which his summer cottage was frequently in danger of being washed away. A typical dream was: "I am on the beach; there is a terrific storm; gradually a tidal wave occurs covering the house; I awaken frightened." He recalled that at the age of ten he was almost drowned and that he often dreamed of tidal waves rushing over him. His father had been in the Galveston flood of 1901 and in the San Francisco earthquake in 1906.

Another dream that pointed to the roots of his homosexuality was as follows. He is in a room with his brother and a woman who has a pistol. He is shot two times and is supposed to be dead. The woman is a government agent. The patient is lying on a couch and feels paralyzed. She says, "You are not dead," and pulls the trigger, aiming at the patient's spine.

Associations led him to recall the close family life at home, a story of a woman shooting her husband, the housework he actually did at home, life with his single brother and a trip to a slaughterhouse in Chicago following which he did not eat meat for a month. Homosexual feelings centered around his brother. The feelings of ineffectuality were related to fear of bodily injury (tidal waves) by agents of the courts (the psychiatrist) and his father.

During the treatment process, interpretations were given sparingly, but the basic castration fears were elucidated to the patient and a thorough ventilation of the social and psychological aspects of his homosexuality was undertaken. After five months, the general depression and anxiety were much reduced, and Jones managed a few heterosexual experiences. In a letter written about this time, the patient indicated his great relief at "being able to walk the streets and not having that desire crop up."

Essentially this case illustrates a lifelong struggle with sexual inadequacy and a strong homosexual drive, with consequent fears of social castigation and strong castration anxiety. The function of therapy here was chiefly to give emotional support to a patient who was threatened with overwhelming anxiety once his problem became known to him. Insight into the neurotic nature of one type of homosexual provided by this case was confirmed in other sexual offenders studied less intensively.

BIGAMY

The psychological characteristics of bigamists are as strongly reminiscent of those of the hysterical swindler as they are akin to those of the sexual psychopath. Study of male bigamists reveals them to be either emotionally immature individuals or swindlers for whom multiple marriages are merely technics for appropriating money from their wives. Bigamy is less a result of excessive sexual passion than it is a search for the ideal wife who represents a mother-figure to the neurotic bigamist. The characteristic history of a bigamist is that of a man who, while separated from his wife because of emotional disharmony or sexual incompatibility, meets and marries another girl in whom he sees the embodiment of all the characteristics he cherishes in a woman; or he may rationalize his impulsive action by declaring that he was answering his second wife's crying need for a protector. The psychological motive behind this apparently romantic or altruistic behavior is that of emotional dependence. The second wife becomes the ideal woman, upon whom are projected the virtues of unlimited love and complete understanding. Only a perfect mother-figure can satisfy these infantile requirements. The force of the rejection of the first wife, who did not measure up to this infantile yearning, is equal to the need for the second woman. Both women are overvalued or undervalued, in the offender's feelings, according to the strength of his dependence needs and the degree of frustration encountered by him in his marital life. The play of unconscious forces, which impel the bigamist to be always in a favored position with regard to a woman, cause him to reject one wife as unsatisfactory and extol another as ideal.

The man who contracts a bigamous marriage through impersonation or deceit displays an interesting variation of the psychological mechanisms outlined above. This type of offense is initiated by a claim of position or wealth. Here the bigamous marriage has as its aim the acquisition of control of the second wife's money. This form of bigamy (cf. discussion of swindling, pp. 23-24) involves an unconscious hostility toward women, in contradistinction to the offense when committed under the influence of emotional need. Actually both mechanisms operate in the offender at the same time—the dependence needs and the hostility toward the woman on whom the neurotic offender's dependence is projected. The money gained is one source of gratification in the swindler bigamy. Another is the witnessing of pain and humiliation in both wives for different reasons. The pattern of unconscious hostility, derived from an infantile conflict, causes the bigamist to be in a special psychological position in which he must injure one of his women. As tension arises from the frustration of an unsatisfactory marriage, a new one is contracted. From the neurotic problem which bigamy poses, it can be seen that the polygamous tendency is interrupted only by the intervention of the law, following a complaint from one of the spouses. In other words, the emotional drives underlying bigamy operate as a continued pressure toward psychological polygamy.

The juncture of neurosis and psychopathic personality is nowhere seen so clearly as in the bigamist. The weakness of the sense of reality toward marriage and the disregard of social and legal responsibility, characteristic of the psychopath, are seen as a direct response to the pressure of emotional needs. This development is observed in male bigamists; it is likewise noted in female bigamists. In the background of the female bigamist, as with her fellow offender, is often a difficult marital situation in which emotional satisfaction has been absent. When another suitor appears with an offer of marriage, the offer is taken without further thought. Children are not considered; laws are disregarded. Compelling emotional needs within the personality of the offender—protection, sexual gratification, need for a kind, affectionate parent-surrogate—demand immediate satisfaction. An example of polyandry in a woman who was married eight times and lived with several paramours illustrates the union of neurotic forces and psychopathic, unrealistic behavior, which are operative in bigamy.

At the age of thirteen, Iris, a fair-haired, blue-eyed girl, became acquainted with a gypsy encamped near her home in Massachusetts. With the consent of her mother, she married him. For two weeks they lived together; there was no sexual life and she left him promptly. It was clear to her at the time that both her mother and father wanted to be rid of her. At sixteen years of age Iris bigamously married her second husband, Joe K., who became the father of her four children. She had been very happy the first several years but brooded over her first marriage. Married life with Joe became tiresome, a constant round of drudgery and care of the children. Her husband earned only a small salary, and she had a yearning for pretty clothes and travel.

The doctor who delivered one of her children talked to her and regretted that "a girl of her age" should have been so harassed. She and her husband were very much in debt, and they talked it over and decided to separate. The home was broken up. Iris went out with this doctor on several occasions. Presently she ran off to New York. There she met a Joseph E. in a hotel room, whom she forthwith married. After six weeks she left him precipitately, returning home without telling her husband of her escapade. Marital life was resumed, a fourth child was born, and a normal course was pursued for a year and a half until she suddenly left home in company with a former schoolmate, Claude, whom she married. After a few weeks she left him. By now Iris had already married four men. When she returned home again, Joe accepted her without question. Soon she developed a relation with Thomas. "It was just an affair but I couldn't get rid of him. . . . I went away again." Disheartened, she went back to Joe, who, unaware of her interim marriages, took her in again. The children had been sent to a foster home, and presently she met a William H., an Englishman, and a Mr. C., both of whom she married in succession. On the occasion of her next return home, Iris had been married six times at the age of 25. She was arrested on the charge of polygamy. After serving fourteen of her fifteen months sentence, Iris ran away from the reformatory to New York, where she met a Fred N. and promptly married him. In the same building in which they lived was another roomer, William W., and during her second month of marriage to Fred he "forced her to marry him," although he knew she was already married. Aside from the eight marriages, there were other liaisons, such as the one with Charles G., with whom she lived for a time in a common-law relationship.

The offender's life story indicated significant factors in the development of her neurotic behavior. She was an only child of parents who, themselves, were in constant emotional difficulties. The rejection by both parents of the child was an outstanding feature in her early life. Her training ran along unusual, almost unnatural lines that reflected the mother's indifference. The latter was particular about having the child immaculately dressed on all occasions and gave her dancing lessons, etc., but kept her from natural and spontaneous association with other children. Her mother's attention was superficial and concerned mostly with externals. The father was distant and never showed her any affection. The parents were divorced when Iris was twenty-two years old.

In Iris' account of her polygamies, the feeling that she considered her liaisons as play-marriages is inescapable. For example, in speaking about Claude, she said, "Claude was good to me; he treated me like a little girl, bought me candy and presents and finally asked if I wanted to marry him. I agreed. It was the only church wedding I had. I had a beautiful white dress, a great big bunch of orchids." Throughout the marriage history runs a note of emotional emptiness. None was satisfactory because no one marriage was real. She spoke of sexual satisfaction only in connection with Jim; in the other marriages sexual feelings played little part in her part of the relationship. She moved from name to name and civil status to civil status. Her husbands were men "who took care of her"; the images of the men as husbands were confused and shadowy. Each marriage seemed to mirror the childlike atmosphere of her first marriage to the gypsy, which her mother did nothing to disrupt. Apparently Iris interpreted her mother's concurrence as an order. The psychological significance of her plural marriages had more to do with her mother than her husbands. Eternal obedience to her mother was an illusory mode of securing a mother's love which was never available, and Iris' marriages were a continuance of the search for a protecting, loving parent through re-enactment of an old pattern of the child-mother relationship.

Bigamy, then, represents a behavioral attempt to correct a neurotic conflict, but true to the fate of neurotic resolutions, such attempts result in further reality difficulties more than in clarification of emotional problems. It is evident that the psychological background of most bigamies is overwhelmingly neurotic in character.

EMOTIONAL REACTIONS OF THE PSYCHOPATH

The acts of the psychopath speak more eloquently than do his words. It is a clinical truism that unstable psychopaths are prone to react with a marked degree of emotionality to even slight provocation. Their intense reactions to the frustrations of reality speak for their emotional lability and the slight degree of resilience in their egos. A discussion of emotional reactions in psychopaths will illustrate those defensive mechanisms in such individuals which underlie their quick reactivity. It is significant that the defensive reactions to be delineated in psychopaths are similar in kind but not in degree to those experienced by disturbed neurotics and even by excited normal individuals at times of emotional stress. The defensiveness of the psychopath is, however, characterized by impulsiveness and vigor beyond that seen in other clinical groups.

It has already been stated that denial, as a behavioral and verbal reaction, represents the ego's withdrawal from painful reality. Such reactions appear in psychiatric practice to range from simple lying to profound depression. Considered in order of defensive intensity, amnesia is the next reaction encountered after direct lying. In amnesia, a specific lapse of memory occurs for the incidents of the offense which ends with the arrest. In spite of the knowledge that amnesias have no legal value in reducing culpability or mitigating punishment, many chronic offenders stoutly insist, even after conviction, that they suffer from amnesias for the period of the offense. It is justifiable, then, to conclude that for the offender, amnesias serve the inner purpose of denial of unpleasant reality. Alcohol often induces the amnesia. Offenders describe the events of the crime as if through a haze; the alcoholic amnesia approaches a fugue or trancelike state in character. Again, the amnesia serves the ego by repressing the memory of the aggressive impulse. But unconscious feelings of guilt countermand the repressing mechanism and direct the offender's behavior so that detection is not too difficult, and subsequent punishment occurs. The amnesia blots out the wish to rob or assault, while from a deeper source, guilt reactions lead to the ready arrest of the culprit. This psychological series of events was well illustrated by a man who shot a victim in an alcoholic fugue but was apprehended as he "stumbled" on the victim a few moments after the deed.

Another type of denial of unpleasant reality can be the assumption of a lack of knowledge through a suddenly acquired stupidity. One form of this is the "hysterical twilight state" described by Ganser among prisoners who exaggerated their memory defects to the point of absurdity. These prisoners gave wrong answers to questions which were characteristically outside the limits of appropriateness. For example, an offender answered "three" to the question, "How much is two and two?" When such a criminal is asked the capital of Massachusetts, he might reply, "Albany"; when asked for the state in which New York City is located, he would say, "New Jersey." The exaggeration of ignorance is clearly a defense against being held responsible before society. Other terms, such as Buffoonery Syndrome or Pseudo-Imbecility, have also been applied to similar pictures where the offender acts in a comical, bizzare and inappropriate way. Thus he may eat an egg with the shell on it; he may throw away the fruit of a banana and eat the skin; he may wear his clothes inside out, and so on. The object of this activity is to demonstrate a degree of stupidity which would render the offender unable to cope with the situation which he faces as an apparently responsible adult.

Malingery (simulation) is another reaction of denial. Experience obtained in wartime has provided an excellent opportunity to study the problems of malingery among psychopaths, immature and neurotic individuals. Malingery has always been considered the result of a conscious wish to feign illness or disability. In spite of the various fields in which malingering appears, its gross structure is immediately recognizable. In a court or prison environment, the acting-out of abnormal or insane behavior has as its purpose escape from legal punishment. In military life, feigning illness provides the opportunity to be excused from dangers of wartime duty. Similarly, malingering by children is employed to avoid the tedium of the schoolroom. The use of malingered or exaggerated symptoms in compensation cases in industry likewise has the real purpose of payment and relief from work. When the purpose for which the symptom was feigned has been achieved, the individual is no longer ill. Even in the case of amputation or other

mutilation, the individual seems to feel better when the purpose of malingering has been accomplished. The generalization, however, that malingery satisfies a conscious wish of evasion requires further scrutiny.

Of the various forms of malingering, some, like amputation of a finger
or poor eyesight, can be discovered by medical examination; but often symptoms are feigned which are impossible to evaluate objectively. To some
degree, delusions, hallucinations, mental confusion, depression, can be confirmed by direct observation. Psychosomatic and neurotic complaints, like
palpitation of the heart, pain in the abdomen, dizziness, malaise, weakness,
headache, visceral pain and a host of others, cannot be objectively proved or
disproved. Even less capable of objective proof are "mental" symptoms like
doubts, phobias, anxieties, obsessions and fears. It has been the practice of
those confronted by a possible malingerer to rely, when objective tests are
unavailing, upon their intuitive feeling about the reality or unreality of a
given symptom. Dependence on intuitive feeling is at best an uncertain
technic, although there is admittedly no other way of dealing with the malingery of neurotic or visceral symptoms. Since the intuition of the medical
officer or physician is the instrument used in the estimation of malingery, it
would be advisable to examine this instrument, especially under the conditions of a military service and under the influence of military ideals.

An important psychological factor in the intuitive testing of the examiner
is the unconscious hostility aroused in the physician-officer by the organization of military life. Military tradition has an influence on the medical
officer in this respect, since his own unconscious anger against cowards is
given legitimate expression by the psychological atmosphere of war. In war,
the majority of military or naval personnel are exposed at one time or another to unpleasant, dangerous or monotonous duties, which they endure.
The ideals for which men fight and their loyalty to their commanding officer
are normally placed before the demands of the ego for comfort or safety.
To do otherwise is to be a coward. Indeed, the corollary which is drawn
from this attitude is the basis of all military codes, namely, that an individual
who does not choose to place the ideals for which he is fighting above personal safety or comfort is criminal in his intent toward his country or leader,
i.e., a traitor. It need not be stressed that from the standpoint of the efficient
working of a military machine this is the only possible view. The individual
who unconsciously or consciously develops symptoms interfering with his
use as a working unit hampers the whole machine. A by-product of this
tradition is the very human impulse to be punitive and to allow the diagnostic "intuitive" sense to be stimulated by this attitude. Malingerers are

considered to be "bad," "unpatriotic" or cowardly men, and medical examiners become themselves imbued with this punitive viewpoint.

The military scene is a significant area where cowardly feelings come to light and where malingery is channeled into the reaction of cowardice. Before pronouncing a man a coward or a malingerer, the underlying psychological problem of the coward should be scrutinized. In the dictionary definition of the coward as a "poltroon" and a "dastard," the evil aspect of the word is always stressed. Since all men are unwilling to be injured or to die if it can be avoided, it appears plausible that a psychological reaction must intervene to enable every normal individual to function in the face of known danger. The prospect of certain death is met with equanimity through a psychological process which can be called that of the hero-position, or hero-idea. This attitude embodies the repression of fear of personal injury, which itself then becomes a source of gratification to the individual. The man who is not a coward unconsciously incorporates the hero-position into his thinking and acts automatically under its influence. Gratification is supplied the hero through sacrifice for the common good. The hero thus plays a masochistic role, of which he is not aware, in which he will be thanked, acclaimed and loved by those for whom he sacrificed himself. In exposing himself to danger, the fear of personal injury or possibility of death is more than compensated by the gratification embodied in his survivors' attitude toward him. This mechanism, although masochistic in form, is not to be considered reprehensible, for it functions in the service of high patriotic and humane ideals. From this analysis it appears apparent that the coward lacks the capacity for identification with the hero-idea to the end that normal fear will be repressed. It would appear that the coward has difficulty in accepting the masochistic satisfaction which comes from sacrifice.

What are the sources in the human personality which lead to the display of cowardice by malingery? What defect in ego structure prevents the use of the unconscious mechanism of masochism which is inherent in the hero idea? Examination of such an individual may give some hint of the dynamics underlying the malingery and cowardice involved.

Robert A., a seaman of twenty-two, enlisted in the Navy "to avoid the Army." After a period at training camp where he was placed in a gunnery school, he was assigned on a U.S. naval vessel for a practice cruise lasting nine days. Reaching port, he immediately went absent without leave for fifty-three days. After being released from imprisonment for this offense, he did return to his ship but went A.W.O.L. again for six months. Several years earlier, Robert had been discharged from the United States Army because of hypochondria and nervousness. He had been married for two months at the time of his present examination. There was a history of a head injury, which was not serious, at the age of ten. His industrial record in civilan life had been poor, and his school work had been fair but marred by truancy.

The prisoner had been restless as a youth and involved in minor delinquencies. Much of his time in adolescence and young adulthood prior to entering the service was spent in idleness. The prisoner complained bitterly of naval life, saying that he was afraid of the sea and frightened at gunnery practice, and threatened suicide unless he was discharged from naval service. He insisted that the only cure for his nervousness and headache was to be returned to his wife. On examination he demonstrated a tremor of the hands and nail-biting and said he thought that the head injury years ago had left some "pus in his head." He developed intense nervousness, stressed suicidal ideas, was unable to work because of headache and spoke about hearing voices at night. The voice was that of his wife saying, "Darling, I want you home." It was obvious that Robert was frightened and determined to be discharged from the service for psychiatric reasons. His wife, an attractive, self-reliant girl, apparently sensed his emotional dependence on her and rejected it by deciding to join the military service herself while Robert was still under confinement.

As a civilian, Robert had always claimed his nervousness would not allow him to work. His parents had been indulgent toward him and thus covered up his immaturity and lack of self-reliance. When he was separated from home for service in the Navy, anxiety developed which had hitherto been absorbed by the protection of his parents, who tacitly allowed him to live a carefree, pleasure-loving life. The imposition of strict naval regulations caused his dependence on women (mother-wife) to come to the surface and control his behavior. The malingery, which took the form of hysterical symptoms, was a sign of the inability of his ego to handle emotional deprivations. Until then, this inability had been hidden from view. The stern realities of a regulated life threw Robert back to a regressive phase of dependence. The fact that his behavior could be described as that of a coward does not detract from the psychological movements underlying the emotional reactions. It was true that Robert's nervous symptoms were present before he entered the service, but not strongly enough to merit medical attention. When he reached military life, his symptoms apparently overwhelmed him. Applying the test of cowardice developed previously, it appears that cowardice, as illustrated in this case, bears a relation to the presence of a neurotic core in the personality. Such an individual is unable to accept the choice of hero-position, which delays immediate satisfaction in favor of future emotional gratification through sacrifice.

In reactions of frightened sailors and soldiers of the type described, cowardice, malingery and neurosis are factors which are simultaneously present in varying degrees. Experience indicates that neurotic mechanisms are always in the background of cases of malingery, whether dereliction of duty is patently a conscious choice, i.e., the result of selfish motives without expressed fear, or the result of an uncontrolled rush of fear. Grossly, the neurotic (hysterical) element can be seen in sudden changes in behavior which are so reminiscent of infantile actions as to indicate their regressive quality to even the untrained observer. In World War II these symptoms were observed at the induction of men into the military service, in the training camp, in special schools preparing for active duty and during and after combat itself. Conflicts between an ego unequipped to assimilate reality and laudable wishes to serve the country constitute the psychological background. Reactions among raw recruits were especially spectacular. Symptoms amounting to near-panic suddenly developed within a day of contact with military or naval organizations. There developed loss of sphincteric control, palpitation, flushing, headaches, feelings of impending dissolution, anxiety dreams, fears for the health and happiness of parents, sudden preoccupation with parents' marital disharmony, dreams of the death of siblings, and so on. Manifestations of psychosomatic symptoms and signs of regression were common. A recruit, age seventeen, a month after being in recruit camp complained that he had frequently cried himself to sleep and had bowel movements several times in bed while asleep. Common also were cases of enuresis. Examination of youths established the fact that enuresis represented the expression of infantile impulses of which the subjects were unaware. Instinctive demands of the infantile ego in youths far outweighed conscious wishes to serve the country, while among older men a conscious dislike of fighting was more likely to have been openly expressed. It was for this reason that neurotic regressive symptoms were common in youthful recruits.

When individuals who have displayed their antagonism toward military service in combat areas are studied, a clearer view is obtained of the simultaneous action of neurotic background and egocentricity in the production of malingery. Men guilty of malingery appear on the surface to be callous to idealism and patriotism. Their personality organizations are not elastic enough to forego certain ego-satisfactions in favor of the common weal. Such cases put the strength of their unconscious demands before ideals of patriotism. In a sense they understand their own personalities well, and the final disposition really rests in their own hands. In such cases the question of discipline comes up for consideration and places the psychiatrist between the horns of a dilemma in treating the man as a "criminal," on the one hand, and a sick (psychopathic) personality on the other. Discipline and punishment would serve their deep unconscious dependency but would not filter through strongly enough to modify the conscious ego attitudes. The apparent split between ego attitudes toward the self and the nation makes punishment unavailing in modifying the military malingerer.

DYNAMIC ASPECTS OF THE PSYCHOPATH

The search for insight into the basic difficulty of the psychopath does not reveal any one specific psychological defect basic to all types of psychopaths. Nevertheless, a common clinical feature stands out repeatedly in the examination of these individuals. This is their inability to absorb the frustrations and limitations of reality situations without doing something about it. Intolerance toward painful or humiliating experiences is followed by a reaction of automatic character. When such persons encounter frustration, the reality involved is apparently immediately excluded from their thinking and feeling. Reality is replaced by action and feelings directed by fantasy. The psychopath lives a life of impulse. It will be recalled that all children conquer the restrictions imposed upon them by the adult world through the magical action of fantasy. As the human individual matures and tests his fantasy powers against reality, he tends to place less reliance on the magical powers of the wish and more on steadily overcoming resistance of the external world through the acquisition of knowledge and skills. Yet in the group of psychopathic deviates the impulse away from reality seems to be given irresistible direction by the character of their fantasies.

In the group of persons under discussion, it is the persistence of fantasy within the personality and its relation to the ego which can be called the psychologic nucleus of the psychopath. Although case studies indicate the universal persistence of this infantile trait in all psychopaths, it is most demonstrable in the so-called hysterical swindler (pathologic liar) psychopaths. Here the omnipotence fantasies are actually lived out in schemes and enterprises characterized by grandiosity. In the lighter variants of this group, the most absurd ideas of grandiosity stand alongside shrewd business sense in otherwise mature men. As Cleckley has pointed out, the disregard of reality, which is characteristic of the plans of such an individual, has been seen to exist in men otherwise successful as professionals or business executives, who sooner or later betray themselves through some crass action which stands at complete variance with their usual behavior.

In the early life of these individuals, emotional deprivation or rejection influenced their ego development to the extent that the resulting ego was hampered in the normal course of identification by the child with the social aspect of either parent. Because the infant could not attain any degree of emotional comfort from one or the other parent, he failed to introject either parent image into his own ego structure. As Greenacre and others have noted, this apparently results in a weak super-ego formation. This general insecurity, which is the cause of an inability to build a social conscience in the psychopath or delinquent, appears to have originated in an early period of personality development.

Case histories of offenders in this book abound in situations where emotional rejection by parents or guardians occurred in early life. These emotional forces persist either as overt memories or as unconscious forces and reach fruition in acts for which there seems no reasonable basis. The emotional sensitivity evoked by childhood rejection, with its reaction of tantrums, rages, humiliation or infantile behavior, is reactivated by current frustrations of adult life. Such individuals have been "conditioned" by their early rejection to live as if they were rejected by society and denied success in adult life. As in childhood, they retreat in adult life through an automatic process to the only source of emotional satisfaction remaining—the fantasy. Reality, which to the psychopath is always unpleasant, is overridden by a feeling of omnipotence carried over from childhood to adulthood and forged into the personality. The surface phenomena of "egotism" and "emotional callousness," so prominent in the adult psychopath are hence defensive reactions against his early rejection built into the character trait of egocentricity. The case of Gustave D., who at the age of thirty-eight had sealed his fate with a sentence of life imprisonment for a fourth felony conviction, provides an example of the effect of early influences on behavior. In the current offense he was arrested after officers observed him entering and leaving four buildings in a suspicious manner. He had in his possession seven pieces of celluloid, two penknives, one picklock and a pin. From his first arrest at the age of eight to the last at thirty-eight, his life had been that of successful thievery, alternating with prison sentences. His career was dotted with burglaries varying in amount from pennies to thousands of dollars. His biggest "jobs" were burglaries of jewelry. One year a burglary netted him $4,000, another year, $1,000, and another year, $2,500. It is interesting that most of his bigger "jobs" were possible because of his alertness and impulsiveness. He recalled an episode where he passed by a cashier's office in a large hotel in which the safe was open. On the impulse of the moment he walked into the office, took $850 in a bundle of cash and slipped out unseen.

Gustave's early life was difficult. Of five children he was the third. His mother was an ineffectual factor in the home even before she was afflicted with paralysis, early in her life. His father beat him; "He used a cat-o'-nine-tails and a belt on me," Gustave said. At the age of six or seven, he would jump out of the window or sneak out of the house at five in the morning before his father returned from work. His terror of his father was extreme. A sister stated to the boy that the day he was born his father, a habitual alcoholic, came home drunk and "raised hell." Once his father found him truant from school and, as punishment, tied him to a wagon and rode him to the parochial school, where he was publicly horsewhipped. Many times the offender experienced ridicule because he wore the castoff clothes of his brothers, and often he felt embarrassed for his parents because they did not assimilate themselves to American customs. Truancy and misbehavior at home resulted in his being sent to an industrial school. At the age of eight Gustave set fire to a barn in retaliation for a beating he received. From this point on, the boy lived away from home, graduating from one crime to another; he was never far thereafter from the toils of the law.

It is a clinical fact agreed upon by everyone who deals with behavior problems that the antisocial histories of psychopaths start in childhood. Some authorities refuse to make a diagnosis of psychopathic personality in the absence of a history of antisocial behavior and lack of adjustment in the home or school from the age of five or six onward. Lauretta Bender in working with problem children is able to diagnose cases of psychopathic children at the early age of six from their unorganized, impulsive behavior, inability to identify themselves with others and obvious difficulty in forming social concepts. These children had been subject to early emotional deprivation due to institutional care, neglect by parents or "critical breaks in the continuity of their relationships to mother or mother substitutes." There is a general agreement among those dealing with both child or adult psychopaths that a fundamental problem is a difficulty in the function of identification with parent-figures.

To attain as precise a picture as possible of the dynamic background of the psychopath's personality, it is necessary to return to a consideration of society's unconscious attitude toward wrongdoers. It will be recalled that in the early chapters it was pointed out that individually and in the aggregate, members of society experience a projected feeling toward the criminal which arises out of struggles with their own unconscious antisocial strivings. A significant aspect of these psychological phenomena is that the psychopath is intuitively aware of society's unconscious hostility which lies behind efforts to reform or treat him. This psychological interaction between the psychopath and society is a prime consideration in treatment. But it is also an important consideration in the dynamic struggle which eventuates in this type of personality disturbance.

The psychopath's distrust of society has a basis in the reality that he was treated badly as a child. Detailed psychoanalytic study of psychopaths shows that the attitude of constant rebelliousness against society is really an ego *defense* against infantile emotional deprivation. The psychopath sees individuals in his adult word in the image of his early denying parents. Bergler has pointed out that the overwhelming feeling of helplessness in the infant who has been orally denied is compensated for by the eternal wish to avenge himself against a society which represents a constantly recurring denying mother. Moreover, Bergler points out that the criminal feels no one believes him capable of exercising revenge on the unjust mother-figure. This reaction develops early in the life of the ego and is related to an unconscious, masochistic urge to continue in the subordinate position to attain security and love for the impoverished child. Continued yearning for emotional nutriment or narcissistic supplies is unconscious to the psychopath since it is a remnant within the nucleus of the psychopath's ego of a state of affairs that existed in the first or second year of his life. Yet this nucleus of emotional forces remains undiminished in its vigor and directs and motivates his entire life pattern of behavior.

These unseen forces, of course, must be interpreted through analysis of a person's emotional attitudes, dreams, and other expressions of unconscious urges. All that can be seen on the surface, even on psychiatric examination, are compensatory behavior elements for these forces. An example of the action of unconscious forces in the psychopath is seen in a youth of 19 who was referred to a psychiatrist by prison officials for incorrigibility, unmanageability and rage reactions. From the age of 10, he had been in constant difficulty with the law. His home life featured an alcoholic father who was constantly involved in criminal offenses, an unstable mother and a life of squalor and criminal associations. During the treatment period this prisoner, then in a prolonged reactive period of rebelliousness and belligerency, brought a dream:

"I found myself wrestling with a werewolf in a playful way, like you would fight with a brother, playing grab-ass. I am home, everyone sits around the table eating but I am under the table with the werewolf. They are not worried, and no one has seen it but me. Then I have a sharp instrument with two points and I am supposed to stick it in a vein to poison myself. A man shows what vein to go into but I fool him and squeeze the poison and blood out of the vein."

The associations to the dream indicated a developing transference to the therapist with emergence of homosexual feelings, and the subordinate position of the psychopathic patient in the family situation. The masochistic nature of his attitude toward the analyst was represented by the werewolf and the needle. While the patient's siblings were eating at the parents' table, he was fed poison (medicated affection) through a doctor's needle. His resentment against his mother prevented him from accepting the emotional nutriment he so desperately craved: "Food (love) cannot be for me; for me there is only death." It is probable that the two-pronged needle represented the patient and his brother and the solution of his sibling hostility: death to both. The depth of his conviction of oral denial and symbolic ostracism from the family and society is represented by placing himself under the table with the werewolf.

In the discussion of the psychopathic personality and its modes of behavior under stress, the presence of neurotic conflicts and neurotic mechanisms has made itself evident in the case material. A neurotic substratum and antisocial aims and ideals are combined in the personality organization. The resulting emotional callousness of the psychopath tends to make his acts appear to be based on willful, i.e., conscious, impulses. This is not actually true. Self-willed as the psychopath's actions seem to be, and overtly unwilling to modify his "bad" behavior as he appears to society, there is a compulsive quality to his offenses which suggests the participation of unconscious neurotic elements. While it cannot be stated categorically from the evidence that the behavior of psychopaths is uniformly under the influence of neurotic conflicts of which they are unaware, it can be said that the egocentricity and disregard of ethical ideals of the psychopath are character traits growing out of defenses against severe early emotional stresses. These personality traits do not appear as preformed behavior patterns which are the result of an abnormal nervous system in psychopaths but evolve within the developing ego. The ego is hampered in its early growth by emotional hunger, insecurity, rejection, domination or emotional overemphasis by either parent. The effect of these emotional traumata is to inhibit the development of identifications. Thus the conscience, or super-ego, is unable to grow on the basis of incorporations of old and new identifications. The super-ego in this group of individuals is confused because the ego-ideal in early life was confused. Emotional insecurity in the home prevented the acceptance of social parent-surrogates in the school, church, etc. These two factors of insecurity and a formless or confused ego-ideal seem to be basic for the well-recognized deficient super-ego of the psychopath.

The particular differences in the development of those egos which eventuate in neurotic, psychotic or psychopathic personalities, respectively, are explained by the concept of ego as an executive organ. As such, the ego is subject both to attack by id impulses and control by the super-ego. In the psychotic (insane) individual the ego is disorganized because the force of instinctive id impulses is disruptive and prevents the ego from maintaining its reality contact with the world. The psychotic presents a picture of disorganization of the functioning ego: he is disorientated, confused, mute, hallucinating and delusional. In the neurotic, the ego is able to function but is hampered because the severe super-ego causes undue inhibition of instinctive impulses. The neurotic, therefore, maintains contact with reality, but his instincts are inhibited. He therefore suffers from inhibitions, guilt feelings, embarrassment and repression of sexual feeling or of social assertiveness. In the psychopathic personality, the super-ego is deficient. Contact with reality is maintained, but the instinctive drives, subject to little or no control, are visited directly upon the social world. The psychopath suffers no inhibition or guilt. His ego is turned in the direction occasioned by unrestrained id impulses. The psychopathic personality appears to the world as emotionally calloused, egocentric, remorseless and impulsive.

The psychopath's tendencies have led to the belief that he lacks insight into the consequences of his acts and has an amoral view of the world. Some authorities consider lack of insight a cardinal symptom of psychopathic personality and an indication of the incurability of this condition. In spite of the apparent truth of this clinical observation, study of the psychopath in a psychotherapeutic situation demonstrates, in even the most desperate individuals, the partial appreciation of the compulsive character of his own impulses. The majority of aggressive individuals have a perception of the asocial bent of their personality patterns, and a number appreciate the social consequences of their impulses. If the personality structure of the psychopath is viewed as a defensive construction starting from infancy, the disregard of ethical standards cannot be regarded as a fixed attribute of the personality. Ethical callousness is the result of a long period of defensiveness against childhood traumata and rejection which becomes consolidated and expresses itself in forms opposing that toward which society strives. The notion of the law-abiding population that offenders belong to a criminal "group" whose ways defy change is based on the perception of the consolidation of such feelings. The psychopath who professes, without show of emotion, an utter disdain for social ideals and sentiments, does it with a blandness which suggests his absorption in a social attitude, evolved out of constant defensiveness, which is his dynamically "proper" view of the world.

Because of the extreme, almost ingrained, defensiveness of the psychopath, deep psychological study of such individuals is difficult, but material slowly developed by workers in this field points more and more to the basic formulation that the psychopath is not different in any essential detail from the so-called neurotic character. The structure of the psychopathic character rests upon the same defenses against strivings for forbidden instinctual gratifications (derived from the early oral phases of infantile development) as those found in many neuroses. The presence of anxiety, feelings of guilt, repression of instinctual urges and substitutive gratifications makes it difficult to view the psychopath as dynamically dissimilar from the symptomatic neurotic.

It is maintained that careful study of psychopaths in a therapeutic relationship where an objective, tolerant atmosphere thaws out their defensive callousness will demonstrate the inner nature of the antisocial attitude of the psychopath. It will be found to be a reflection of a coalesced attitude, an identification with others who also have defended themselves since infancy against emotional deprivation, and a denial of ethical principles laboriously erected by our Western civilization. It is less a characteristic embedded in the personality as a constitutional trait than a constantly maintained reaction against what appears to the psychopath to be a menacing society. Unfortunately, the psychological atmosphere of our current social life, with its approbation of legal institutions, is not psychologically suited to remove this constantly maintained character reaction. Hence, the criminal's identification with the antisocial view of life cannot be replaced by a broad, mature attitude of adjustment without the intervention of subtle and continued psychological technics.

When the dynamic view of the psychopathic personality is added to the clinical description, we become aware of a somewhat different attitude toward the problem. The picture which emerges tends to lie close to that of the character neurosis, except that the symptoms are more outspoken and expressed in a social direction. The acceptance of the dynamic view of the psychopath has one practical value for the criminologist, namely, the inadmissibility in his thinking of a specific type of "criminal psychopath." Since criminality is the result of the abutment of a personality in action on a legal code, merely to apply the term "criminal psychopath" to the recidivist or chronic criminal begs the question of the genesis of the individual's criminal actions in terms of his psychological life.

The total concept of psychopathic personality rests upon the standards of social adjustment as they are accepted and defined by the vast majority of individuals. But society itself maintains a view of these criteria which is relative to each member's unconscious identification with criminal impulses. Another unconscious influence on social criteria is that of the emotional connotation of words applied to antisocial behavior. The semantic element, the psychological effect of emotionally-toned words like "psychopathic," "inferiority" or "criminality," has been hinted at in the pages describing the growth of the psychopathic personality concept. This latter influence in part grew out of the ethical implications of the idea of psychopathy's forerunner—moral insanity—and should not be underestimated in an analysis of the psychopathic behavior pattern.

Just as the semantic value of words may have influenced society in its judgment of criminals, so there may have been a reciprocal semantic influence on criminals themselves. This hypothesis was suggested by Cleckley's observation that psychopathic personalities are in a real sense cases of semantic dementia: they use words without any true understanding of them. It is not unreasonable to suppose that the psychopath appears to have this semantic defect because of his reaction to the emotional connotation of words flung at him. This semantic superficiality, rather than being based on an inborn constitutional trait, may have been a diffused reaction to the mass of feeling that has filtered through the centuries from society and its legal representatives to the criminal. Emotionally-toned words act as an invisible boomerang thrown by society to the criminal and curving back again with redoubled force. The reflection of society's attitude toward evildoers joins with the inner emotional rigidity of psychopaths and thus reinforces their antagonism to society.

5

Emotional Immaturity and Crime

There is an intimate relationship between psychopathic personality and emotional immaturity. Elements of immaturity are found in every psychopath, and behavioral representations of psychopathy are found in every immature person. It has been stated that almost every act of a psychopathic personality is a source of discomfort to others in the environment or is in conflict with law and custom. This situation is true, to a lesser degree, of emotional immaturity. The purpose of this chapter is to trace the relationship between emotional and social immaturity and antisocial conduct.

Emotional immaturity is a term readily understood by those who have attained a perspective of life experience. That emotional immaturity parallels youth and is an inevitable accompaniment of physical immaturity is an accepted fact. Although standards of maturity vary with racial and cultural influences, political philosophies and even with historical eras among the same peoples, the attainment of a certain level of manhood or womanhood implies the adoption of mature attitudes of social living. In the past, maturity was often measured by the rule of "common sense," and parents and educators appreciated immaturity in adolescence and treated it with indulgence or impatience. Emotional maturity was generally expected to occur with the passage of time, when young people would "settle down." But serious students of the problems of youth, juvenile court judges, clergymen and teachers were aware that the maturing process did not always develop on schedule. Chronologic age, it was found, was not a reliable standard for measuring emotional and social maturity. The investigation of the structure of the mature personality placed emotional immaturity in the category of a symptom of personality abnormality. Adjudged as a symptom of maldevelopment of the personality, emotional immaturity has emerged as a factor of major importance in human misbehavior.

Emotional immaturity frequently occurs to a demonstrable degree among youthful offenders and in psychopaths, two groups which contribute heavily to antisocial problems. In youth, where immaturity is a natural concomitant of inexperience, the social consequences of immature attitudes range from harmless mischief to antisocial conduct. Among adult psychopaths who have suffered an arrest or deviation in the course of their emotional development, immaturity leads almost inevitably to conflict with society.

The alarming increase in the participation of youthful individuals in serious crime in the past two decades is the outstanding reason for the present recognized need to analyze the contribution of social and emotional immaturity to criminal behavior. In 1930, the study by the Wickersham Commission of the prison population of adult penal institutions showed that 54.8 per cent of all inmates had been less than twenty-one years of age when imprisoned. Reports promulgated a decade later by the American Law Institute (1940) indicated that the largest single four-year age group among apprehended felons was that of the offenders from sixteen to twenty years old. Criminal statistics show that the youthful offenders make up more than half of the total number of serious offenders apprehended, a ratio markedly out of proportion to the numerical incidence of youths in the total population. The problems of youth, and therefore of emotional immaturity, were brought to the fore in an emphatic manner by conditions of the postwar period (World War I), the depression years and the world unrest preceding World War II. The aftereffects of World War II are expected by many observers to result in criminal behavior among adolescents and youths to a serious degree.

IMMATURITY DEFINED

There has always been a tacit acceptance of the fact that maturity is defined according to the viewpoint of the most stable population. According to the views of the stable majority, standards of maturity can be defined as those which allow a maximum of achievements and enjoyments to the individual without conflict with law or custom. In psychological terms, maturity involves the acceptance of the realities of life, the breakdown of infantile fantasy aims and the shifting of emotional interests from infantile and adolescent objects to those of adulthood. More broadly, maturity means (Adolf Meyer) "dependability, a span of outlook and vision, i.e., insight, a capacity to accept illness, disappointment and frustration, an adjustment to emotional as well as sexual married life, a capacity to recognize limitations and an ability to appreciate and respect one's own place in the scale . . . Maturity means also a philosophy of objectivity about the past, i.e., a capacity to use the past." *

The conflict between immature aims and the limitations set by mature standards, as embodied in laws and convention, is the direct cause of the frequency with which youths become lawbreakers. What then are the indices of immaturity which lead to conflict and how do they develop? Examination of the points of conflict between mature and immature attitudes in social

* Reprinted from Meyer, Adolf: Our Children; A Handbook for Parents, ed. by Fisher & Gruenberg, New York, Viking, 1932, chap. 15, pp. 167-168.

areas is aided by a consideration of the developmental process through which the personality acquires maturity.

Observation of infants tends to support the view deduced from psychological study of adults that the human personality owes its origin to the pressure of social influences on human instincts. With due regard for the present uncertainty among psychologists about the precise nature of the instinct, the concept of an "instinct" as a preformed set of apparently unlearned reactions is used here to facilitate thinking. The first move of the infant toward its environment, the effort to gain nutriment, signalizes the start of the process of personality formation. The preformed set of reaction patterns served by the muscles about the mouth and throat used in nursing became intimately associated with feelings or emotions representing pleasure or satisfaction. Almost from the beginning, however, the infant organism is restricted in its nursing environment (mother). These restrictions, as a consequence, modify the emotions invested in the preformed patterns involved in feeding or other activities. The restrictions of the adults may be contrary to the innate primitive tendencies or "wishes" of the new organism. A conflict thus arises which is usually solved by the infant adopting the restrictions of the adult world. These restrictions become insensibly and gradually internalized and assume the force of inhibitions within the individual. The social result of this psychological mechanism is the "adjustment" of the infant to its environment. The successful completion of this process provides the basis for a "good" character.

As restrictions similar to those surrounding suckling are extended to other areas of infant activity, new attitudes are as insensibly developed. Under the guidance or teaching of adults, further emotional modifications occur in the infant which, as new areas of the body become subject to training, may be contrary to the primitive organism's "wishes." For example, toilet training in a child imposes new "teachings" that are in reality restrictions of the infant's tendency to do that which gives pleasure or to evade parental demands. In this case again, prohibitions become internalized in the form of inhibitions. Later, at the behest of social convention, injunctions are applied to the infant's interest in other areas of the body, or to activities arising from the use of its physical equipment, e.g., the use of the arms and legs as aggressive organs to injure others, etc.

The prolonged exertion of social pressure on instinctive tendencies has several results in terms of personality reactions. The infant may accept the restrictions imposed by the adults and adopt acceptable forms of behavior; he may reject the prohibitions and develop unacceptable forms of behavior; or he may be sidetracked into reaction formations which show up in later life as symptoms whose origins are obscured (unconscious) to the individual. The example of the resolution of prohibitions directed against feeding activities may be cited. The infant with few conflicts about his eating activities will develop acceptable behavior in later life regarding activities surrounding the oral zone, i.e., speech and food. The infant with unsolved conflicts centering about the oral zone will develop unacceptable behavior—he will be greedy or verbally aggressive. The emotional feelings concerning the activities of his oral areas will not be smoothly blended in his personality with adult realities. Other individuals with a fixation at this point will develop neurotic symptoms and reaction formations such as smacking tics of the lips, peculiar attitudes toward food or neurotic speech disturbances.

The acceptance or denial of enforced prohibitions depends upon the emotional atmosphere imparted to the infant when its wishes are curbed. The main purpose of adult control of children in the earliest years is that of attaining obedience. Obedience in the home extends to demands for obedience in many areas of the child's social life. He must be kind to other children, forbear quarreling with brothers and sisters, relinquish his desire to touch a myriad of objects that belong to the adult world and conform to a stringent ordering of his life in many details. Ordinarily, the parents' affection in the form of rewards removes the sharpness of these constantly repeated frustrations. However, in some instances the anxiety of the parents that arises from their guilty awareness of their own arbitrary position of authority is perceived by the child, who reacts to authority with knowledge of its half-hearted nature. Again when parents or teachers accompany their training efforts with emotional coldness, the young organism accepts his training with reluctance. Children who have been taught to accept adult discipline without the lubrication that is provided by parental love show lack of assimilation of authority in their resultant behavior patterns. The emotional overtones which are contributed to the child's personality by the parents' love or lack of love become evident in automatic patterns in later life.

As the prohibitions directed at the growing organism expand to include social areas, reaction formations toward social ideals develop which become manifest in attitudes and in behavior. The personality incorporates these new attitudes as imperceptibly and holds them with as much tenacity as it did in the case of body function attitudes and reactions. The source of early social injunctions in the family unit is usually the father. Reaction formations built on rejection of such prohibitions therefore are directed at the father or substitute figures, i.e., legal agents and institutions. Attitudes of hostility to authority in later years spring from the early reaction to the parent whose social teaching was misinterpreted by the child as punishment, an interpretation made plausible because of the absence of tokens of affection accompanying training efforts.

The meaning of education is the control or modification of immaturity to the end that conflict with society is minimized or removed. In youth, social immaturity is brought under control in the home, school and church by constantly exerted pressure, through precept, example and exhortation. The child's early patterns of acceptance of social teachings, formed in the home, require continuous re-emphasis as the individual is brought into contact with practical problems of living. During the period of scholastic training, education of the emotions extends from home to school as an intangible but active force. It is only later that youth obtains intellectual insight into the reason for the mature individual's insistence on habits of disciplined living. Education of the emotions is a lifelong process, and society exerts a never-ending influence alike on youths and adults. Law and custom remain inexorably active, continuously molding the personality in terms of mature standards.

Some adolescents do not accept the prohibitions which are necessary for the development of a mature viewpoint or recognize the need for a capacity to endure frustration. They behave according to standards evolving out of their own emotional economy. Similarly some adults reject the standards of mature reality in accordance with their persisting emotional immaturity. These adult individuals retain personality peculiarities to a degree that does not conflict with law. Remnants of immaturity, expressed in eccentricities of dress, nonconformism or voluble antagonism to authority without criminal behavior, are not uncommon. However, where rejection of standards of maturity is persistent in the behavior of the total personality, a psychopathic reaction pattern can be considered to exist. Psychologically, social immaturity portrays the early stage of psychopathy, but the significant point is that not every immature youth becomes a psychopath. The striking circumstance of the decline of immature attitudes with the passage of years suggests the possibility of attaining insight into the basis of psychopathy through the study of immaturity.

Interest in immaturity at this point is confined to its appearance in the sphere of antisocial conduct, where immature behavior and attitudes precipitate criminal acts. The endeavor in this chapter will be to obtain a more intimate picture of the relationship between persisting immaturity and criminal behavior. Many criminal offenses among adolescents and adults have this basis, e.g., the so-called "inexplicable" offenses, crimes among first offenders and offenses which seem unplanned or without obvious gain.

The problem will be approached by viewing areas of social relationships wherein immaturity stands out conspicuously in its relation to criminal acts. They can be grouped conveniently into attitudes toward (1) society and authority, (2) activity and aggression, (3) the body and its adornment and (4) sexual life. These contactual areas between the individual and society loom large upon the adolescents' emotional horizon and contain the greatest variance in attitudes in comparison with those held by mature individuals. The attitudes of immature persons generally touch on specific emotional elements in the crime involved. For example, in a burglary by an immature youth, there may be found an infantile attitude regarding clothes and adornment. In a robbery of a homosexual, the immature attitudes toward sex are involved; in assault, the relationship to activity and aggression is in question.

(1) IMMATURE ATTITUDES TOWARD SOCIETY

Boys and youths express their attitudes toward society most clearly in the coalesced feelings of gangs. The immature person, because of his basic feeling of inferiority, tends to gather with a like-minded group wherein his attitudes are understood without explanation. The gang toward which he gravitates is very often the first social institution which he finds congenial to his wishes and tastes. He finds in the group a common body of feeling toward authority, the one disturbing reality in his life. Gangs are in essence elements foreign to civilized living, entertaining attitudes toward community ideals antithetic to those of mature persons.

In sociologic discussions of gang life much attention has been given to the external stimuli to gang formation, such as the example of the glorified criminal in the cinema, the comic-book gangster or even actual association with criminal groups by boys in slum areas. A more important factor in the formation of gangs is the psychological need of boys to express concretely their community of emotional interests. The impulse toward gang formation arises in adolescents out of the need to express antiparental or antisocial tendencies. The individual who finds it hazardous openly to espouse such feelings gains strength in company of like-minded youths. The gang fosters the free voicing of aggression in its members. The gang has a psychological value to the individual since in it aggressiveness is socially acceptable, whereas the home fosters suppression of aggressive or rebellious tendencies. Boys in a gang can pelt a tradesman who protects his merchandise from theft or revile a police officer for unwarranted interference with their mischief when they would be fearful of individually voicing their defiance of law.

The tone of gang psychology is set by requirements of initiation. It is based upon the reversal of adult social values. The initiate must give some token of subscribing to the fundamental tenet of the gang, which is anti-authoritarianism. The gang code insists that if a youth does not steal, he is unworthy of "belonging"; if a boy shows a liking for books or is ambitious or obedient to parents he is anathema; if he enjoys the arts he is at least regarded as "peculiar." This transposition of mature ideals has its basis in the individual emotional problems of the gang-member and in the general rebelliousness of boys.

Rebelliousness is a natural trait in children of our culture. It varies in degree according to whether parents discourage it vigorously or allow its emergence. Ordinarily childhood or adolescent rebelliousness stems from a hatred of authority, often of the father. Even the nondelinquent child senses an attitude which is repressive beyond the dictates of discipline. A parent's ill-advised commands directed against motor activity or adventurousness may stir up deep resentments in the boy who is used to obeying. In a child who is not used to obeying, open rebellion occurs. If the parent takes strong punitive measures, the child's manifest rebelliousness is curbed, but enduring resentment takes root and may blossom, under prevailing gang attitudes, into subsequent criminal activity.

The direct translation of rebelliousness into overt acts is shown in the case of a youth sixteen years of age, a member of a loosely organized group of boys who engaged in burglaries in the neighborhood. In the company of two other boys, George burglarized a candy store near his home, taking $35.00 in cash. Because of truancy and other difficulties in school, George had spent a brief period at a reformatory. Tall, slender, well-built, of average intelligence, he was the second oldest in a family of five boys, the oldest of whom had been previously sentenced to the reformatory. The father, a stern man, impatient with his sons' contrary behavior, was arrogant and abusive at home and could not tolerate his children's rebellion. He treated George with pointed silence and would not allow him or his older brother to eat at the same table with other members of the family. Even before the instant offense, George had such fear and hatred of his father that he often spent nights sleeping on near-by roof tops. He said he was positive that his father considered him worthless.

The youth was placed on probation for the burglary but continued his rebellious behavior. He left home and resumed sleeping on roof tops and sometimes in basements near the scene of the burglary for which he was apprehended. He was suspected of stealing bottles of milk in the building. Although motivated by great hostility, George also showed the opposite emotion of deep dependence on his father. He could not remain in his home but he never went far from it. By keeping in close proximity to his home and by his return to the scene of his crime, George demonstrated the ambivalence behind his conflict, which expressed itself in apparently contradictory behavior. The youth wished to punish his father but succeeded only in punishing himself. The deep need for parental understanding and love confused his motives and behavior. These two phases of emotion, love and hatred, are present in the rebelliousness of all immature youths. Open rebelliousness accompanied by unconscious dependence on the authoritative person against whom the aggression is directed is a common finding.

Gang feelings, which solidify around many types of criminal activity, also center about noncriminal attitudes. Solidarity among gang members is seen in slang, mannerisms, clothes customs, gestures and even facial expressions. Often the psychological elements which each member of a gang contributes are crystallized in a social code surrounding community activities. The code applied to the imbibing of alcoholic beverages provides an example of the coalesced feelings of immature persons. Drinking at bars has its own etiquette and ritual. The elements of this rigid procedure feature nonchalance and avoidance of obvious expression of anxiety. For example, payment for drinks is always made before they are consumed. Change placed on the bar is never picked up and coins are slapped on the bar in a clicking manner indicating a mild disdain for money. A drink is offered to a stranger only by referring the offer through the bartender, in which case the recipient raises his glass in a salute before he drinks. The bartender is the master of ceremonies, the social arbiter of etiquette and the judge of all disputes or wagers.

The discussion of drinking habits among the immature brings to the fore their special attitudes toward friends. Friends are considered in a utilitarian light: friendship is valued as an opportunity not for giving to others but receiving. "A friend is a fellow who helps you out in a pinch," explained a youthful offender. The reason for this attitude rests upon the inherent difficulty in making social contacts, which is a consequence of emotional rigidity in the immature person. Underlying inferiority feelings cause each contact with a strange individual to assume the proportions of an anxiety-producing event. The apparent nonchalance of the immature individual toward those not in his group proves in reality to be a defense against timidity. New social contacts arouse anxiety because they threaten self-exposure, and any device which allays the anxiety of feared exposure is seized by immature persons and incorporated into their social practices. Alcohol, for this reason, is a valuable social aid for immature individuals because it acts as a lubricant to their emotional rigidity. Close adherence to the code of the group is another form of ego-protecting mechanism. The utilitarian attitude toward friends acts as a barrier against the emergence of inferiority and inhibits the free flow of emotion between friends. Expression of emotion is denied by the immature. It is conceived as an unmitigated weakness. This view accounts for the disdain of gang members for "polite society," which openly acknowledges the emotional support received from social intercourse between friends.

The immature individual who yearns to belong to a gang or club is in the same psychological position as any person who wishes to be regarded as an integral part of a living social group. The difference between the mature adult in his social grouping and the immature adolescent is merely that of the direction of social aims pursued. The drive for identification with a group, whether it be a poolroom gang or an exclusive gentlemen's club, stems from an ultimate emotional need for human interdependence.

The effect of culturally limited homes and neighborhoods on adolescents is an important factor in the formation of immature attitudes toward the community. The social notions of such individuals are haphazard and unformed. Their fund of information is poor, their interests provincial, their attitude toward learning defensive. Most individuals from areas of low cultural levels automatically accept their social deprivations. They allow themselves to be emotionally disfranchised. Feelings of inferiority prevent such individuals from utilizing community sources of emotional support, such as settlement houses, "Big Brother" organizations, churches, etc.

Other adolescents adhere to short-sighted social values for other reasons. They do not suffer from a lack of cultural stimulation in the home; rather they actively reject these influences. These persons vigorously deny the standards of social maturity set down by generations before them. Here rebelliousness appears to be aimed at the prescribed drudgery which ends in only moderate success in life. Without an intellectual awareness of the persistent effort which mature reason decrees, immature individuals move impulsively into activities which promise to change their personal fortunes quickly. In their impatience, which is so characteristic of immaturity, they reject the normal pace of social growth. Yet, impatience with set standards occasionally leads to social changes of immeasurable benefit to humanity. Rebelliousness and impatience, although evidences of immaturity, are not always necessarily antisocial in result. Psychiatry, which assumes the responsibility for defining the indices of adjustment, must also reckon with this fact. Social immaturity becomes a problem of psychiatric significance only when rejection of accepted social philosophy leads to antisocial acts.

Experiences of psychiatrists among the American forces in World War

II demonstrated that psychological mechanisms were active in immature, rebellious soldiers and sailors which were analogous to those operative in the antisocial behavior of immature civilian offenders. It will be advantageous in the discussion of rebelliousness to recall the description of personality development set forth earlier in this chapter. It was pointed out then that the manner in which the infant met the restrictions imposed by its environment determined the later adoption of social or antisocial attitudes. It was noted that necessary restrictions of the infant's wishes (instinctive tendencies) provoked rebellious reactions in the average child which, for all practical purposes, were suppressed in the process of incorporating the parent's prohibitions in the child's ego. In spite of this block to the persistent expression of antagonism to authority, all children retain some spirit of rebelliousness toward their parents and elders. This residual feeling of revolt becomes the mainspring for the independence characteristic of adolescence and youth. When rebelliousness continues and is crystallized in a pattern of antisocial behavior, we speak of immature and psychopathic behavior. What determines the persistence or rejection of reasonable authority depends upon several factors in the individual's development. A broken home with absence of parental guidance, or a home with disinterested, neurotic parents plays an outstanding role in the rejection of mature standards by youth. Emotional rejection may come from either parent, but it is the father, the representative of the social world, who is the figure against which rebelliousness is most often projected.

Authority is the crucial aspect of a military organization which handles large numbers of men without primary consideration for their individual wishes or impulses. The psychology of rebelliousness against commands is clearly seen in deserters from military service. Immature men in the army and the navy were stimulated early in their military careers by the novelty of duty away from home, by competitive reaction to their friends and by the promise of adventure. When confronted by the rigid discipline of the military service, they became defiant of authority and discipline and reacted by running away. Studies of this group demonstrated an admixture of neurotic elements and a negativistic attitude toward authority. Military offenders who stated that they hated officers and military service gave evidence of neurotic attitudes toward their parents. Early emotional reactions to the father were projected to officers and to the impersonal authority of regulations. Strong dependency needs, however, lay back of this attitude of arrogance to authority. Antagonism was demonstrably a defense reaction which hid from the individual his unconscious passive, dependent elements. Conscious submission to those in control was considered a weakness by the man. The psychological stimulation for desertion from military service was found in the main to rest on the unconscious force of ambivalent feelings of antagonism and dependence projected from parent-figures to those in authority.

An example of this situation is seen in the case of Roy, an 18-year-old seaman who was in the Navy five and a half months before he went A.W.O.L. for fifty-nine days. During his first seven weeks at training camp he adjusted well, but at a specialty school during the next few months he became nervous, was unable to concentrate and did poorly in his work. While in transit with a draft of men to a seaport, Roy's train passed through the railroad station of his home town, where he impulsively got off the train. When he arrived home, he immediately sought out and caressed his two dogs, whom he declared he loved "as much as I love my mother." He felt emotionally comfortable at home, spent his time with his mother and with girl friends. Under the rationalization that he went home "to straighten things out before he went to sea," was a strong wish to be with his mother and to "settle things" with his father, i.e., ameliorate his guilt toward the latter. He spoke constantly of his wish to become engaged to a girl so he could "have" somebody when he went to sea.

On examination Roy was restless and talked with an overcompensating sense of self-confidence which, under probing, revealed a dependent, insecure youth. He was contemptuous of naval regulations and showed disregard of the importance of his desertion from the service. His attitude was flippant, egocentric and intolerant of authority, although his intelligence and interest in mechanics were above average. His mother was evidently overprotective of her only child, and his father was apparently a neurotic person with whom the youth had been constantly at odds over minor matters. Roy complained that his father was a stingy, petty individual. Both parents had tried to fashion the life of this boy, one in an indulgent way and the other behind a screen of rivalry. In spite of their careful attention and oversolicitude, Roy achieved little emotional nourishment from the atmosphere of his home. Roy's great fondness for his dogs and his obsessive drive for a fiancée were indications of the displacement of his emotional craving to objects other than his parents. The impulse to disregard regulations and flout authority was related to emotional deprivations that were carried over from an early period of life and activated by the demands of the military service.

(2) IMMATURE ATTITUDES TOWARD ACTIVITY
AND AGGRESSION

Rebelliousness, as a trait of emotionally immature individuals, bears a relation to the intensified degree of physical activity characteristic of the young. The neural and muscular systems of children and youths are physiologically attuned to activity. It can be assumed, therefore, that behavior patterns involving aggression are necessarily influenced by the organic predisposition of youth to motor activity. This relationship is one that is generally understood, for no one disagrees that aggressive bits of behavior appearing in sports among adolescents are normal phenomena. Increased capacity for expending energy resulting from sudden puberty stimulation of glandular activity is balanced by the psychic correlate of feelings of unlimited potential achievement. This mental attitude of invincibility contributes a heroic caste to adolescent exploits and projects the youth into difficult reality situations which appear to be easily surmountable under the influence of his illusion of power. In the immature individual the psychological correlate of recently acquired physiologic power is the factor that pushes youth into criminal acts.

Hyperactivity and the feeling of omnipotence and achievement characteristic of adolescence, both require consideration when they overstep the bounds of normality. The hyperactive behavior of immature individuals bears a close relation to the restlessness of certain troublesome children. These are children whose motor energy oversteps the limits of ordinary play. The chronically hyperactive child behaves in a characteristic way: he tears books, teases playmates constantly, indulges in sex play, lacks concentration, loses interest in games or goals quickly, and talks with a "push" of speech which often surprises adults with its apparent brilliance. Such a child mimics adults, nags constantly and has a persistent desire to inflict pain on parents or siblings (especially girls) by punching, pinching, spitting or pushing. The hyperactive child is a human dynamo in constant rebellion against the normal limitations of activity which parents and society impose.

This group of behavior symptoms, considered in the past as due to willfulness or mischievousness, can be designated by the term *hyperkinetic syndrome,* which when persistent is a distinctly abnormal condition. Ordinarily hyperactivity of moderate degree fades with the growth of the young organism and is properly considered a phase of maturation. The persistence or accentuation of such hyperactivity, however, indicates a possible relation to a structural or functional disturbance within the nervous system. The first intimation of such a hypothesis came from the history of the behavior of the cases of chronic encephalitis which resulted from the sleeping sickness epidemics of the 1920's. Neurologists noted in this disease significant motor disturbances, including constant, uncontrolled choreiform and athetoid movements. Other cases appeared in which restlessness was the predominant symptom. American observers reported these postencephalitic children as "destructive, restless, (who) want to be their 'own boss,' and seem to have excessive sexual curiosity." Psychiatrists described the activity as a throwback to "infantile forms with a disregard for external controls." Later it was not an uncommon experience to see this chronic misbehavior pattern appear in children with a history of an attack of encephalitis in the past who were otherwise apparently well. The similarity of hyperactive children to psychopathic individuals with their restless, disrespectful, asocial, impudent attitudes was remarked by many authorities.

The occurrence of hyperkinesis as an aftereffect of sleeping sickness suggests a possible relationship between the hyperactivity of immature boys and hyperactivity due to organic disease of the nervous system. It is possible that individuals whose hyperactivity persists into early manhood may have a basic structural predisposition to movement because of an organic defect, either congenital or the sequela of disease in the cerebral tissues. Hyperactivity can also be considered a passing phase of emotional development in which motor activity is a response to strong anxiety based on guilty feelings or reactions to emotional deprivation. If the former is the case, we may expect immaturity in youthful offenders to disappear when the neural tissues in the body eventually gain balance after puberty. If the latter is true, i.e., that anxiety and unconscious emotional needs are expressed in motor terms, there would be little cessation in the criminality of these individuals throughout the course of their lives unless restraint of these forces occurs through successful therapy. It can only be a matter for speculation how much of the tendency toward destructiveness is emotionally conditioned and how much is due to the original energy disposition with which the biologic machine is endowed. At this point it will suffice to point to the close relationship between hyperactivity, as seen normally among children and some adolescents, and excessive activity in immature personalities and psychopaths which may lead directly to the commission of criminal acts.

The urge toward movement and muscular activity in the young individual receives its most obvious expression in the criminal field in motor car larcenies. Although the theft of an automobile is listed as Grand Larceny in the statutes of most states of the Union, investigation shows that the great majority of auto thefts serve the purpose of pleasure through movement rather than that of financial gain. The great number of such crimes represents primarily a gratification of the adolescent urge for motor activity. The technic of the usual motor car larceny provides a nice demonstration of the psychological elements involved. These may be indicated in the following composite case culled from experience with hundreds of such crimes committed by youths in a metropolitan city.

After preliminary observance of an empty automobile, several youths seat themselves in it, talking of the cost of the car and the thrill of driving. Presently one of their number, toying with the ignition switch, starts the motor by crossing the wires. The first satisfaction derived is that of driving slowly through the neighborhood in the commandeered car. This feeling of heightened social prestige gives way to the urge for speed. As hyperkinetic impulses assert themselves, the drive becomes a joy ride which increases in tempo until it is terminated by apprehension of the car by the police or by an accident.

The motor car, like the airplane, is the modern symbol of speed. For the immature person behind the wheel, the psychobiologic drive toward movement becomes a compulsion which is unhampered by mature considerations of danger or propriety. Speed mania can be definitely regarded as resting on an immature attitude toward activity. Driving a car entails movement without an object, an intransitive act encompassing an identification of the driver with the apparently unlimited power of the mechanism he controls. Cases of compulsive joy riding like the following are extremely frequent in every criminal court. This case concerns a youth of twenty-three, arrested twice for driving without a license, who was apprehended for stealing a new car which he drove as fast as 108 miles an hour on the highway. He boasted that he never drove less than 100 miles per hour in any car where possible. "It's in my blood to drive fast," he explained.

A graphic instance of the compulsive aspect of speed mania which resulted in a charge of grand larceny for theft of a motor car was seen in a man of twenty-eight, regularly employed as a chauffeur on buses running between two large eastern cities. He was without previous criminal record, suffered no accidents during eleven years of driving and bore an excellent reputation. On the evening of the offense he had been drinking and noticed an ambulance with the motor running standing in front of a hospital. He climbed in, rang the bell and careened wildly down a busy thoroughfare. "For some reason I can't explain," he said, "I got into the ambulance and drove away . . . The bell was the main thing, I guess."

Frequently car thieves are easily apprehended because their joy rides finish with destruction of the vehicle they steal. There is conceivably a psychological meaning to the wreck which frequently terminates the stealing of a car. The speed of the machine is absorbed into the psyche of the driver and tends to express his aggression as well as to serve the pleasure instinct. An act of aggression without an object, like movement without terminus, is a frustrating experience. The terminal smashup, often caused in part by alcoholism, is frequently an unconsciously determined act which is aimed at removing the frustration of objectless speed.

An indirect expression of the immature attitude toward activity is to be observed in the *runaway reaction*. Although this phrase is commonly used in reference to child behavior problems, the runaway tendency is regularly seen in adolescents and may be traced to the immature adult, where it reaches its most extreme form in the nomadic psychopath. The "running away" of young adults is not always immature, for in certain instances leaving home has had laudable results in exploration, pioneering and the spread of commerce. In the ordinary course of development of adolescents the runaway tendency is rationalized as "wanderlust." During the last century, the "wanderjahr" of the student or the year "before the mast" of the less advantageously placed youth was recognized as a salutory period in the character growth of the individual. However, if the romantic and intellectual elements are substracted from wanderlust, the emotional substrate is observed to be closely akin to that of the hyperactive, immature individual. The runaway reaction is impelled by the ego's perception of emerging aggressive feelings toward the parents and the parent-symbol institutions of the environment, and the ego's wish to escape the result of these potentially destructive impulses.

In the case histories of immature offenders and recidivists, a history of elopement from home at an early age is a very common finding. Flight from home is a sharp reaction to intolerable emotional strain in which the modality of hyperactivity, actually or figuratively, is used as an instinctive mechanism of defense. The psychic pain arising from rejection, humiliation, frustration or emotional deprivation in the home environment drives the sensitive child or adolescent into flight. Moreover, elements from less visible levels of the ego contribute to the neurotic compulsion to run away. Among immature persons, leaving home is quite evidently charged with strong emotion arising from the powerful forces of anxiety. Unconscious urges arising from the Oedipus situation, which promote antagonism to the father that the ego of the individual cannot tolerate, also stimulate flight from home. The fantasy of renunciation of parents is operative in these cases. In older youths of the predelinquent group, hostile impulses toward the parents, which are hidden in the renunciation idea, are so overwhelming that they can be relieved only by an attempt to escape. But the immature personality rarely gains anything from the resolution of his conflicts through flight, because the mechanism of renunciation is rooted in unconscious dependence on the parents from whom he so obviously wishes to escape.

The fantasy of injury to parents, observed among young children in the familiar plaint, "You'll be sorry when I die," is an inverted expression of the child's need to be loved and the wish to be taken back into the bosom of the family. The same mechanism applies in youths who are sensitized by humiliation and emotional rejection and whose dependency wishes are hidden under a shell of apparent hardness. In such situations hostile feelings toward the parent, compensating for yearnings for love, can be so intense as to lead to a denial of name, religion or any affiliation that may constitute recognition of family ties.

A nineteen-year-old boy of Jewish origin, living under the name of Geoffrey Earl, was arrested after a series of burglaries. Two years prior to this arrest, Earl had run away from home, sailing on a merchant ship as mess steward and wiper in the engine room. The long trip took him around South America and up the west coast to Vancouver, thoroughly satisfying his wanderlust. On his return to New York, his money spent, he set up a cold-water flat in a slum area, intent upon never going back to his family or using his own name. He wanted to remain Geoffrey Earl forever. His dream had been to return home from the sea in ten or twenty years with money and live in splendor while his family remained in squalor.

Within a short time he committed twenty-two burglaries. He stole especially works of art, violins, jewelry and men's clothing. He considered himself clever; his burglarizing technic was to walk out of an apartment audibly waving good-by so that passers-by could hear him. Later Geoffrey felt that he had disgraced his family and wanted to conceal from his parents the fact that he was a "petty crook." The pattern of his criminal exploits was fashioned by his attempt at solution of his emotional problems. Geoffrey wanted to be a successful burglar who outwitted his victims. His crime motive was a reaction to an intense feeling of hostility against his father.

It is significant that the flight mechanism utilized by the immature to resolve their mental conflicts, is closely related to a predilection for fantasying. Play, for the normal child, is replete with examples of motor impulses intimately associated with fantasy images. It has long been known that the imagination of many individuals, especially immature persons, characteristically has a motor component. There is an equally intimate connection between fantasy images and the illusion of unlimited power. Again, spontaneous games of children provide graphic illustrations of the alliance between the imagination, motor activity and emotionally-toned illusions of tremendous strength. On the wings of imagination, boys destroy gigantic enemies, decimate imaginary armies, erase continents and soar across oceans. The residuals of the imaginative drive which persist in immature persons beyond the age of childhood retain a threefold character of fancy, activity and power. The combination of these elements, which gain expression through the imagination in a manner that is so specifically a feature of emotional immaturity, obstructs from view the limitations of reality which the mature person readily perceives. In ordinary experience, the closer these tendencies of omnipotence feeling and physical prowess are associated, the clearer immaturity appears to the observer. One consequence of this phenomenon is that the youth or young adult whose fantasy requires gratification easily falls into criminal activity such as car thefts. His motoric tendency pushes him over the limits of reality, less because of his wish to be antisocial than because of the impelling quality of his imagination, in which fantasy is linked to hyperactivity.

The mechanical influences of our present-day life, rather than decreasing the effect of fantasy thinking among all levels of our population, promise to increase it. The impetus toward wishful thinking provided by today's space-devouring and time-devouring developments is conceivably a psychological factor in the persistence of immaturity. Technologic developments which lift the work of the world out of human hands have an inhibiting influence on man's ego and a stultifying effect on the psyche of man. The dwarfing of the individual in our civilization stimulates wishful thinking in the liliputian feelings so engendered. Fantasy, with its timelessness and infiniteness, becomes a natural antidote to frustration. In a complex world where hitherto daring ideas quickly become transmuted into reality, fantasy daily moves closer to reality. The confusion in the immature mind concerning fantasy, speed, power and time tends to support a disregard of reality considerations. Another factor moving in this direction is the daily literary diet of millions, the comic strip, which feeds the fantasy with intimations of the power of cosmic rays, electronic energy and radio-controlled robots. A recent excerpt from a pictorial magazine explained of an imaginary figure, who embodied the apotheosis of fantasy, power and speed, that he came

out of an imaginary planet less than two years ago. He is Superman, a character who combines the best talents of a Robin Hood and a god, and every day his feats of strength, speed and benevolence bring thrills to millions of newspaper and comic magazine readers. Superman is the extension of their (authors') dream, and proof that Americans still like their fantasy raw. (*Look Magazine*, February 27, 1940, pp. 15-17.)

The psychological sustenance which immature persons of our day draw from their environment is a mixture, neither totally fantastic nor yet completely realistic.

Allied to the prevalent currency of fantasy in the minds of the immature is the tendency toward substituting aggression for wishful thinking in the psychic economy. Aggression has always been an integral component of the human urge toward activity but it has been curbed by definite delimitations woven into social traditions and legal codes. Physical aggression is only morally permissible in self-defense. The law has incorporated this evaluation of aggression by providing lesser degrees of assault and homicide on the plea of self-defense. Physical aggression on all but the strongest provocation is looked on askance by those who hold mature attitudes. To display aggression without reason is indicative of an attitude not tolerated by civilized persons.

The emotionally immature person, on the other hand, expresses his derision or hate openly, resorting to blows without adequate provocation or the need to defend himself. Significant psychological elements are observable in this distinctly characteristic type of aggression which is seen among immature persons. Gratuitous fighting, spurred on by intolerance, arises from a deep-seated feeling of insecurity in which every contact is imagined to be laden with contempt or possible injury. The intolerance to humiliation may concern racial dissimilarities, those of age, dress or sectional differences in the same city or country. Any one of many factors can serve as a screen on which to project a defensive reaction to an implied threat of contumely or implication of inferiority. The tension engendered by the threat of inferiority, which is inherent in any competitive situation, demands immediate solution for immature persons. A casual meeting of such individuals looms as a possible encounter with one who challenges their emotional security. The immature individual anticipates the defense he imagines he will be called upon to make by preparing himself for aggressive action. Physical combat serves to ease his fear, as the functioning muscular organization absorbs his anxieties.

The compulsive urge to strike out defensively or the corollary fear of being struck immediately when they are confronted by a situation that presents potentialities of injury, is described by many adolescents. Ordinarily a mature individual faced by potential danger will estimate the time allotted, the forces to be met and the strength he has at his disposal. The immature individual, however, is spurred on by the instinctive elements mentioned above. An unwillingness to fight immediately is rationalized as a failing, an indication of a lack of adequate masculinity. In this attitude the immature youth has the support of the common association between aggressiveness and masculinity, on the one hand, and between passivity and femininity on the other. Adolescents naturally fear to expose the possession of so-called feminine traits of passivity or submissiveness when the world holds up as an ideal the dichotomy, masculine-aggressivity and feminine-passivity.

A striking example of the extension of this feeling of inadequacy into aggressive criminal behavior is that of Harry, eighteen years of age, born in this country of foreign parentage, who was convicted, in company with two others, of the murder of a gas station manager. When the latter resisted the attempted robbery of the till and raised a cry, he was instantaneously shot. The offender, the second of three children, had had difficulty in school, although his intelligence measured average. At the age of fifteen he was transferred to a probation school because of truancy, misconduct and poor scholarship.

Harry vividly described his reactions when angry. "When I get angry I get steamed, can't control myself. My face gets hot, my ears get hot. I get shaky and scared. If I fight with a fellow I fight nice and easy after the first few blows. I would have to get hit to feel good. The first few blows make me feel satisfied." In anger, Harry's anxiety could only be quieted by immediately hitting the opponent or by being struck by the latter.

Psychiatrists have been aware of this apparently anomalous situation in which receipt of a blow relieves anxiety, thus allowing the emergence of an aggressive response. To be struck first satisfies strains of passivity which the individual involved is the last to recognize. Keiser and Schilder, in studying the psychologic meaning of aggression in murder and assault cases, encountered a substratum of passivity in even the most aggressive criminals. The swaggering front and "masculine" attitude represented an overcompensation for internally perceived but abhorred "feminine" traits. On a still deeper psychological level, the fear of being considered nonmasculine was expressive of strong castration anxiety and often a fear of exposure of latent homosexual elements. Anxiety arising from this source gave rise to the immediate attempt to counteract basic softness of character by an aggressive front. Adult criminals particularly display this reaction. In the example to follow, the reaction occurred where it would least be expected, in a professional prize fighter.

John Jacks, twenty-six years old, a competent prize ring fighter, was arrested on a charge of sodomy. His offense occurred in relation to several boys ranging from nine to thirteen years of age. Jacks had been in four hundred boxing bouts, was a world's middleweight championship contender, a clever, aggressive puncher who had never been knocked out. In the ring he was constantly on the aggressive, but among his associates he was known to be plagued by the fear of being hurt or touched when his back was turned.

A hero to the children in his neighborhood, Jacks always had a string of adoring boys following in his wake. With these, which included several of the complainants, he was at ease. With men, his uneasiness was demonstrated constantly in a tense, paranoid attitude. During psychiatric examinations, for example, he was jumpy, careful always to face his interrogators, anxious and suspicious. Among boxers Jacks was known to be sensitive toward the imputation of homosexuality. His aggressive tactics in the ring, where his earnings were high, were in reaction to feelings of inadequacy and strong fears of possible injury to himself. Jacks' overt perception of homosexual urges, signalized by the instant offense, came at a time in his career as a prize ring fighter when he was less able to carry his defensive aggressiveness to his opponent. Homosexual impulses broke through and rendered the overcompensating physical aggression ineffective. The persistence of the fear of being considered physically weak and passive represented remnants of immature attitudes that were observable in the offender's life pattern as well as in his offense.

(3) IMMATURE ATTITUDES TOWARD THE BODY

Immature attitudes toward the person have been discussed in relation to offenders who committed assault in reaction to strong feelings of humiliation. The prominence of anxiety and sensitivity in the emotional life of immature individuals concerning the body and its appearance also extends to bodily adornment. Psychological traits which bear a causal relationship to antisocial behavior are discerned in the examination of immature feelings toward adornment of the body. The manner in which the skin, for example, is regarded by any given individual is a highly personal matter, varying with the neurotic components present in his make-up (narcissistic investment) and his social viewpoint. Nevertheless, enough uniformity of attitude toward clothing and skin adornment such as tattooing is visible in immature persons to suggest several generalizations in this area of social psychology.

It is a psychiatric truism that everyone has an enormous amount of emotion invested in his body covering. The skin is known to encompass much of the interest normally maintained in the body image, that pictorial representation of himself which each individual carries in his mind. This observation leads to the complicated problem of narcissism, body image and its place in the ego structure of the normal and neurotic personality. For the present purpose, it is to be noted that an imperceptible passage of emotional investment occurs from the body itself to the skin and hair and finally to clothes. Normally this process of narcissistic displacement occupies a period of years and is not noteworthy, since it receives its form from the pressure of accepted social styles. However, among immature persons the transition of emotional interest from body to clothes is spectacularly presented by the sudden attention to clothes exhibited in the boy or girl emerging from puberty. The love of extravagant and colorful apparel, unusual costume or distinctive manner of wearing clothing, deplored by conservative older persons, is evidence of the narcissistic displacement from body to clothes. These arresting changes, which take the form of never-ending fads observed among adolescents, bespeak the psychological process through which libidinal investment in the body expands to include body coverings. Although the psychology of clothes is itself a large and fascinating chapter in contemporary social psychology, only those immature attitudes toward the body and its coverings which show a clear relationship to delinquency will be traced here.

It is universally recognized in our culture that much feeling is attached to clothing. Although clothes admittedly have a prestige value, it is tacitly understood by mature persons that they have little social worth without integrity in the wearer. Garments, in addition to their utility value, have several psychological meanings for the individual. One of these is the neutralization of feelings of insecurity. Indeed, many social institutions are based on this need "to belong." The uniform or insignia of an organization, especially if laden with sentiment or tradition, represents a socially approved amalgamation of the reaction against insecurity of those who wear it. Youth is notoriously fond of badges, buttons, class pins or other accessories that carry a connotation of occupation or social class. Nor is this tendency to gain emotional security from group-linked clothes limited to youth. The presence of this trait in adults as well as the immature is demonstrated by secret fraternal organizations which employ distinctive insignia with esoteric meanings. The universal emotional investment in bodily adornment, which operates in all strata of society, is of particular psychological significance in the individual who feels inferior. To the latter, bodily adornment answers an emotional need that is not easily satisfied in other ways.

Adolescents accept clothes as a final symbol of prestige to a much greater degree than do mature individuals. The youth from a low economic level, who has no immediate possibility of identification with any occupational or social group, feels this lack keenly. He can get along without travel, amusements or sexual gratification, but he cannot exist without clothes, the outward symbol of his social hopes. Among Negro boys, the *clothes need* is found to be at its most intense, and therefrom results the extremism of color and design seen in the garments of these individuals. This is understandable in terms of their greater economic and social frustration. For immature individuals clothes are predominantly regarded as a socially allowable investiture of narcissism and a method of raising self-esteem.

Experience shows that immature persons find it intolerable to be seen without distinctive clothes. This may so lower their self-esteem as to lead directly to crime. "If you don't have clothes it hurts you inside," said a nineteen-year-old Negro boy who had robbed the owner of a cheap hotel of his watch and currency. "You feel bad inside; you can't go dancing or do anything. Sometimes I stay in the house crying." The utility value of clothing is disregarded, and only the prestige value functions in immature offenders. Criminologic experience with youths of the underprivileged class proves that this need can be more pressing than food or shelter. Frequently the urge for adornment leads directly to a burglary or robbery, where enough money to meet a specific need, like a suit, coat, etc., is desired. Once this is attained, the impulse to crime fades.

There is another type of bodily adornment, tattooing, which is worthy of consideration because of its frequency among immature individuals. It is well known that Lombroso, in his studies of criminologic anthropology, linked tattooing to criminality. He pointed to the fact that criminals, like primitive man, were egocentric and self-adorning. Current experience agrees that tattooing, although not specific in criminal offenders, is unquestionably closely related to emotional immaturity. In spite of Lombroso's accurate observation that egocentricity was a factor in tattooing among criminals, diverse psychological elements are found to underlie this practice which require more explanation than is provided by description of the self-adorning tendency of the savage.

From a descriptive viewpoint there are two types of men who have designs tattooed on themselves. One is the older, clearly exhibitionistic individual, usually a virile type of man, often a sailor, who was satisfied with his early designs and has added to his collection slowly over a period of years. At the extreme end of this group is the professional tattooer and the circus performer. The second group comprises the younger men who wish to bolster their feelings of inferiority by identification with strong men. Often designs on the skin of this latter group express obvious anthropomorphism, with pictures of stalwart warriors, snakes or lions, weapons or Indian braves. It is in this group that strong psychological currents underlying tattooing are visible. The social taboo against self-adornment in men is keenly felt in these individuals. They will often say that the tattooing made them look "vulgar and rough." Their decision to have the tattoo design applied was made impulsively, often on a dare while intoxicated or under the pressure of the suggestions of companions. For besides breaking the social taboo against marring the skin, a disinclination to injure the narcissistic organ, i.e., the skin, had to be overcome. Many young offenders have confided that fear of being called a coward was the chief or only stimulus for being tattooed.

It is possible also that latent homosexual factors operate in the social atmosphere of the tattoo process. The very symbolism of the tattooing needle and fluid—the infliction of pain by an older man, the tattooer—and the masochistic attitude in the subject, who disregards pain during the painful, tedious process, suggest the participation of unconscious homosexual factors. More striking in this connection is the fact that in the days of sailing vessels sailors frequently tattooed each other on their long voyages. Modern prison officials frequently encounter the occurrence of tattooing among inmates, performed within prison walls with crude pigments and instruments.

The figures commonly tattooed are diverse in design, but their content provides a nice illustration of psychological factors of immaturity. Frequently seen are pictures implying sexuality. In most cases pictures of sexual objects simply proclaim the heterosexuality of the man. This is illustrated in the case of Roland, twenty-one years of age, who had a nude figure of a woman tattooed on his right thigh and a girl's face on the right arm. For a month he was proud of the pictures and then began to feel remorseful. To counteract this feeling, Roland had a cross tattooed on his left arm under which the word "mother" appeared. Roland said he wanted to keep all the "sexual stuff" (girl's figure and head) on one side of the body and away from his mother's name and the cross on the opposite side. The cross with his mother's name served to compensate for the sexual implication of the female figures. In his choice of tattoo figures Roland bore his sexual guilt figuratively on his sleeve.

A third common type of tattooing illustrates direct representation of infantile sadistic elements. These include pictures of skulls, serpents, daggers and knives, often with a liberal accompaniment of blood. The choice of such designs bespeaks the strength of the castration fear in the immature individual and his defensive, exhibitionistic reaction formation. Thus James, a mental and emotional defective, eighteen years of age, pridefully demonstrated a design on his arm depicting a large dagger cutting through a cuff of skin from which blood dripped.

Pictures of Chinese dragons, skeletons or skulls, beneath which lies the inscription "Death before Dishonor," also are common. In such designs can be discerned the basic ambivalence of fear and its antithesis—swaggering bravado. Tattoos which deal with death, such as that seen in the case of Roland, quoted above, are frequently represented by the picture of a cross with the word "mother" beneath. In sexually suggestive designs the same ambivalence is to be noted—sexual striving and castration anxiety derivatives. The portrayal of adventurousness and piety, sadism and religious (masochistic) fervor, gaiety and sobriety, all reflect the basic tendency toward expression of ambivalence. Indeed, the presence of conflicting impulses can be sensed in anyone with more than one tattoo design. In all such cases, the immature individual is portraying his advance toward adult impulse gratification and simultaneously his retreat into fear and guilt.

Contrary to Lombroso's notion, tattooing seems more a manifestation of a neurotic conflict depicted on the body surface than an atavistic regression to a primitive love of adornment. The striving for narcissistic gratification which is displayed in tattooing, mixed with sexual and exhibitionistic elements and opposed by guilt feelings, seems to have some relation to the narcissistic investment in clothes. The movement of narcissism from skin to clothes, a natural development during childhood and puberty, appears to be reversed in the act of tattooing. It is as if bodily adornment were not sufficient to portray the conflict raging within the immature individual.

In these two areas, tattooing and the feeling for clothes, the psychological basis for immature attitudes toward the body becomes patent. This principle is, in essence, that the person is used not for its own value but to serve as an instrument to express unconscious attitudes toward the self, especially feelings of inferiority or compensatory virility. Similar findings appear when one examines the great respect of immature individuals for physical prowess and overpowering physique. In addition to admiring the reality value of strength, the immature individual weaves various unconscious conflicts and compensatory reactions into his attitude toward muscular strength.

(4) IMMATURE ATTITUDES TOWARD SEX

Immature attitudes, as has been explained, originate in neurotic roots in the personality and then undergo consolidation into characteristic group feelings. Those neurotic symptoms which are most often concerned in the development of immature attitudes are inferiority feelings with attendant anxiety. The process of elaboration from individual neurotic elements to immature characteristics is clear in the case of sexual attitudes among immature youths. These attitudes are colored by the universal guilt feelings which accompany the rising interest of adolescents in sexuality. Masturbation, which is often the first excursion into sexual expression among adolescence, usually causes a moderate guilt reaction. In neurotic youths, however, guilty feelings may develop into a depressed emotional state with a sense of isolation and feelings of unworthiness. These symptoms, derived from sexual guilt, determine attitudes toward sex among the immature. The formalistic expressions into which such attitudes fall have a readily discernible stamp and tend to acquire the value of rules of social conduct for the immature group.

On the surface the immature person is crass and derogatory of all tender emotions toward sexual objects. Women are viewed purely from a utilitarian standpoint. Sexual activity is believed to be degrading for women, and their sharing of sexual pleasure is looked on askance. Girls and women serve the momentary purpose of discharge of sexual feelings. The immature man demonstrates his defensive misogyny by dissociating the relief of physiologic sexual tension from romance. From a criminologic point of view, the readiness with which robbery of prostitutes is contemplated and executed attests the basic disdain for women felt by these persons. The complex interreactions which the adult world recognizes as "love" carry a connotation of weakness to the immature. Girls, with their intuitive sense of the need for romance and love in the sexual relationship, are a threat to the ego-security of such individuals. Immature males' denial of love appears to be a defense against an admission that women may be equal partners in sexual pleasure. Such an admission is denied by the repressing force of the youth's ego in the interests of preventing the exposure of intolerable feelings of inferiority. The feeling of inferiority has its strongest expression in fears of sexual inadequacy.

The anxiety which underlies an immature distrust of women is demonstrated unmistakably in a universal myth concerning the psychiatric examination. This myth arises when the psychiatrist makes inquiry into the sexual life, the emotional relations to parents and siblings, or any intimate feeling in the immature offender. The story, as told by young offenders, concerns a fantasied plot, attributed to the examiner, to expose the hidden sexual desires of the immature person. The examiner is reputed to pose the test question, "Suppose you were alone on a desert island with your mother and sister and wife; with which one would you sleep?" A variant of this perennial plot states that a nurse was brought into the examining room and instructed to disrobe in order to tempt the offender and ascertain whether his sexual impulses could be successfully suppressed in the presence of authority. As the story is retold by succeeding offenders, the situation is elaborated to show how the teller parried the examiner, bested him or even beat him physically for daring such a proposal. The story, common in all institutions where psychiatric examinations are made which involve what youths term "personal questions," is kept alive by the offender's own anxieties, aroused by psychiatric questioning.

Behind the defense mechanism of projecting blame for sexual interests to the psychiatrists can be seen sexual guilt arising from a deeper level. This myth is a clear expression of unconscious sexual guilt, which is aroused by the examiner's probing into the inner thoughts of immature individuals. The tension which is observable in the situation of the psychiatric examination is a reflection of the fear of the immature offender about being placed in a disadvantageous position by an older man who is assumed to have powers of peering into the youth's mind. Probing into the emotional life is equated by offenders to an assault upon themselves and their accepted sexual attitudes. One of the results of psychiatric contact, therefore, is the development of quantities of sexual guilt. Under the influence of guilty feelings, the original sexual impulses are reversed and depicted as emanating from adults in the form of tempting women who are teasingly displayed but protected by the cruel, denying father-figure of the examining psychiatrist.

There is a second type of defensive reaction stimulated in immature offenders when they are in contact with older, mature men which bears a relation to the sexual attitudes of the former. This attitude arises from anxiety caused by the threatened emergence of passive homosexual feelings. The immature individual projects his own fear of discovery of homosexual elements in himself into a situation where he is interrogated and in this way develops further tension when he confronts a more mature man, as in the instance of a psychiatric examination. To the offender, this contact is fraught with possibilities of personal injury, as indicated in the frequent statement that offenders physically beat the examiner when he makes the proposal described above. Fear of physical injury is merely a reflection of the newly aroused anxiety of unconscious homosexual origin. One immature offender expressed this fear by explaining that his employer, a man of fifty, looked at him in a way that indicated homosexual interest. "It is well known," the offender averred, "these old fellows become fags . . . he used to look at me with hypnotizing eyes . . . I used to close my eyes when I left the shop."

Ordinarily the fear of the perception of homosexual feelings in immature youth is covered by an aggressive intolerance to anything suggesting homosexuality. One of the patent sexual attributes of immature individuals is their obvious resentment of true homosexuals and instinctive derision of any display of femininity in men. The faintest implication of homosexuality is met with quick physical retaliation, as if against an insult not to be borne. The contempt felt for sexual deviates rests on the insecurity experienced by immature youths concerning the possible imputation of perverse sexual aims in themselves. Widespread social disapprobation of homosexuals aids in the development of this feeling, but the aggressive attitude toward them stems from a deep fear of discovery of some such moiety in the personality of the immature person. The police have long been aware of the common practice of extortion or outright robbery of homosexuals, committed under the moral protection of the general contempt for sexual degenerates, which is shared alike by offender and public.

*   *   *

The relationship between emotional and social immaturity and psychopathic personality is of great practical importance and theoretical interest. There is much overlapping in the two conditions, and experience with psychopaths demonstrates the presence in them of marked immature, defensive mechanisms. There is a gradation, which the careful clinician may observe, from immaturity among normal youths to that among immature adults and finally to psychopathic personalities. A further complication is that reactions which form the picture of immaturity can be readily pointed out as neurotic defenses (to castration anxiety, inferiority feelings, ambivalence to parents and Oedipus derivatives), whereas the same reactions having similar social results are not so readily and obviously demonstrated among psychopaths. The statement, however, that those defensive character formations which are called immature constitute an integral part of the psychopath's make-up, can be made with certainty.

This account of immaturity expressed in the foregoing social psychological areas does not exhaust all the facets of immaturity as a personality abnormality. Examination of normal life activity often brings to light examples of the reappearance, sometimes dramatic and unsuspected, of remnants of immaturity in otherwise adjusted adults. Many of these immature fragments not only eventuate in criminal behavior but are observable also in social life. Hallmarks of the immature, such as impracticality, impatience with limitations of reality and reliance on fantasy aims and satisfaction, are reluctantly relinquished by all mankind only under the continued pressure of reality. That emotional immaturity is a factor in antisocial conduct was proved by Sheldon and Eleanor Glueck in their statistical study of the aftermath of criminal careers. They found that the chief factor in the decrease in criminality with advance in years is that of maturation. As the result of the impingement of social pressures on the psychological elements that make up emotional immaturity, the average offender gradually loses his antisocial tendencies. Those who deal with manifestations of immature behavior in criminality are in a position to evaluate the vital social implications of immature attitudes.

6

The Neurotic Offender

The majority of individual offenders convicted of felonies cannot be correctly diagnosed as either psychopathic or emotionally immature personalities. This large group of occasional offenders display no unusual reaction to their early training, retain no observable social hostility in their character formations and are apparently adjusted in their social relationships. Yet study of these ostensibly normal persons frequently demonstrates that a remnant of neurotic conflict or a derivative of unconscious impulses is the activating force in occasional criminal acts. In this group can be found the neurotic offender.

The neurotic offender, in contrast to the psychopath, becomes a criminal in response to a solitary aberrant impulse. The criminal act embodies a symbolic and indirect gratification of a completely unconscious impulse which is not part of the pattern of daily behavior. Many of the crimes of the so-called occasional or accidental offender are patently the "acting out" of unconscious conflicts. But such offenders are not neurotic in the ordinary clinical sense. In such persons the unconscious conflict finds expression in a forbidden act rather than in a neurotic symptom. Psychological conflicts, causing behavior at sharp variance with the individuals' accustomed social performance, are only exposed through study of the content of the criminal act.

The operation of neurotic complexes in the personality of the offender is observed in specific crime groups like those of theft and homicide. Even the various types of theft preserve a distinct psychological architecture of their own, e.g., embezzling, fraud, larceny, burglary, robbery and extortion. The unconscious choice within the crime group depends upon the personality disposition of each offender and the deeper neurotic conflicts involved. Only a careful analysis of each offender and each crime will yield clues to the psychological relationship existing between them.

NEUROTIC MECHANISMS IN BURGLARY AND ROBBERY

Burglary and robbery are two recurring types of larceny familiar to the public. The personalities of those who commit these offenses vary as widely as the crime technics differ. Burglary is the theft of money or property accomplished by entering a building or dwelling in the absence of the owner or under the presumption that it is empty of occupants. The essential nature of burglary, that of entering a forbidden place, is expressed by the statutory definitions of its varying degrees, such as Breaking and Entering, Unlawful Entry, Attempted Unlawful Entry, etc. The burglar may be a youth who breaks a window of a store or trips the lock on a door of a dwelling. He may be a chronic criminal who invades a loft or jimmies the safe in a cashier's office. In any event, his theft is preceded by first removing locks, bars or other safeguards set up to prevent any depredation such as he contemplates. In each case the burglar exerts force to overcome the safeguards which prevent his gaining access to those articles of value he covets.

In contrast to the burglar, the robber achieves his larceny by direct use of force on the person of the individual who, he assumes, has money or valuables. The robber is often armed with a weapon for use against a victim, whereas the burglar uses his instruments to break into the home or building from which he is expressly excluded. It is obvious that burglary is accomplished in a totally different atmosphere from that surrounding robbery and that the burglar operates in different psychological modalities than the robber. The burglar is furtive, whereas the robber approaches his victims directly, confronting them with demands for money. Burglary is a stealthy crime while robbery is an aggressive one.

Taken as a behavioral whole, the common underlying characteristic of burglary is passivity, and judged by the technic employed, burglary is a passive crime. Although the crime is legally stated to be an act of aggression against society, the basic character of burglary is that of stealth. Stealth is aggression under cover, the aggression of a passive individual with a feeling of inferiority. In some burglars submissiveness is not easily recognized as a basic personality trait. The presenting attitude of the young burglar who is caught and brought to the courts is often an overcompensated truculence. The surface manner of such boys belies any notion of submissiveness. Their very stance, shoulder squarings and expression of insouciance are significant of their compensatory aggressive attitude.

A second clue to the psychological nature of the crime is provided by an attitude which apparently disregards the realities involved. Youthful burglars are literally shocked when a minor depredation, such as breaking into a candy shop, is designated as a crime. Police and the courts are considered persecuting objects. The young offenders regard themselves as external to the crime from the standpoint of criminal motivation. Beneath this childish denial lies a significant psychological attitude: it is the acceptance within themselves of an inferior, passive position in life. They are unable to perceive the social meaning of their acts because of the influence of an infantile feeling that what is "taken" is theirs by birthright. Denial and protests against legal action represent the unconscious wish that the police, their symbolic parents, regard the burglary and theft with parental benevolence.

These emotional factors are readily visible in minor burglaries, for example, the so-called "lead pipe" burglars whose thefts are of objects nominally of little monetary value; old water tanks, pieces of scrap metal, old stoves, sections of lead or brass pipe from abandoned houses, etc. This group of burglars, found almost uniformly among dull or mentally defective boys and dull adults of a low cultural level, typifies the crude pattern of simple theft and illustrates the essential emotional meaning of burglary. The low value of the objects taken, e.g., the abandoned house from which they steal, and the clearly defined air of poverty of the crime merge with their own feelings of self-depreciation. Such offenders often readily admit the relative worthlessness of the objects stolen, as if expecting society's approval to follow from the very nature of their offenses. Such an attitude bears the psychological implication of marked inferiority feeling in the offender. Rather than assert themselves to the point of acquiring what they wish, they are attracted by castoff objects.

Many common types of burglaries appear to run counter to the theory expounded in these pages. For example, the common school burglary seems to be motivated by the aggression and arrogance of students. But study shows that the underlying psychological mechanisms also prove to be reactive to feelings of unworthiness and inferiority. Burglary in these cases is an expression of aggression against the school or store, the symbol of the parent. Significantly, the stores burglarized are often confectioners' shops, barrooms or restaurants—symbolic repositories of nutriment. These crimes represent a symbolic effort to participate in the community of family life and share its common property. The individual's childhood deprivation is the unconscious stimulus for theft from a barred or closed building. The burglary is an attempt to correct a historical situation in the emotional life of the offender, long since lost to memory. Such burglaries tend to neutralize deep feelings of inadequacy by enhancing self-esteem in the offender through the same maneuver that expresses his parental hostility.

A similar mechanism underlies a type of burglary common among men living in furnished rooms, hotels or clubs. In this group of burglaries an offender enters the quarters of a friend or neighbor and rifles it in the latter's absence. The details of this variety of burglary, like that of the marauding student, suggest an unconscious resolution by the offender of an unsatisfactory psychological design that obtained in his original family group. The crime is psychologically motivated by the reinvoked family situation in which deprivation, real or imagined, led to early rivalry with brothers. Irrespective of its actual reality value, the burglary represents an unconscious attempt to satisfy wishes for a share in the family life. Clothes and money symbolize love or its physical correlate, nutriment, which was denied in infancy. Although the psychic wound of parental deprivation has apparently been healed, burglary is its distorted expression. The depth of these unconscious forces is indicated by the rationalization offered as a frequent explanation by offenders: "A friend of mine owed me some money, so I took his clothes."

The psychological meaning of the crime of burglary then is a passive expression of fundamentally aggressive impulses. It has been indicated that the choice of burglary as a technic of theft implies a note of furtiveness in the offender's make-up. Characteristic stealth in the appropriation of hidden articles in the absence of the owner is in reality suppressed aggression toward parent or parent surrogates. The hostility is clearly in reaction to infantile feelings of deprivation. This form of handling aggression is unquestionably neurotic in nature. The appearance of subverted aggressive tendencies in burglary is reminiscent of the manner in which anger was suppressed in infantile reactions to frustrations or deprivations. Childhood aggression, impossible of direct fulfillment, was transformed and distorted into symptoms or misbehavior. The neurotic burglar re-enacts the early pattern of aggression in adult life but turns it against society. It is possible to demonstrate the psychological conflicts and unconscious forces motivating the crime of burglary in the occasional offender with relative clarity.

Barry, thirty-five years old, arrested for the first time, was charged with burglary of a woman's suitcase taken from a locked storeroom in the basement of his rooming house. He had never seen the woman nor had he any financial reason for the theft. On the night of the burglary Barry had been drinking alone in his room while awaiting friends. He remembered nothing after the first few drinks except that his landlady had suggested, on his inquiry, that he could find some additional furniture for his room in the basement. The next morning he awakened to find himself fully dressed but feeling the effects of a large quantity of alcohol. The suitcase was in his room. Two days later the landlady discovered the bag, which contained 60 dollars worth of wearing apparel and stock certificates worth 360 dollars. Nothing was missing from the bag when claimed by the owner, although some of the feminine attire apparently had been disarranged. Under questioning Barry did not recall any activities having to do with his theft of the suitcase.

Disturbed by his first conviction, the offender was furtive, bewildered and visibly under tension during the psychiatric interview. He was a quiet individual, subdued in his manner and almost feminine in his social approach. When psychological investigation of his offense was proposed, he was eager to co-operate in order to learn how he had become involved.

The case study disclosed the following history. Barry was born in a small midwestern town. His father was a farmer and in later life a manual worker in a near-by town. The mother was a dressmaker. Boyhood was typical of small town life. All clothes for the children of the family were made by the mother. The defendant recalled that when he was seven years old his clothes were "store bought." The house furnishings were very plain, and apparently the family lived frugally, if not on the edge of poverty. The offender had a brother two years his senior and a younger one, "a natural-born athlete." Barry and his older brother were similar in tastes, appearance and physical structure. The younger brother, markedly extrovert in make-up, was in marked contrast. After school the offender worked in a local tailor shop. As a child he was admired for his artistic talent. In high school he was shy, retiring and had few friends. He did not graduate because two months before commencement he was suspended for a minor infraction. Lack of a high school certificate humiliated him, but he felt that later European trips and art studies in Paris offset this educational lack.

When Barry was about twenty years old he met a girl in Chicago with whom he lived and who, he felt, was a real companion to him. He thought an idyllic relationship existed, but when he went to Paris to study the girl married a doctor who "just came along." This disappointment caused a decline of interest in women. Following the period of study in Paris, Barry engaged in dress designing for a fashionable New York shop.

Psychological analysis was initiated. Early in the treatment Barry was anxious and timid in his verbal productions. Soon he reported copious dreams. These were characteristically full of vivid color and reflected his love of artistic form. Running through the dreams was constant reference to gold in the form of trimmings on dresses which he was designing and gold braid on uniforms. His associations to the dreams indicated strong feelings of ineffectualness and inadequacy related to the discrepancy between his economic position and his talents. Frequently his dreams had to do with injury to himself and to his parents and siblings. In relation to these thoughts he spoke of an auto accident seven years previously, when he had sustained injuries. Recollection of the accident evoked great anxiety and free associations reverted to the earlier family situation. Hostility, which he freely expressed against his parents and brothers in dreams, revealed infantile frustrations. A characteristic dream was:

I tell my family I cannot eat with them. They are as they were in my childhood. I get on a bus with a friend. It's the wrong one. We jump off and run back to find two men run over. I take the cap of one; they are officers and dead. I run to my room in fright.

As the psychological investigation proceeded, a new element arose, namely, his fear of being cheated. He complained of his fellow workers, that he was not getting his financial due, that he was in a rut economically, and contrasted this with the more satisfactory periods of his life—the idealized romance in Chicago, his lionization as a child prodigy, the promise of his Paris days, etc. About this time his elder brother came to visit him, and his dreams and associations reflected his old rivalry with the brother under the parental roof. Feelings of poverty and of being robbed and cheated were commonly expressed in this period of the analysis. The tendency to decorate the dresses he worked on with gold and to furbish his dream figures with brilliant colors and rich decorations was prominent. This trend was in compensation for his deep feelings of poverty and inadequacy. Once he dreamed of a large frog in the form of a vase of the most brilliant emerald hue he had ever seen. He frequently complained about his mother's drabness in early life and argued that as a competent designer he could take issue with her on the question of trimmings.

The patient's choice of vocation was apparently influenced by unconscious wishes to correct his dissatisfaction with his mother. He identified himself with women, the recipients of adulation and riches, but felt himself ineffectual and weak in competition with them. Nevertheless, Barry had reactions against the passive trends which impelled him in a feminine direction. Anxiety centering around this conflict influenced much of his life and provided the motivation for his offense. His lifelong complaints of ineffectuality appeared as the surface symptoms and intensified the patient's general dissatisfaction.

From this dynamic point of view, Barry's offense became intelligible. The theft was a symbolic restatement of the mother-child relationship which existed in early life. The clothes and money, which Barry stole under the influence of alcoholic amnesia from a woman he had never seen, symbolized a retrieval of his infantile birthright. Fear of women and the hostility engendered by old fraternal rivalry kept alive his feminine strivings and therefore the neurotic conflict which prevented him from claiming his due according to his abilities.

Following four months of treatment, Barry was released from active supervision, and a year later he married a woman slightly older than himself, deep-voiced, with fairly distinct masculine reactions. This marriage to a loving but predominantly positive woman seemed to follow as a renunciation of a neurotic search for femininity. There were no further difficulties with the law after nine years. He had given up alcoholism and had made a good economic adjustment.

Although the occasional crime of the neurotic offender is subject to psychological explanation on the basis of early family environment, the question arises whether the professional burglar has a similar motivation. These individuals rarely show psychopathology on direct examination. They embark on a career of crime at a time of economic necessity and continue in it for the profit involved. Professional burglars are men of mature years, accepting the advantages and risks of this type of work as one accepts those of a legitimate profession. Many professional loft or house burglars are family men whose children maintain a good standing in the community. Rarely are their children or neighbors aware of their true "business." These men are never outspokenly aggressive, even when apprehended. The only intimation obtained of the existence of motivating psychological factors is interpreted from emotional depressions arising from guilt feelings following an arrest.

Study of their emotional conflicts does demonstrate early emotional factors upon which the apparently conscious choice of burglary as a profession depended. The influence of sibling rivalries, of reaction to infantile deprivation and of stealthy hostility to the parents, is less observable but just as active in the case of the professional thief as in the neurotic burglar. Professional burglars live in a furtive atmosphere and express themselves in subverted behavior. The explanation usually given—that their criminal careers were due to circumstance—is a rationalization. Whatever compulsive or neurotic elements exist are woven into their characters and sealed over with a façade of resignation to the particular form of antisocial expression adopted. Acceptance of a criminal pattern of life by chronic offenders provides them, in actuality, with a feeling of security. They sink into the anonymity of burglary to protect unperceived neurotic impulses. In chronic offenders the recurring impetus to burglaries, which persists irrespective of the monetary gain, gives strong evidence of a neurotic basis to their acts. The compulsive quality of burglary is particularly convincing in recidivists whose criminal careers as burglars continue over years without involving a single instance of frank aggression, such as in robbery.

The chronic burglar who has consolidated his neurotic impulses into an antisocial personality is in fact a psychopathic individual. The psychodynamics underlying repetition of crime among psychopaths involves the same mechanisms as are found in the occasional neurotic offender. The difference between the two groups of criminals resides in the fact that emotional deprivation and rejection very early influence the ego of the psychopath to cause an incomplete development of the conscience. The neurotic offender struggles with his impulses, while the psychopath's ego incorporates and expresses them in antisocial acts.

While the technic of burglary reflects neurotic elements in the personality of the offender, robbery appears to express only the conscious wishes of the criminal. The crime of robbery bears the stamp of outright aggression. The robber confronts his victim and demands that the latter yield his money or valuables. To support his demands, the robber usually displays a weapon or employs a threat of injury to the victim in the event of noncompliance. There is no secret of the robber's aggressive intent, no subversive expression of his wishes. From a psychological point of view the crime of robbery represents less neurosis than is found in the burglary. The impulse behind robbery is an unmodified expression of the wish to take, an unconscious, uncontrolled impulse which is primitive in its essential nature. It is obvious that the personality of the robber, which mediates this predatory impulse, differs from that of the extortionist, who utilizes the element of borrowed authority in his technic, the embezzler, who dips into the magic symbolism entailed in the written name, and the burglar, who employs furtive methods in his crime.

In spite of the generalization that robbery is a grossly aggressive act, upon examination individual robbers show widely varying mental mechanisms. The actual technics of robberies indicate a lack of unanimity of psychological motivation in all robbers. The man who arranges an armed "holdup" of a shop proprietor differs in his personality make-up from the pocketbook snatcher or the offender who feigns possession of a revolver and uses a toy pistol with the knowledge that he can do no harm to his victim. Although the technic of robbery is a pre-eminently aggressive one, the inner core of the personality of the robber does not always match this implied description. Deep feelings of inferiority and passivity are startlingly common among convicted robbers.

Scrutiny of the emotional reactions behind robbery suggests the occurrence sometimes of more fear in the robber than in his victim. Especially is this obvious when a weapon is utilized. The offender who carries a gun betrays fear that he may not be aggressive enough to carry out his intention to rob. The anxiety, clinically demonstrable in almost every case of robbery by a young person, stems from an inner conviction of powerlessness in the absence of a weapon. The perception of this inferiority feeling, combined with the imminence of an aggressive act, stimulates quantities of guilt that often impel the offender into a panic. Shooting occurs in armed robbery because of a sudden gust of panic, usually after the robbery has been successfully completed.

It can be seen that the upsurge of hostile impulses aroused by the implication of resistance of a robbery victim is based less on the fact that the situation actually calls for defense than on reactions within the robber. As has been pointed out, aggressive impulses in robbers which are based on unconscious feelings of inadequacy evoke acute feelings of guilt. The ego is caught between the rush of infantile rage loosed in the robber and the adult wishes of the conscience for control of aggressive impulses. Guilty feelings, unknown to the criminal, often motivate him to carry his act to a point where drastic punishment may result to him, i.e., apprehension for murder with the possibility of subsequent long imprisonment or the death penalty. In this connection the frequency of emotional depression among convicted robbers in prison attests to the prevalence of guilt in this group of offenders.

Psychiatrists are familiar with neurotic patients who, burdened with guilty feelings, are unconsciously impelled into foolhardy or forbidden acts in the effort to obtain relief. Relief from guilt is afforded these anxiety-driven individuals by the punishment which their ill-advised acts entail. The resultant punishment, in whichever form it assumes, whether through apprehension by police, loss of prestige or actual failure of achievement, provides relief for disturbing feelings of guilt. The guilt precedes, rather than follows, the unapproved or forbidden act. In actuality, the forbidden act or crime is set in motion because of a need for punishment, which, in turn, provides masochistic satisfaction when received. This mental mechanism, completely unknown to the individual, is found in many neurotic persons. It is only exposed by an analysis of unconscious factors which operate to produce continued misfortune in neurotics and inexplicable offenses among neurotic or occasional criminals.

Paradoxical as this need for punishment among criminal offenders may seem, it is readily observable in actual case material. There is no other explanation for the prison-wise offender who, knowing of the long sentence awaiting him upon arrest, still dares another armed robbery. Again and again one sees calloused robbers, out of prison only a few weeks or months, engage in bold armed robberies, even though faced with possible life imprisonment. Contrary to common opinion, many recidivists serving long terms agree that they feel at home in prison. The security they experience is in part compounded of guilt feelings and the relief obtained from expiation through punishment. The criminal is without perception of this phenomenon: his explanations are rationalizations that higher stakes imply greater risks, that the world offers greater rewards for courage, and so on. These explanations are masks for unconscious forces which drive the offender into behavior calculated to bring him to conviction and subsequent punishment.

There is another aspect of the need for punishment not evident on the surface. This is the unperceived dependence of the criminal on a stable emotional figure, symbolized by the father-figure of the judge or warden and, in a sense, by society as a whole. The neurotic dependence need which underlies aggressive acts against society can be observed in the criminal's reactions after apprehension and sentencing. Public recognition of the robber's plight seems as important to him as gain from crime. Among aggressive youths, especially those who fall under the influence of the "hardened gangster" attitude, public recognition for their daring is an important stimulating factor in their crime motivation. Interest in the press stories of their offenses and its effect upon their reputations among their associates are obviously a screen for the unconscious wish to exhibit their guilt to the public. The apparent bravery of robbers has a double psychological value: it invites interest and stimulates fear of them in the public, and at the same time exposes their dependence on, and need for, a protecting father-figure, represented by the court or officers of penal institutions. The crime itself serves the first need; the criminal's subsequent arrest and imprisonment serve the second.

The neurotic robber is often sensitive to his social place among his fellows. He has a strong need to uphold prestige values, as he perceives them. In the robber's community, prestige rests on clothes, motor cars, drinking, the company of women or easy money. Antisocial groups are united by specific social values and cultural attitudes, just as the social community has prescribed allegiances. The impact on the offender who feels inferior of these prestige requirements is a common impelling force toward robberies and burglaries. The criminal scurries under the pressure of anxiety to conform to the standards of conduct and prestige laid before him by his group.

Feelings of inferiority are the mainspring of many robberies, especially among the immature. In addition to unconscious inferiority feelings, organic defects or constitutional deficiencies may give rise to inferiority neuroses, which lead to compensatory aggression reflected in robbery. Shortness of height is one of the structural anomalies which stimulates prestige sensitivity among youths. Illustrative is a boy of sixteen, arrested for an armed robbery, whose short physique entered significantly into the psychodynamics of his robbery. He was the butt of his companions' jibes; his short stature, lack of athletic prowess and poverty disturbed him. Poverty and the ever-present feelings of insecurity gave him the idea to accumulate enough money through robberies to create a "$25,000 trust fund" for himself, so that in the future he would never need suffer indignities from anyone.

NEUROTIC FACTORS IN LARCENY

The crime of theft, with its various subdivisions, comprises the largest group of felony offenses. The common forms of theft—swindling, fraud, embezzling, grand larceny, forgery and conspiracy—have differing psychological modalities which are clearly observable in the technics employed in these crimes. All forms of theft are united by the common idea of monetary gain without the expenditure of effort in a legitimate calling or business. The essential meaning of theft is the acquisition of money or articles of value to which the offender has no rights; its psychological meaning is modified by the need to employ deception, trickery or dishonesty to accomplish this wish. The particular conditions under which each type of theft is committed depend to a large degree on psychological factors in the offender. It has already been shown how the psychological forces in the burglar and robber fashion their choice of a particular criminal activity. It will also be demonstrated that varying forms of larceny reflect the presence of neurotic elements in the offender.

A consideration of the psychology of larceny recalls the involvement of psychological elements that lie close to those in normal individuals. Neurotic roots of larcenous impulses are closely related to acquisitive tendencies present in everyone. These tendencies have been carefully regulated by law and commercial practice, and controlling devices which have evolved are accepted by the law-abiding individual. In Chapter 2, in the discussion of Antisocial Impulses in Society, the universality of submerged predatory impulses existing in the law-abiding population was indicated to be due to residual cravings of the personality which escaped complete repression during the infantile period of social training. Larceny, like trade, was found to rest, in its psychological essence, on the persistent operation in the individual of infantile patterns of "wanting." Unlike the impulses behind legitimate commerce, however, larcenous impulses are not under the constant action of controlling influences. This is clearly the distinction between the normal wish of law-abiding individuals to profit by commercial enterprise and that of persons guilty of any form of theft. From a scrutiny of the psychological meaning of the repression of acquisitive impulses in business life, the basic dissimilarity between the personalities of law-abiding and antisocial individuals becomes evident. It is well known that possibilities for control or lack of control of larcenous tendencies are reflected in many areas of legitimate commercial activity, such as credit, installment buying, buying for speculation, etc. Therefore, an examination of several little-discussed but generally understood psychological aspects of commerce would be illuminating in a discussion of the psychology of larceny.

There are distinguishable several motives which lie behind gainful activity. The first is that of *profit*. It can be accepted as a truism that without the motive of gain (including wages) there would be no commercial activity.

The second motive is that of *self-esteem*. Every worker, from the intellectual to the manual laborer, has an ego investment in his work. The worker experiences pleasure in labor in proportion as his work satisfies the needs of his ego to be recognized as an effective social unit. Ordinary life experience profusely demonstrates this assertion; the professional's ego feeds upon his reputation and knowledge, the businessman gauges his effectiveness by the consumer's recognition of his prestige and economic importance; the entertainer is sustained by the applause of his public; the mechanic obtains personal gratification from the efficient operation of his equipment.

The third motive for gainful activity is that of *service*. The service motive encompasses the pleasure given others by the product which is used or enjoyed. Satisfaction derived from giving service contains a mixture of reality values and psychological elements. The reality elements of service are reflected in larger gains and greater self-esteem. The psychological elements are sublimations of masochistic tendencies in the one who serves, made acceptable by traditions of work. Secondarily, the service motive reflexly supports the self-esteem motive. The narcissistic reflection from the pleasure of serving others falls back upon the worker himself in terms of heightened self-esteem. Moral education has recognized the operation of these forces. Thomas Carlyle wrote, "There is a perennial nobleness in Work; in Idleness only is there perpetual despair." *

The three psychological factors considered to be operative in gainful occupations may now be related to the psychology of larceny as exemplified in the professional thief. For both the reputable businessman and the thief the element of gain or profit is uppermost. For the thief the elements of prestige and self-esteem are also of vital importance. The larcenist has his own group of friends who exchange their experiences, successes or failures, and are sensitive about their reputations. Candid revelations by professional

* Reprinted from The Works of Thomas Carlyle, vol. 3, Past and Present, New York, John B. Alden, 1885, p. 189.

larcenists indicate that, like the reputable worker or businessman, antisocial persons derive true self-esteem from their criminal activity. A professional thief knows the conditions favorable to his trade just as the businessman understands problems in production and merchandising. The larcenist knows what time of day would be most profitable to steal, understands the psychology of his victims and knows how to prosecute his calling with a minimum of failures, i.e., arrests.

When, however, the larcenist is examined in relation to the service aspect of his activity, its absence is immediately noted. Does the difference between the psychological approach of illegitimate and legitimate enterprise lie here? Experience contradicts this, for everyone has a basic satisfaction in serving well. Hawkers who sell an item on the street which implies an illusion of service are themselves inwardly aware that they are unfair to the public. In every walk of life it can be observed that men who make and sell cheaper products are less satisfied than those who make the best: writers would rather write classics than magazine articles; dance band leaders wish to write symphonies, etc. Careful study of those who profit through shoddy methods of business will demonstrate the presence of feelings of guilt at not having served well.

The explanation of the larcenists' lack of response to the service motive is to be sought in the manner in which the acquisitive tendencies of the growing human organism were modified during social development. Emotional education carried on from the cradle to adulthood by parents, the church, schools, the press, and later other avenues of public propaganda, is predicated upon a philosophic construct as compelling as if it were a fact. This assumption is that larcenous impulses are absent rather than successfully repressed in the law-abiding population. A sense of honor and the social pressure surounding duty have fixed this assumption into the code of civilized life. The realities of law and the vigil of its ever-present agents add weight to this resolution.

Actually this assumption is an "as if" postulate. We act "as if" we do not want another's wealth, social position or reputation. The entire credit structure, without which commerce would be impossible, is intimately related to the assumption that everyone agrees to suppress his larcenous impulses in daily transactions. This tacit agreement is the basis of all commercial and social intercourse. The public reaction of rage and disappointment when an international banker like Insull or Kruger abuses his position of trust is partial proof of the constant play of this powerful social force for which integrity is another name. Business is aware of the constant need to refresh this attitude; numerous governmental agencies and business organizations exist that control irresponsible businessmen who reduce their service to a minimum or increase their profit unconscionably. The result of constant education in this direction is the complete repression of acquisitive tendencies in law-abiding persons. Adoption of the principle of suppression of larcenous impulses becomes the ethical rule of commerce.

The larcenist cannot subscribe to the idea that each of us lives in a special relation to the other in regard to our acquisitive impulses. The larcenist rejects the pragmatic use of the "as if" philosophy in our social commonwealth. He cannot give up instinctual gratification, symbolically represented by thefts, in exchange for the rewards inherent in social adjustment. Due to specific emotional factors in the early life of the child who becomes a thief, the balance at which emotional education is aimed is never achieved. The child that could not give up instinctive wishes and receive the parent's love in return cannot, as an adult, give service to his fellow men and receive their gratitude. His identification is with the social element whose life philosophy is not predicated on the assumption that we can renounce our instinctive demands in the interest of our fellows.

In larceny, as in many situations involving the play of neurotic factors, reality provides a basis for ready rationalization of unconscious trends. The credit structure of commerce often unwittingly aids the emergence of larcenous impulses. The many thefts which rest upon false financial statements provide examples of what Sutherland has called "white collar criminality." Offenders, in their efforts to keep business afloat, deceive their creditors by submitting accounts of merchandise sold and moneys received far in excess of actuality. The inability of the credit larcenist to subscribe to the universal renunciation of immediate gratification is based on a neurotic urgency for fulfillment. The possibility of gain through trade precipitates the unconscious demand for immediate gratification, and the credit larcenist's behavior is directed by this emotional force.

Frequent thefts of jewels and other luxury articles by agents who receive such articles on memorandum for possible future sale illustrate this point. Dundon, a prosperous-looking man of forty-six, was convicted of grand larceny after having pawned $20,000 worth of jewelry obtained on memorandum from several dealers. Dundon had been both a theatrical manager and jewelry broker. In the present offense, he secured jewelry worth $20,000 on the pretext of having already secured customers for the jewels. Immediately after pawning the pieces he went to Paris, where he had leased a theater with the intent of importing an American theatrical production into France. His arrest for the jewel larceny occurred in London while he was arranging an English presentation of the same play, before the French production had been started. His actual income was never very high, but he lived on and gloried in his reputation as an entrepreneur. Dundon's pockets were filled with newspaper clippings and notes indicating intimate contacts with international theatrical celebrities. The personality of the offender showed obvious expansive elements indicating the readiness with which he could identify with the magical power implied in jewels.

The attraction of precious metals and jewels resides in their high monetary value. Beyond this reality there are psychological elements which subtly stimulate the acquisitive elements of potential jewel larcenists. Jewels have always been endowed with magical properties, and this added psychological value strikes a responsive chord in the jewel thief. Folklore indicates that jewels have been omens of luck from time immemorial, and that their possession controlled human destinies. A suggestion of this primitive imputation of magic to jewels creeps into the attitude of those who habitually deal with precious stones. Precious metals and stones are invested with a supernatural aura suggesting that they lie beyond the vicissitudes of fortune of their human owners and transcend their monetary value. The concentration of great value in a tiny precious stone acts as a magnet to those in whose behavior fantasy of magic plays a strong part. The unconscious values given these objects stimulate the conscious actions of many individuals, who yield to the temptation of stealing jewelry consigned to them in a legitimate business transaction.

The promise of profit through investment or speculation carries a magic similar to that surrounding precious jewels and stimulates the same fantasy trend in many offenders. Stock market larcenists who, in misappropriating customers' securities, hoped to make up the deficit through stock market speculation, demonstrated the operation of feelings of magical influence in their embezzlement. Methods of security sales familiar to America of the 1920's and early 1930's played upon the public's fantasy of omnipotence. In this unconscious wish of the prospective customer (victim) was a factor as important in stock market larcenies as were the designs of the offender. When public faith in the miracle of riches-for-all through stock market speculation faded, the convictions of this variety of offender decreased in number.

Stock market larcenies provide a view of variety of frauds which encroach in their technic upon legitimate business practices. Offenders in these cases depended on their astuteness in selecting names of financially powerful men, who were claimed to be associated in their dubious ventures. Often names of noted financiers were falsely attached to prospectuses of stock issues to serve as bait for the victims. The psychological background of this variety of theft comprises the appropriation by the offender of another person's identity through the mechanism of identification. This mechanism has been observed also in cases of extortion by impersonation. The impersonation, although consciously utilized as a trick, was impelled by the need in the offender to attain prestige through identification with a revered name. Such larcenists demonstrated in this way their tendencies toward magical thinking.

It should be stated, however, that reverence for names to which a connotation of wealth is attached is not an inconspicuous aspect of normal social psychology. Business and advertising rely upon this mechanism to a considerable degree.

Criminologic representation of this form of identification is illustrated in the case of a mother and son who assumed the name and credit rating of nationally known millionaires. Terrence, a youth of seventeen, was brought up as a Little Lord Fauntleroy by his mother. The father was a weak, submissive character who played a secondary role in the household. As a child, Terrence is alleged to have attracted the attention of a wealthy woman, Mrs. R., who befriended him and at her death left him a cash bequest of $15,000, in addition to large gifts of jewels. On the basis of this anticipated fortune, mother and son lived on a credit level of opulence. In the exclusive clubs which they frequented, the mother was introduced by the son as his aunt, the "Duchess," while Terrence himself adopted the name of William J. K. Vanderbilt. The pair, living on credit, continued this gay deception for several years. In retrospect, exhaustive inquiry by the court officers did not yield any clues of the gift of $15,000 to Terrence or of the existence of a Mrs. R. At the time of the instant arrest for larceny, Terrence, stating that he "wanted something halfway decent for mother," had purchased an expensive ring for her from a fashionable jewelry establishment, using a worthless check signed with the name of William J. K. Vanderbilt. The ring, valued at over $1,000, had been immediately pawned by the offender.

Eight years after the offense just described, Terrence was apprehended for a similar embezzlement utilizing the name of another wealthy and socially prominent family. The technic of his crime, the usurpation of a name revered in the social world and the fraudulent receipt of credit and jewels through the use of this name, followed precisely the same pattern in both offenses. Repetition of the offenses indicated the compulsive neurotic character of the thefts. Reality gains from the thefts were apparently of an importance secondary to the satisfaction of emotional needs in the offender.

Experience with the occasional larceny offender confirms the fact that many thefts are the behavioral expression of unconscious drives. However, the emotional problems involved are not always as patent as in the case detailed above. Occasional offenders usually give every appearance of sobriety and adjustment until an offense occurs which proves to have been a socially disastrous attempt to solve an unconscious conflict through behavior.

This situation is exemplified by the case of Blackrock, a man of mature years who, while president of the nation's largest stock exchange, was convicted of grand larceny of funds approximating two million dollars. For several years preceding his conviction Blackrock had been securing bank loans by pledging his customers' securities without their knowledge. The money so obtained was poured into two business ventures: a distilling company which manufactured a relatively unknown alcoholic beverage and a vast agricultural project of nebulous character. The distilling company absorbed with total loss $1,600,000 worth of securities belonging to individuals and institutions of which the offender was a trustee. The agricultural project, a large-scale production of humus expected to be a potential source of great wealth, likewise failed dismally. After two years of frenzied borrowing and juggling of losses, Blackrock's peculations of several millions of dollars were uncovered.

It may be asked how a man of unusual intelligence, outstandingly successful in his business career, mentally well, in habits the essence of responsibility and stability, whose education and training were realistic and complete, could become involved in an obviously unsound enterprise. What unseen personality quirks led this distinguished banker into misappropriations totaling five million dollars? What prevented his conscience, sharpened by years of experience with financial problems, from holding his larcenous impulses in check? Apparently some force was active in the offender's personality against which Blackrock's training, education, seasoned judgment and experience had no power. That force, which exerted so overwhelming an influence on the conscious actions of this financier, was an unsuspected omnipotence fantasy which lay at the core of his personality. An understanding of the operation of this psychological force in the offender involves an analysis of the relation between guilt and conscience in individuals who have the imposing task of controlling large enterprises.

The psychiatric examination of Blackrock revealed no noticeable guilt or expression of emotional depression: there was only fortitude in the face of punishment and dignified regret for his defections. The explanation for the lack of demonstration of guilty feelings appeared to lie in the reality circumstance of Blackrock's position in the financial world. This position fitted his ego wishes so closely that little room remained for guilty feelings. In the development of his personality, the ego-ideal or standard of individual attainment, created unconsciously by the offender, was suffused with the characteristic feelings of power and invincibility. The patrician spirit of his environment and the aura of infallibility surrounding his position as financial mentor were influences that forged a personality where super-ego and ego-ideal were almost synonymous. The sense of omniscience so developed out of his cultural and psychological atmosphere excluded the formation of the usual taxing conscience.

An analogy will illustrate the mechanisms in the hypothesis advanced to explain Blackrock's larceny. If the offender under discussion were a lowly clerk in a banking house conspiring to steal hundreds rather than millions of dollars, guilt reactions would undoubtedly have developed because of the discrepancy between impulses to appropriate money and restrictions of the conscience or super-ego. When, however, desires of the ego coincide with the reality position of the individual, there is little discrepancy between the ego and super-ego. The person who controls vast wealth is in actuality in a different position with regard to restrictions imposed on him by his conscience than one who is relatively deprived. As in the case of Blackrock, the individual with strong fantasies of omnipotence who is actually in a position of power borrows nourishment from his social and economic reality to sustain his conviction of infallibility.

This feeling of invincibility in bankers is transmitted to their clients as faith in ultimate wealth. The strength of this feeling is proportionate to the depth of the man's confidence in himself. In the last analysis, attitudes of invincibility depend upon the reality-testing which the individual's fantasy of omnipotence has undergone during his life experience. It is surprising how omnipotence fantasies occasionally can remain active among skillful, prudent investment counselors who have been successful in amassing fortunes for their clients. In such individuals a dichotomy develops in their mental processes between their practiced judgment and their daydreams, which in many cases leads to embezzling of vast fortunes entrusted to them.

Neurotic elements in the personality of embezzlers are often so hidden that no maladjustment or inefficiency in their business relations is demonstrable until a peculation is uncovered. The press is rarely without a news story of the embezzlement of a bank or large business firm by a trusted, efficient employee. In each case careful examination shows a residual infantile grandiosity encompassed in a psychological identification with wealthy employers or with the impersonal figure of the corporation. This unconscious identification is present in all persons to some degree, for, as has been shown in a previous chapter, the fantasy of participation in unlimited wealth is a representation of the infant's original egocentric conception of his universe.

Accountants and bookkeepers are often in a position where the illusion of wealth is stimulated by their identification with the corporation whose financial secrets are known to them. Through this identification, the power of the corporation becomes their own and their narcissistic feelings swell to a point commensurate with the financial power of the organization.

The principle of identification with large enterprises in embezzlers is illustrated by the case of an accountant who falsified the books of a large hosiery mill to the extent of $1,800,000 without visible benefit to himself. The "paper" larceny, which occurred over a long period, appeared inexplicable, for a thorough investigation showed no actual gain to anyone from the accountant's false statement of swollen assets. An explanation of this embezzlement can only be given in psychological terms. The accountant, a competent man of excellent reputation, gratified his own infantile tendencies toward aggrandizement by his identification with the corporation. His comment on the crime was that he had felt confused and overworked and was driven by a "certain complex about the company. I watched it grow . . . it was like a baby to me." His identification allowed him only surreptitious gratification, for in his falsifications he hardly dared slip over the threshold from wishing to having.

Instances of theft from large corporations are bound up with the psychological relationship between the individual and an organization symbolic of opulence and bounty. The infantile wish to share the wealth belonging to others is a repetition of the anticipation of unlimited parental love. In adulthood this wish assumes the form of an immature illusion regarding rewards for work. An individual under this unconscious influence longs for paternalistic affection from his employers more eagerly than he wishes for monetary recompense. Offenders in this group have not yet accepted the impossibility of achievement of their magical wishes. The point of complete maturation in such offenders has been delayed to the degree that unsuspected neurotic inclusions in the personality direct their behavior toward larcenous acts.

NEUROTIC FACTORS IN AGGRESSIVE CRIMINALS

When subjected to psychological analysis, many aggressive crimes are also found to rest on a neurotic background in the perpetrator. The accidental or occasional offender who is guilty of assault or homicide, may not show the neurotic basis of aggressive acts in daily life. It is only through emotional explosions culminating in assault or homicide that the occasional offender reveals his neurotic drives and conflicts, which are ordinarily repressed in his daily activities. Probing into the personality structure of these individuals prior to the offense undoubtedly would have disclosed emotional sensitivities which subsequently become exaggerated to the degree of motivating homicidal attacks. On the other hand, among psychopathic individuals who display primary aggression, neurotic elements, although present, are demonstrated with difficulty.

One frequently recurring psychological conflict underlying "accidental" murders in men relates to the fear of exposure of sexual inadequacy on the part of the offender. Such persons are under a constant strain to defend their sexual virility, and the highly charged emotion surrounding their sexual fear is brought to attention only in a situation where allusion is made to sexual inadequacy. The resultant behavior, specific and forceful, is set in motion by a psychological mechanism that can be conveniently called the "cuckolding reaction." The emotional energy of this reaction is derived from emphasis on the high social value given sexual potency in our civilization. The universal attitude toward potency is reflected in myths, folk customs and religious rituals bearing on a respect for fertility of the soil. Conversely, disdain for sexual impotency has been embodied among the peasants of the Mediterranean and Central Europe in the "cuckolding" sign, made by thrusting the thumb between the first and second finger and holding clenched hands aloft athwart the forehead. Originally the hand position simulated the position of horns on a goat, an ancient symbol of sexuality. The effect of the cuckolding sign is to thrust the barb of social contempt at the one toward whom the sign is pointed. The social significance of the cuckold symbol is the exposure of sexual inadequacy in such a person to the community. Cases of impulsive murder often reflect the psychological effect of this social phenomenon on the offender.

The situation behind a charge of manslaughter brought against a thirty-four-year-old Russian peasant who clubbed a man to death is a simple example of the cuckolding reaction. The offender came home after an hour spent at a barroom to find his wife in bed with another man. The fact of adultery was patent enough to demand action, but the implication of sexual inferiority provided the motive power for the crime. Knowledge that his wife should find sexual pleasure with another man was humiliation enough for the offender. But the psychological stimulus for the homicide sprang from the fact that the wife's infidelity exposed the offender's own sexual inferiority to the victim. The code under which the offender lived called for an immediate solution of this intolerable situation: he seized a wooden club and with a blow fractured the skull of his wife's paramour. In the offender's cultural group, the imputation of sexual inadequacy was not met by the equanimity which any other biologic disturbance would merit. Individuals in other social groups, more controlled, might have handled such a blow to the ego with socially sanctioned methods such as divorce or separation, or through a nonlethal blow, outburst of verbal rage or alcoholism. Indeed, in no social group do men meet exposure of sexual inadequacy with complete objectivity. The neurotic kernel of sensitivity to sexual inadequacy is a powerful influence in social, even criminal, aggression among men of all cultural levels.

Although accepted patterns of behavior in triangle situations undoubtedly play a role in accidental murder, the basis of such reactions is predominantly a personal, psychological one. Frequent murders in triangle situations provide nice illustrations of the reaction of sensitized persons. The provocateur who exposes the offender's sexual inadequacy must be wiped out to avenge the humiliation. The stronger the unconscious conviction of impotence in the cuckolded person, the potential murderer, the more vicious will be the resulting attack. When a person is suddenly confronted by a secret which the ego has striven to hide even from the self, defensive behavior of heroic character results. The instantaneousness of the aggressive act in so-called crimes of passion, a circumstance which suggests the frequent characterization of the act as "instinctive," depends upon the influence of ever-present unconscious inadequacy fears in the offender.

The specific defense mechanism developed in the offender against exposure of sexual secrets determines the fact and even the form of the homicide. For example, in a triangle situation where the cuckolded man is young, his impulse is to kill the erring woman. On the other hand, when the cuckolded individual is older, the erring man is more frequently the victim. The reason for this selectivity appears to be psychologically describable.

To the younger offender the woman is the more serious psychological threat, since her misbehavior reawakens his feelings of sexual incompetence. The young offender has given his secret of sexual desires to the woman and has achieved emotional ease through her expiation of his guilt. When the woman of his choice betrays his secret through entering a triangle, his sexual guilt with its accompanying anger mounts to fury. The wife or sweetheart has shared the secret of his sexual desire with another man. The intolerable situation, rendered peracute by its reflections from an earlier infantile (Oedipus) situation, can only be remedied by killing the woman in the triangle.

In the older offender the cuckolding, with its implied sexual incompetence, is closer to actuality. The wife's infidelity is interpreted as a betrayal of the murderer's weakness to another man. The social exposure of his secret, aided possibly by latent homosexual feelings released in witnessing sexual activity by another man, demands immediate retaliation. The offender can only regain his ego equilibrium by killing the man who has impliedly exposed his sexual incompetence to society. Whether the external stimulus be the direct observation of a sexual act or a hearsay report of the partner's infidelity, the homicidal attack in a triangle murder is a reaction to the humiliation of being placed in a cuckolding position.

The operation of the cuckolding principle in aggressive crime will be illustrated by two cases of murder which occurred under markedly different circumstances. One was that of a twenty-two-year-old ecclesiastical student who shot his wife and an older clergyman after witnessing them together in his hotel room. The second case was that of a reputable businessman who killed his younger partner following a mere inference that the partner had attempted sexual intimacy with the offender's daughter. In both cases, unconscious psychosexual factors, receiving stimulus from reality circumstances, swept the offenders into sudden crimes of passion.

Gregory was a youth of twenty-two who had come to America from Hungary, the oldest son of an orthodox Rabbi. As a boy, Gregory was a sensitive and nervous individual. Soon after his father's death, he underwent religious conversion from Judaism to Christianity. Esthetic, scholarly in bearing, he became immersed in an ecclesiastical atmosphere while preparing for the Protestant clergy. During his training period he met a girl, barely sixteen, with whom he became infatuated. They married in the West and, after a few months of happy life together, traveled to the east coast and registered at a metropolitan hotel. The evening of the murder the couple had dinner with a clergyman of another denomination, an old friend of Gregory's wife. Gregory, returning after an errand, waited outside the door of their hotel room long enough to ascertain that the voices he heard within were those of his wife and another man. He burst into the room, to find his wife and the clergyman in an embrace. Striding into the room, he quickly took a gun out of a drawer, saying, "You kissed each other and you are going to Heaven." He fired the revolver point-blank, killing both.

The offender was a neurotic individual whose early attachment to his father had been pathologic in intensity. His father's death had been a severe shock to him; it was then that he forsook his religion. He had always been idealistic, and his loss convinced him that the only purpose he could have in life would be to spread good fellowship and humanity through the world.

The idealistic goal Gregory had chosen acted as a cover for strong feelings of inferiority. His neurotic conflict had been characterized by mixed hostility and dependence on his father. The shock of exposure of his wife's infidelity flooded to the surface when he witnessed his open betrayal and exploded into an aggressive act. The figure of the older clergyman, the cuckolder, was a double factor in the psychological motivation of this impulsive murder. He not only cuckolded the younger man in actuality but at the same time symbolized the punishing and potentially castrating father of the old conflict. In this case both the wife and her accomplice in the offender's cuckolding received the full force of his retaliation.

Less obvious were the emotional forces in the second case, in which Ingram, a mature man, murdered his business partner, Roe, in a moment of fury. For several weeks a crisis had been developing in their business which involved accusations of financial peculations by the victim. The day of the offense, the younger partner, Roe, had terminated several minutes of heated conversation by abruptly going to the basement of the premises, muttering a common imprecation of sexual nature. Ingram then stalked to the stairway leading to the cellar in the rear of the store. As the victim, returning, reached the third or fourth step, Ingram lifted his revolver and fired six shots directly into Roe's body. He then handed the empty revolver to his cashier and instructed her to telephone the police. The officers, on reaching the drug store, were greeted by the defendant, who readily assented to his guilt. When taken into custody, the offender calmly admitted that he had reached the determination to kill Roe previous to the shooting. This determination grew out of information received from his daughter, employed as a cashier in the same store, that the deceased had at one time innocuously flirted with her. In actuality the offender's behavior, though apparently deliberate, cloaked a state of extreme excitement.

In discussing the offense Ingram described an increasing emotional irritation within himself because of the suspicion that Roe had been depleting the funds of the firm. His rankling anger mounted as his twenty-nine-year-old daughter reported the flirtation by the partner. Ingram's smoldering anger increased during the days preceding the murder to the point where he felt exhausted. He recognized himself as being in an emotional haze the day of the shooting. "It was," he explained with heat, "just the idea that he (the victim) had attempted another shameful act." Unable to restrain himself, he approached Roe for an explanation, which the younger man evaded with the sexual vulgarism indicated. The offender stood at the head of the stairs with the gun in his hand awaiting Roe's return. "I asked God to stay my hand but it was not to be." The shooting was done in a haze of cold fury and humiliation, yet he shot deliberately and accurately. When the firing ceased, his agitation suddenly left him and the excitement which had suffused him disappeared. He was calm and poised when the police officers arrived.

Ingram's life on casual view indicated complete adjustment. His reputation in the community was excellent. Conscientious in business, the offender was a typically righteous, intelligent citizen who endeared himself to his business associates and friends. Ingram's attitude during the detention period was typical of his life reactions. He reported that he slept well because "My conscience is clear." The offender accepted his self-appointed destiny of righteousness. In explanation of his lifelong devotion to goodness, the offender related how, in his own home, he had established a "peace psychology."

There were indications, however, that Ingram's overrighteousness was a compensation for unconscious sexual (incest) fantasies which had no place in his conscious thinking or code of behavior. The offender's unnecessarily frequent condemnation of Roe's promiscuous tendencies, although the latter was a younger, unmarried man, represented Ingram's active, but unconscious, sexual fantasies, behind which lay fears of sexual inadequacy. Another reaction formation to unconscious feelings of sexual inadequacy was seen in the offender's engrossment with revolvers and target practice. One of Ingram's boasts was that he carried a gun for twenty-seven years under a license from the police department. Regular pistol practice with the police officers became his hobby. The underlying motive for the excessive humiliation Ingram suffered through the alleged business irregularities of his partner was the unconscious fear engendered by fantasied sexual competition. The mass of feeling involved in this conflict was displaced onto Roe. Hence the exaggerated reaction to Roe's flirtation was raised to the point of a fantasied sexual assault by the obsessed offender. The story of the flirtation related by his daughter touched off an extremely sensitive spot in the offender's make-up; i.e., his unconscious incest fantasy. The "bad" man who thus challenged the offender's paternal righteousness unwittingly stirred up unconscious incest fantasies for which there was only one defense. Ingram, the peacemaker, had to rid the world of a "wolf." Belittlement of his self-esteem reached a point of intolerance, and Ingram's impulses erupted violently. Removal of the threat of virility in the person of the younger man resolved Ingram's inner struggle, and on the surface his conscience appeared untroubled.

Humiliation centering about lowered social prestige is a common psychological stimulant for crimes of passion. A derogatory remark relating to race, skin color, social position or economic success in life may be sufficient external stimulus to lead the person so singled out into acts of violence. The belittling remark occasions a murderous impulse aimed at removing an intolerable condition, due chiefly to a basic severe sense of inferiority.

The acute drop in prestige occasioned by name-calling occurs only in individuals conditioned by neurotic sensitivity to feel the intolerable mental pain of belittlement. Even so minor a provocation as being called a "show-off" at a neighborhood charity affair was the signal for a thirty-four-year-old man, without previous criminal record, to shoot two of his playful tormentors in a blind rage. Felonious assaults and homicide cases following social humiliation demonstrate the same deep-seated psychological dynamics as were observed in cuckolding reactions operative in the triangle murder.

The crime of assault presents, in the main, psychological problems closely similar to those of murder. Consideration is given the fact, however, that the crime of homicide or assault depends also on accidental factors. A moment's reflection will show that the variation of a quarter of an inch in the entrance point of a knife into the victim's body spells the difference between life and death. Obviously the psychological force behind murderous impulses cannot be matched with the eventuality. An attempt to kill may result in only minor assault, and a wish merely to disfigure a victim may result in death. Aggression displayed in cases of assault bears a relation to hidden neurotic conflicts not necessarily inherent in the external situation.

Assault and homicide, however, are not the only antisocial forms of "aggressive behavior." In crimes against property, e.g., arson, aggression is a common modality for the expression of human feelings. It is expressed through a lower level of personality integration. Aside from cases where arson is a deliberate act planned for the purpose of gaining revenue from fire insurance or to destroy evidence of prior crimes, fire-setting occurs as isolated offenses contingent upon specific psychological difficulties in the offender. The more blatant mental disturbances are found among fire-setters chiefly because primitive expression of aggression is more apt to be found among mentally dull or insane persons. The remaining large number of arson offenders have been explained by the concept "pyromania," a disorder in which the compulsion to set fire is irresistible.

ARSON

Considerable thought has been expended in attempts to shed light on the psychology of criminal fire-setting. Most investigators have adopted a psychoanalytic explanation of arson as an archaic, regressive means of expressing unconscious aggression in the individual. Some workers recognize that an "arson impulse," considered a natural tendency in childhood, persists in adult arsonists. They point to the finding that, among children, fire is a

primitive weapon partaking of magical power, a psychological symbol denying their actual powerlessness in an adult world.

The motivations which set arsonists into action are, broadly speaking,
related to attention-gaining and revenge-seeking motives, reactions to specific
psychological difficulties in the offender. In the actual case material a complex of interrelated emotional factors are present. Attention-gaining and
rejection are frequently found in adolescents in escapades such as setting
off fire alarm boxes, burning barn doors or other types of malicious mischief.
Such offenses, having a psychological background similar to the cherished
childhood fantasy of a conflagration of the schoolhouse, contain elements of
revenge directed toward society in general. The undistorted expression of
social aggression is most clearly seen in dull individuals.

An example is that of George S., an adult of borderline defective intelligence, who set fire to a loft building and caused the destruction of 10,000
dollars worth of yarn. George was a dull, inadequate individual, an "industrial inefficient." He worked as a Western Union messenger until he was
forty years old and remained satisfied with his adjustment. When his in-laws
came to live with him, they objected to the ignominy of his wife's social
position, and a rupture resulted within the family. Dissatisfied with his lack
of economic progress, his wife finally ejected George from the home. Immediately he started to set small fires in the neighborhood, continuing his
acts until the present offense led to his arrest. His anger against his
"troubles" spread to a series of childish acts of vengeance. George's description of his offense was clear: "I had been drinking to forget my troubles. I
was cold and I came to a clothing store and decided to get an overcoat. I
kicked in the plate glass in the doorway and went in. I found the store
filled with yarns and thread. Then I suddenly got mad and pulled the yarn
off the shelves and lit a match . . . until it blazed up." The arson in this
case served as a final desperate measure to gain attention and affection. The
blaze was literally an answer to George's wish for warmth and his yearning
for a return to the security of his home.

The crime of arson has two psychological components—starting the blaze
and extinguishing it. The second aspect of arson, the impulse to put out
the fire, is equally significant in the criminal psychology of arson. Setting
a fire partakes of patent aggressive motives, while extinguishing it involves
impulses arising from deeper levels of the personality. Fire marshals are
aware of the close relationship between fascination with fires and sexual
excitement in male arsonists who compulsively return to watch the fires they
set. This criminologic axiom is understandable in terms of the unconscious
meaning of fire-setting and the corresponding need to put the fire out. In

these compulsions both sexual (fire-passion) and aggressive (urination-domination) impulses are involved.

In the early stage of personality development, emotional charges surrounding the genito-urinary function contribute aggressive influences to the final personality structure. The usual repression of emotions surrounding this aspect of bodily function results in the sublimated expression of aggression in a socially prescribed manner. Ambition, for example, is a character trait developing from repression of aggressive-urinary elements in personality evolution. Where there is a neurotic fixation on the level of urinary function, aggressive impulses remain connected to the several aspects of the genito-urinary apparatus. The infantile satisfaction of extinguishing fires through urination or, in the case of the neurotic arsonist, seeing the fire extinguished by firemen, is an unconscious remnant of the wish to dominate. This wish is mediated through the archaic (unconsciously determined) relation between the urinary function and impulses of mastery.

These psychological factors are observed directly among neurotic arsonists. One youth, who had spent all his time in the fire station and was suspected of starting many fires, was convicted of impersonating a fire marshal. He developed marked anxiety when he was restrained by order of the court from frequenting firehouses while on probation. Association with fire equipment and those professionally interested in fires gratified his deeper impulses for mastery. However, anxiety developed in the probationer when he was restrained from the gratification of these neurotic impulses. He became tense, restless and complained of what, to him, was unnecessary privation. The youth could see no relationship between his offense and the restraint imposed by the court. The identification with the fire fighters was complete; in his fantasies he expressed his aggressive impulses through displacement of all his emotions to the position of fire marshal.

Also striking was the case of a dangerous pyromaniac who set some seventy fires over a period of several years. This offender's arsonous impulses were stimulated by alcoholism. He stated freely that his greatest delight was surreptitiously watching the firemen put out a blaze which he had started. The offender asserted that when drinking he became sexually aroused. Setting the fire and watching the blaze being extinguished gratified his sexual desire. Offenders of this group have been known to experience sexual satisfaction through spontaneous orgasm or open masturbation while watching a fire of their own setting.

Clinical observation of this group of cases allows the general statement that there are definite neurotic patterns actively directing the arsonists' offenses. It is questionable whether the neurotic arsonist can be dignified by the special diagnostic designation of pyromaniac. The case material studied indicates that several types of neurotic reaction, rather than one definite, perverted impulse, may lead to the crime of arson.

PSYCHOLOGICAL FACTORS IN FEMALE OFFENDERS

An appraisal of the psychological problems of women convicted of major crime involves social and cultural factors not operative among male criminals. For example, it might be suspected that adumbrations of the favored position women occupy economically would be visible in the infrequency of criminal offenses among women as compared with men of like mentality, cultural and social background. The numerical disparity* between male and female robbery and burglary offenders immediately brings to mind certain external factors. The law's protective attitude toward women unquestionably acts as a deterrant in their criminal activities. Further, married women in an economically dependent position do not have the same type of financial responsibility as men. Again, certain felony categories, such as sodomy, rape or exhibitionism, practically do not exist for women. A relative reduction in the capacity for physical aggression affords an explanation for the negligible number of assault, robbery and burglary cases committed by women. A psychological correlate of this biologic fact is that rebelliousness against parental control is expressed among girls by leaving home or by early marriages rather than by antisocial conduct.

The question presents itself, Why do not emotional pressures in women result so frequently in antisocial behavior as in men? An obvious answer is that neurotically determined impulses among women have differing social consequences. Rebellious tendencies in young girls take the form of sexual misconduct rather than aggressive behavior. Behavior based on immature sexual attitudes brings girls into the misdemeanor courts on charges of wayward minor, illegitimacy, prostitution and so on, whereas immaturity in boys leads to burglary, vagrancy, robbery, rape or homosexual escapades. Social attitudes even more than laws have given a "felonious" meaning to the results of antisocial behavior in men, whereas immature misbehavior in women encompasses less serious connotations. In addition, social influences

* In New York County over a period of 13 years (1930 to 1942 inclusive), 4 per cent of the total convicted felons were women.

DeVine, in a survey of 3700 county and city jails in the United States, found 7 per cent of the population to be females: DeVine's survey included felonies, misdemeanors or other lesser offenses.

Of all felons serving time in 1930 in N.Y. State institutions, 1.2 per cent were women.

comprising impalpable but strongly felt negative attitudes regarding women and crime are reflexly felt by women themselves. Traditionally, women are not thought of as harboring criminal impulses. Rather, they are considered more indirect in wrongdoing than men. Women have been considered powers behind the scenes, motivating evil rather than executing it, dealers in intrigues rather than in direct attack.

In support of the influence of particular social attitudes toward women, the clinical behavior of female offenders discloses subtle differences from that of male prisoners. In the masculine environment of court and jail, women offenders exhibit defensiveness against expression of social aggression. This type of defensiveness is a direct transference of their feelings from society to the legalistic environment. Whereas the male offender defends himself by being aggressive and blustering or unco-operative or surly, his female counterpart is bewildered, frightened and either diffident or casually talkative in her responses to questioning. The very behavior of female offenders—their bundling themselves in their outer garments, their disinclination to co-operate—betokens a protectiveness against a world that confronts them with their misdeeds.

The technic and mechanisms in the various crimes committed by women are comparable to those in men, with certain psychological differences. Theft will serve as an illustration of the presence of distinctive psychological features in female criminals. In an earlier chapter the dual psychologic meaning of theft was discussed: stealing encompasses both reality and neurotic values to the offender. This duality exists among female as among male larcenists, but a strong impression is gained that in the former, infantile acquisitive impulses are not so deviously represented. In the frequent thefts of clothes committed by female houseworkers who are jealous of their mistresses, less neurotic guilt attends the crime than is found in male larcenists. Infantile motives in larceny undergo little repression or distortion and appear to arise directly from the situation in which the crime is committed. Nor do such situations obtain only in ignorant or underprivileged women.

These trends were observed, for example, in the case of an unmarried woman of mature years, well-educated in languages and fine arts and highly regarded as a teacher and governess. For several years Mary C. had systematically stolen a total of 8,500 dollars from her employer, a wealthy widow, for whom Mary acted as companion and governess to two sons. At the time of conviction Mary, who was fifty-two years old, had never married because an accident to her spine in youth prevented her from having children. Her father had often told her that she was physically unattractive and should never think of marriage. On her father's advice she had tried to supplant her maternal instincts by scholarly pursuits. Earlier in life the position of governess and teacher had given her emotional gratification. She was known among her friends as one who always did something for other people without looking for a return. Mary's interests in later years had turned to spiritualism as a compensation for emotional deprivation. After growth to adulthood of her two charges, to whom Mary was much attached, Mary's mistress made plans to live alone on an annuity from her deceased husband. Mary's thefts directly expressed her envy and hatred of her employer. The latter was left, after her life's work, with two grown sons and an income, but Mary had only the bitterness of an unsuccessful life to fall back on in her search for emotional ease.

In discussing larceny among women there are several larger social and psychologic issues to be considered. Experience indicates that the psychology of women lends itself to a less ready development of guilt toward money matters than among men. The impression is gained that money, as a symbol of purchasing power among women, is somewhat less laden with inhibitions of a neurotic nature. The institution of installment buying in this country illustrates this tendency. Economists point to the tremendous increase in consumption of household goods resulting from the influence of advertising designed to appeal to women. It may be that women's readiness to accept the use of things before full payment is made has some relationship to their historically and culturally conditioned attitudes toward property. Women were conditioned, in a world wherein control of trade and industry was in masculine hands, to attach greater amounts of cathexis (emotional charge) to the use of property rather than to property rights.

If it be true that women are less responsive to the restrictive voice of prohibitions in money matters, it might logically be expected that they would be involved in larcenous acts more frequently than are men. The situation, however, proves to be the reverse. It is difficult to explain this finding in spite of the demonstrable fact that guilt feelings are strikingly diminished in apprehended female larcenists.

The paucity of guilt feelings in female larcenists is even clearer among shoplifters. Clinical contacts with female larcenists support the impression that they are relatively comfortable emotionally in the face of thefts of money or articles of value. Feelings of righteousness and blandness of attitude is a regular finding in the shoplifter. It must be added, however, that the male pickpocket's attitude presents a striking analogue to that of the female shoplifter. In both groups the influence of an infantile expectation of ownership of stolen goods can transparently be seen. Unconscious wishes for participation in parental wealth, encapsulated in the ego, permit little insight by the offender into the social meaning of shoplifting. Such offenders do not consider themselves criminal. A widow of thirty-eight who supported several children by the proceeds of her "work," which averaged as high as 200 dollars a week, complained, "The store detective is a sadist. He gloats on making people miserable. . . . Let those who are going to be house drudges do it. I must make a living."

In considering crimes involving aggression by women, certain aspects of women's criminal psychology appear. For example, robbery demonstrates that impetus toward crime among women has deep psychological roots. Casual experience indicates that most female robbers are thrust into armed robberies by male companions. Yet the passive dependence of women on men does not result as frequently as is thought in identification by women with antisocial male partners. In fact, female robbers are often impelled in their crimes by unconscious hostile impulses against men. Girls who assume the swaggering aggression of their male companions in a robbery, assault or murder actually have an emotionally thin relationship with their male codefendants. When there is professed a great depth of love between the man and woman in a major crime, it is usually a rationalization of unconscious hostility and independent antisocial impulses in the woman. The love relationship, when it is present, often is a shield for unconscious impulses against men on the part of the woman.

Support for this hypothesis is seen in those prostitutes who make a practice of robbing their clients. The behavior of such offenders is obviously in conflict with their prostitution; they inflict injury upon men whom they serve sexually. Stealing represents a wish to deprive men of their power (money) and is thus a symbolic act of castration. Behind this neurotic drive is a clearly discernible rejection of passivity and womanhood joined with aggressive castrating tendencies toward men.

Other varieties of aggressive crimes among women, such as murder and assault, are based on the familiar psychological modalities of humiliation, jealousy, frustration and emotional sensitivity. Unconscious factors behind these reactions, however, have a specific character. As stated above, these impulses function to render men powerless, either symbolically or in actuality. This mechanism, a derivative of castrating tendencies recognizable in certain types of robbery, is also operative in infanticide and criminal abortion, varieties of homicide peculiar to women. Criminal abortion and, to a lesser degree, abandonment of infants by women, are psychologically related to infanticide. Because women are closer to children biologically, infanticide is most repugnant to the public sentiment. It is probable that the maternal impulse to infanticide is much more common, especially among mothers of illegitimate children, than is indicated by records of criminal convictions. Unquestionably death wishes against the unborn child or newly born infant may have emotional justification, in view of the humiliation and social guilt which the unwed mother suffers. Nevertheless, cultural and personal attitudes of positive nature toward children conflict with feelings of humiliation. In cases where the mother is under no cloud concerning illicit sexual relations, death wishes against the infant are mainly of unconscious origin. In either event, destructive tendencies in the infanticide offender are found to have a specific meaning in terms of the emotional life story of the individual.

Examination of the psychodynamics of those guilty of infanticide indicates that old emotional patterns based on parent-child antagonisms bring unconscious death wishes to the surface, and these are displaced to the newborn infant. Sometimes murderous impulses against infants are defensive reactions to incest fantasies toward the offender's father. L. Bender, in her study of child murderers, recognized that in cases of infanticide by women, the mother was psychologically identified with the child victim. The act of murder proved to be a symbolic suicide aimed at easing the pressure of a burdensome reality situation. This mechanism has been confirmed in criminologic material. A case of infanticide committed by a young mother of twenty-one illustrates the frequent psychological meaning of this crime.

The offender, Bertha M., had started a casual correspondence with a sailor whom she had met through a "Lonely Hearts Club" advertisement in a magazine. After several years of correspondence the young man visited her for ten days. Their romance developed rapidly and their engagement was announced during his visit. The sailor fiancé returned to service in foreign waters while Bertha arranged a prolonged visit to a relative in New England to await the sailor's discharge from the service. During the waiting period Bertha met a man at the summer resort, and a brief flirtation developed during which sexual relations were consummated. When her sailor returned, Bertha married him. Both she and her husband, Bertha claimed later, were unaware that she was already pregnant. The offense occurred four months after her marriage. During the course of a family party Bertha suddenly left the group, returning to her home on a pretext. She felt ill and in a dazed, confused state when she arrived at her home. Bertha remembered neither the pain nor the bleeding of the spontaneous birth which occurred within an hour, as she lay in her apartment alone. Still apparently mentally clouded, Bertha managed to grasp the infant and strike its head against the bathtub several times. Later, under pressure she recounted these incidents as vague memories. When alarmed relatives arrived, Bertha was found in bed, comatose, her dead infant swathed in bloody underclothes and towels in a pail in a corner of the bathroom.

Study of the offender revealed her to be strikingly immature in her emotional make-up. Bertha had always referred her problems to the parents. Her father, an engineer in the military service, who had been away from home for long periods of time, still exerted a strong influence on her. She was aware of being in a dependent attitude. Some of this crept into her speech during psychiatric interviews.

Several clearcut trends were apparent in Bertha's situation. Mixed with these yearnings were unconscious feelings of dependency and love for the father. It is quite probable that for Bertha the marriage to the sailor represented a flight to her father. The long absence of her husband-to-be after their engagement confused her. It represented a denial of love awarded, and her ego demanded that the resulting frustration be neutralized. The casual affair with the father of the murdered infant during her waiting period was an impulsive act aimed toward the satisfaction of this emotional craving. Her affair occurred under the influence of an unconscious fantasy of reunion with the father, in which guilty feelings evoked by unconscious incest wishes also played a role. These deeper emotional forces, which disturbed Bertha more than she realized, clashed with the actual problems that the pregnancy created. As she was caught in a dilemma, her guilt feelings and the anticipated anger of her husband forcibly conflicted with the need for a man's love and protection. The solution of the terrible social plight which Bertha faced was too painful for her ego to entertain. Hysterical amnesia blotted out memories of the infant's birth and of the subsequent crime. The infanticide was motivated by both a real social dilemma and a serious underlying neurotic problem. The unconscious conflict had actually exerted an influence, of which the offender was totally unaware, on the course of her love life and on her subsequent offense.

Psychological trends disclosed in the study of women convicted of infanticide are repeated in unmistakable form among female abortionists. While felony convictions for criminal abortion in most jurisdictions predominantly involve midwives, occasionally male physicians are found among this group of offenders. Among men, the motive of criminal abortion is directly related to the large amounts of money involved. In women convicted of this crime, on the other hand, psychological elements are perceptible. The female abortionist demonstrates a particular defensiveness that is intimately connected with the nucleus of the underlying psychological conflict.

Female abortionists are so similar in structure, attitude and background as to be recognizable as a "type" in criminal court practice. They are found to be evasive, shrewd and defensive. They minimize their offenses, even after apprehension, to a point beyond reason. The evidence entailed in discovery of instruments such as catheters, curets or anesthesia equipment is swept aside by them as insignificant. The tenacity and lofty contempt of these offenders for what is considered good legal "evidence," is tenacious beyond that observed in other criminals.

In explanation of this behavior, the hypothesis comes to mind that elements in this marked evasiveness derive from an emotional need to suppress the activity surrounding childbirth from the eyes of men. This attitude in the offending midwife is peculiar to this group of women. Committing abortions, to such individuals, has the meaning of a symbolic rejection of children. Coinciding with the professed wish to lift their patients from a position of social humiliation is a strong feeling of hostility to the patients they consciously agree to help. Admission to the authorities of details of the offense would stir anxieties that dip into unconscious layers and stimulate ambivalent feelings in the offender. Only complete denial of the offense will suppress these turbulent emotions and serve to repress unconscious hostility toward their clients from the eyes of the court and the world of men.

This mechanism is illustrated in the case of a Scotswoman, Bess W., who at the age of sixty-eight was convicted upon her seventh arrest for abortion, the first six of which resulted in acquittals. She had married a widower at the age of twenty-six; there were three stepchildren but no children of her own. Upon the death of her husband she remarried, at the age of twenty-nine; again there were three stepchildren of this marriage. Her life was spent in caring for these six children. Her attitude of resigned bitterness was swallowed up in the bustle of home life. When her stepchildren grew up, she developed an interest in midwifery and practiced it actively for more than ten years until her final conviction for criminal abortion. It was evident, through a study of her attitudes in operating on young girls who came to her to be aborted, that she was symbolically injuring them. Her unconscious hostility was directed against these patients who, in contrast to herself, were women successful in the biologic role of childbearing. As a midwife, she was in reality aiding young women in distress. On another level of her emotional organization, Bess was denying the fact of their biologic potency and vanquishing her rivals (patients) in the function of childbearing. In one stroke two motives were served; the conscious wish as midwife to help socially unfortunate women and the unconscious, hostile impulse to injure her more prolific sisters in the competitive biologic struggle.

7

The Cure for Crime

The approach to crime and criminals urged here has been essentially consonant with the aims and philosophy developed by medical discipline. Medicine considers all human behavior and function susceptible of explanation by scientific principles. Psychiatry adds to medical knowledge an emotional attitude essential for its successful application. It is an attitude based on a firm belief that biologic and psychological riddles can be solved by the slow, steady application of knowledge derived from experiment and study. Applied to criminal conduct, this attitude assumes that crime—man's perpetual plague—could be wiped out in time as medical plagues have been systematically attacked and eradicated during the past two centuries. Knowledge of man's personality in action and of the psychological interreactions between the criminal offender and the social body against whom he offends, has accumulated sufficiently to encourage the further use of this discipline in attempting to cure criminals.

Adoption of medical attitudes in therapy of crime and criminals presupposes the assumption of the broad viewpoint of multiple causation, discussed in Chapter 1. In physical medicine, medical scientists are aware of the delicate interrelations between the chemistry, pathology and physiology of their patients. In the field of crime, the psychology and psychopathology of society also are considered, since crime, though it originates in the individual, is expressed in and through society. The sick patient suffers alone or possibly indirectly involves a few members of his family. The criminal, on the other hand, though he himself may be forced to endure the consequence of his offense, primarily inflicts injury and suffering on his society. Criminals are closest in this respect to neurotic patients who secondarily and unconsciously injure those who are in an intimate relationship to the patient. It is evident then, that plans for treatment of criminals require a broader horizon in the therapist's preparation than obtains in the consideration of medical patients.

PSYCHOTHERAPY AND THE THEORY OF CRIMINAL INTENT

Treatment of behavior problems, as in medical conditions, entails the use of a hypothesis which will provide a rationale for therapeutic measures adopted. The key to successful management of sociopsychological disorders rests on an attainment of etiologic knowledge of the disturbances treated. In the case of criminal conduct, it would be presumptuous to suppose that all factors underlying any criminal act can be known precisely. However, a sufficient number of facts are understood at present to base a working hypothesis upon them.

An hypothesis of crime causation is subject to certain limitations. It must be realistic in relation to the law, which has long assumed responsibility for the care of criminals and prevention of crime. The criminal law embodies an attempt to compress all the myriad contingencies of human behavior into rules which govern the conduct and punish the misconduct of men. In spite of defects, the law meets the continued need to judge and dispose of criminals. Hence a theory of treatment of the offender should lie within the structure of legal institutions and criminal jurisprudence. One aspect of legal reality which underlies trial and sentencing of offenders is the pervasive consideration of criminal intent.

The criminal law concentrates its attention on that aspect of criminal mentality which concerns evil intentions motivating wrongdoing. The philosophical premise on which the law judges the intentions and conduct of men is that of freedom of the will. This doctrine holds that unless individuals suffer an absence of reason because of mental deficiency or insanity, they are able of their own will to choose the proper course to pursue and to do what is right or wrong in accordance with their conscious choice.

In spite of this immutable standard of conduct, in actual judicial practice the principle of determinism rises to become a formidable factor in treating criminals. This principle states that a human action is caused by physical, mental and environmental forces not under the individual's control. Every sentencing judge takes into account, automatically or explicitly, the circumstances of each offense and the history of the offender. The effect of poor environment, a history of previous criminal activity, the probability of suggestive influence of more experienced criminals, the presence of nervous disorder or personality disturbance in the culprit are all considered in relation to the punishment meted out. Ratiocination of this nature becomes an automatic function of the experienced judicial mind. One legal authority commented, in speaking of treatment of offenders, "The judge . . . is not restricted to a myopic view of the criminal act."

The law's focus on the criminal as a psychological entity is mediated by the fundamental tenet that criminality cannot exist in the absence of criminal intent. But the court is limited in its interest in the offender by the need to satisfy both statutory law and social conscience. Psychiatry is privileged to probe deeper into the question of criminal intent. Medical and legal disciplines alike address themselves to the basic criminologic problems of criminal intent. Although couched in different terms, the law's "intent to do evil" and psychiatry's "emergence of antisocial impulses," are two facets of the same phenomenon. The long history of criminal law shows a gradual increase in awareness of the importance of criminal intent in offenders and a tacit agreement with the psychological view of criminal acts. Thus various degrees of a crime, as first and second degrees of murder or first, second and third degrees of rape, were established to conform with varying degrees of intent and the exhibition of varying intensities of effort corresponding to that intent.

INTENT AND IMPULSE

It is obvious that if psychiatry is to help solve problems in crime, it must illuminate the obscure question of criminal intent. The origin of antisocial impulses, the obstructions or aids to their emergence, the various mental mechanisms by which these intentions are mediated, is the concern of criminologic psychiatry. The attainment of precise knowledge of the complex behavior constituting crime, derived from study of convicted and sentenced criminals, involves certain difficulties, e.g., those of sampling. It is impossible to be sure that offenders who are apprehended and hence available for study, are the criminals responsible for the majority of serious offenses suffered by society. Another factor in this statistical uncertainty is the variation in criminal activity in any given offender: chronic offenders may be convicted of widely different crimes in different periods of their careers. Innumerable criminal records portray offense profiles in which there is a first conviction for burglary, a second for assault, a third for rape or murder, etc. Among youthful offenders, burglary is an extremely common first offense, but the offender may either cease his criminal behavior after one offense or continue in burglary or other crime. Thus the study of an offender at one period in his career may elicit psychological elements reflected in a totally different crime at a later period. This unavoidable variable in the relation of psychology to specific crime groups does not necessarily prohibit the assumption that emotional conflicts motivate criminal acts. Sufficient uniformity of impulse is present in any given recidivist or occasional offender to provide a distinct picture of his antisocial behavior pattern, just as the personality of a man is recognizable as an entity, continuous throughout his life.

Each personality, whether normal or severely psychopathic, exhibits many types of mental mechanisms in behavior. Each individual is host to a network or a syncytium of impulses under varying degrees of control, of which only the strongest become evident on the surface in behavior. Case material quoted throughout this work demonstrated the presence of a plexus of impulses, inhibitions and reaction formations in each personality diagnostic group. Thus neurotic features were found in those clinically diagnosable as psychopaths, emotional immaturity was found in neurotic individuals, and neurotic and socially immature elements were found in normal individuals. Behavior is directly influenced by the complex mixture of emotion, instinct and impulse operating within man.

A criminal act results when an impulse contrary to the expressed restrictions of civilized life cannot be withstood. Society's restrictions notably relate to impulses of aggression, anger, covetousness, revenge and sexual gratification. In primitive days responsibility for exacting retribution for personal injury or death was in the hands of him who suffered. In time the state recognized its role of protector of individual rights and assumed, through law, the function of curbing or punishing those who gave vent to their impulses. The area of criminal acts therefore enlarged, as greater and greater control was exercised over antisocial tendencies. Because of the increasing responsiveness of the state to the welfare of its members, society in modern times has given the individual less latitude than formerly for the exercise of those wishes and drives which cause unhappiness to others.

The thread which ties together all antisocial acts into the recognizable entity of crime is a series of *human impulses*. These drives are the true causes of crime; the numerous social and economic factors which modify antisocial behavior are merely contingencies of such acts. This view of crime causation does not deny that multiple contingencies such as the influence of physical disorders, nervous diseases and endocrine changes in the individual, or poverty, criminal association, political corruption, enervating cultural atmosphere and improper housing in the social environment, are factors. It does state that from the standpoint of treatment we must come to grips with that function in human psychology—impulse—which is a first cause of antisocial behavior.

Objectively viewed, the impulse life is the significant inciter of criminal actions. How would the conflict between impulse and restrictions appear to the criminal if he were fully cognizant of the forces within himself? What, in other words, would a subjective view of the cause of crime demonstrate of the actual inner situation? Analysis of the criminal's emotional state indicates that his conflict is in the relationship between the reality demands of civilization and his impulses as an individual. This is the problem the offender has to meet. His reactions to this conflict are psychologically close to those adopted by children. Offenders speak the language of children, which is that of behavior. The burden of what they tell can be expressed in simple terms: "to take, to grasp, to be angry, to hate and to strike." In children it is the language of consciousness, in adults the current of the unconscious. Both groups are antisocial in an environment which from the cradle onward has taught and continues to teach them to throttle these socially intolerable impulses.

The psychological situation of the criminal in society is analogous to the relationship between the infant and the parent. Criminals defy the State, on which they are dependent, as infants defy the parents who nourished them. The general aim in treating child behavior problems is to understand the language of the child, to fathom the meaning of defiant independence, under which lies emotional dependence. Similarly, in the criminal the meaning of rebelliousness and aggression, beneath which lie unrecognized and unconscious pleas for help, requires understanding. An intelligent therapy for criminals can be developed on the basis of this knowledge of the inner meaning of the criminal's defiant behavior. The resulting philosophy of therapy will control and yet aid the offender. It will not be a vindictive treatment, where the "intent" to commit a crime is taken at face value—as defiance meriting punishment, but a process of treatment through legal, social and psychiatric agencies which operate through an understanding of the causes of misbehavior. Only a technic that circumvents the punitive attitudes and unconscious prejudices of everyone toward lawbreakers and emphasizes the motives behind crime can be of lasting benefit to the offender.

The task of applying psychotherapy to offenders requires more than unremitting activity of professional psychiatrists, psychologists and social workers with individual offenders. It requires the education of society to an appreciation that criminal acts are not due to an irretrievable and fixed evil intent but are an expression of transient impulses. Crime as behavior is the failure of the ego's struggle to control aggression, hates and frustration reactions. Crime is less craziness or inexplicable badness than a neurotic disposition of the ego which hinders its adjustment to a multifaceted, restrictive reality.

Civilized society, which has never been unaware of its need to struggle with antisocial impulses in its members, uses religious influences to restrain open expression of aggressive feelings. Indeed, ethical teaching was and is a sufficient curb on antisocial impulses to prevent the largest majority of people from committing criminal acts. Since the task of this chapter is to indicate the possibilities for treatment of criminals, the tried and approved

methods of handling criminal impulses must be considered in conjunction
with those therapeutic principles enunciated by modern mental science.

The teaching of ethics is accomplished in several ways, each method
efficacious to some degree. In one of these, religious dogma emphasizes
the need for ethical behavior in securing a personal immortality for the
individual. In another way, ethical teaching, influenced by religious principles of forebearance, places a restraint on social impulses out of respect for
one's fellow beings. A more generalized ethical teaching, to which all human
beings are subject, is the moral view of "goodness" for its own sake. Success
and happiness in life are the material rewards for restraining impulses the
expression of which may constitute danger to others. Moral education is
aimed at bringing to light the social disadvantage of allowing evil or antisocial impulses to eventuate in action. Education of this nature utilizes the
conscience, as the ego struggles to control unrestricted instincts. Eternal
ego vigilance is necessary to keep them under control, but their discharge
in dreams and fantasy, or their sublimation in play, sports or drama all
through life, is proof of their ubiquity in our mental life. In spite of this
never-ending struggle against the pressure of unrestrained, egocentric impulses, ethical teaching meets with success in law-abiding persons. The
passage of individuals from immaturity to maturity is itself eloquent testimony of the eventual suppression of antisocial impulses in most human
beings. These psychobiologic facts provide justification for that emotional
education called psychotherapy, which is aimed at resolving criminal impulses in offenders.

THE TREATMENT PROGRAM

A vital preliminary aspect of a treatment program for criminals is the
education of the public to a psychological orientation toward crime. Society
must be educated to view crime as a psychological illness, a disorder of the
impulse life.

It is to be expected, on the basis of what the long history of society's attitudes toward criminals teaches, that this educational process would con-
sume many years. The history of penology gives a clear indication of the
depth and tenacity of conscious and unconscious attitudes toward the criminal. Retribution and vengeance are difficult feelings to modify. The
education of society should proceed concomitantly with the emotional education, i.e., treatment of the individual criminal. That the material of this
dual project lies in an area beclouded by moral views need not detract from

patient analysis and study of antisocial impulses, even though they be expressed in repugnant or terrifying conduct.

Another prerequisite for a program of treatment of criminals is the reorientation of public attitudes toward individualization of treatment. Just as the insane during earlier centuries were lumped together in the minds of the populace as a group of souls lost to the domination of Satan, so have criminals been regarded as an alien group among law-abiding people. The populace, unacquainted with offenders, carries in its collective mind a composite picture of the criminal as unmistakably different from the rest of society. Earlier impressions of a "criminal type" must be eradicated from the social consciousness because connotations of this nature have an impeding effect on the total treatment effort. Those who care for the young should relinquish the view that a child or youth in trouble has thereby irretrievably cast his lot with the criminal group in society. A forward-looking step in this program would comprise teaching parents to adopt a sensible attitude toward the petty thefts, sexual misadventures, runaway reactions and rebelliousness of their children. This teaching would inculcate the idea that such misbehavior was representative of emotional disturbances rather than of moral turpitude.

The prevention of serious crime later in life devolves upon educators and parents, in whose hands the personalities of children are placed to be made or marred. Parent education in mental hygiene, under the guidance of trained psychiatric and social personnel, must be pursued through every avenue of approach—the press, the radio, parent-teacher organizations and civic clubs. The adult education field provides a promising area for training parents and parents-to-be in an appreciation of the emotional background out of which future criminals evolve. Open discussion of major life problems, the psychology of marriage and family life and the emotional tensions within the family constellation constitute a real aspect of the mental hygiene program of crime prevention. Anxiety on the part of the public toward trained social workers, psychiatrists and psychoanalysts is in general still too acute for the former to bring all their emotional problems to these specialists. The natural leaders to whom many of the populace turn with their troubles are the clergy. The training of future spiritual leaders needs to be heavily weighted with a sociopsychological viewpoint. If the ministry, already endowed with a considerable degree of psychotherapeutic influence by their parishioners, were more fully educated to think in terms of the social consequences of distorted emotional drives in individuals, a strong band of allies would be brought to the field of crime prevention.

The emotional influence of the schoolroom on the development of a social conscience in children and youth is second only to that of the home. Education as a force in crime control must be suited to the emotional as well as the intellectual needs of the children. Widespread use of aptitude and projective (e.g., Rorschach ink blot) tests, as well as intelligence tests, would demonstrate the educational needs of these individuals. Retarded and emotionally immature children require an appropriate education in social living which encompasses technics of emotional control. The child is not always so balanced in mental development as to profit only by the bare routine of classroom work. Emotional reactions require as much attention as scholastic deficiencies.

Cases encountered among younger offenders have indicated the presence of specific educational problems which produced frustration that was reflected in social misbehavior. These are children who display wide discrepancies between verbal and performance function or suffer from retarding factors like reading disabilities (strephosymbolia) or confusion of handedness, which interferes with their literate education. Such persons require special teaching technics to help them learn. In the competitive environment of the schoolroom, such disturbances in learning react upon the personality of the growing child to evoke inferiority feelings that often find expression in delinquency. The sensitivity of dull children or of those with reading handicaps to the social stigma of their illiteracy has not been appreciated sufficiently. Unable to develop interest in fields beyond their capacities and without the capacity to verbalize their feelings, these individuals fall into patterns of abnormal behavior—truancy, mischievousness and petty larceny. The vast experience of the military service in World War II with illiterate or semiliterate men forcibly demonstrated the behavioral importance of problems of uneven learning. Many men reacted to their social disadvantage with inner humiliation and outward misbehavior such as insubordination and desertion.

The contribution to self-esteem of familiarity with and mastery of words cannot be overestimated in the developing personality. Education in our grade and secondary school has always revolved around verbality, i.e., ideas clothed in words. It was the recognition of this tendency that changed the face of pedagogy during the past half-century with the establishment of manual training and vocational classes. Many youths who feel at home around machinery are confused and embarrassed amid mathematical formulae or abstract ideas. These individuals react to the verbal atmosphere of the schoolroom with feelings of inferiority and indifference, often solving their conflict by running away from the area of pressure. It is probable that scholastic emphasis on studies involving verbal functions almost exclusively is a factor in developing neurotic reactions in youths and boys who have predominantly nonverbal mental functions. Admonitions by school teachers to the effect that disinterest in literacy condemns the pupil to a lifetime of plebeian labor are familiar to pupils of every generation and reflect society's prejudice in favor of verbality. The sociopsychological connotation of this horrendous prophecy had an economic background. It was related to the industrial organization of the country, which allowed the laborer or semi-skilled mechanic to be exploited by the verbally minded, glib or tongue-entrepreneur. The executive, the salesman and professional were held up to pupils as models for a socially successful life. However, in recent years, the rise of technology and the growing importance of the skilled mechanic has been recognized by modern school systems in their inclusion of scientific and mechanical subjects in the curriculum. Nevertheless, dull or nonverbal and immature individuals, from whose ranks many beginners in crime are recruited, are sensitive to the emotional connotation of disapproval directed at those who work with their hands.

The training of emotional reactions of such children in schools directed by psychiatrically trained psychologists would provide a broader educational front, aimed at relieving frustrations, adjusting youths to their capacities and minimizing rebellious attitudes. A further and necessary extension of this endeavor includes the illumination and correction of personality maladjustments in the teachers themselves, in view of the strong unconscious influence they exert on their charges. The extension of pedagogy to include emotional as well as intellectual education has the most far-reaching potentialities and could constitute an outstanding achievement of two related disciplines, education and psychology.

The efforts of legal and sociologic leaders to modernize the treatment of youthful offenders are embodied in the Youth Correction Authority Act and have been discussed in detail in Chapter 3. The principles underlying this model legislation, when adopted throughout this country, would bring into active play all the social and educational facilities which the community can offer. Each social agency and institution for training and correction of youth would eventually be co-ordinated, with the advisory help of a staff of psychologists and psychiatrists. Probation departments and juvenile courts would function in co-operation with welfare agencies, the first line of defense against the development of young criminals. Workers in these fields are first to receive complaints of mischievousness which presage delinquency and crime in later life. Clinics for the treatment of problem children on the strength of the Youth Correction Act principles would be enlarged and strengthened with psychiatrists as supervisors for parole and probation workers.

Extension of these forward-looking ideas of delinquency treatment leads to still larger tasks. One of these is that of activities in the community for pre-delinquent youths. Recreational direction in settlement houses and supervised activity in community playgrounds are potent forces in shaping the energies of adolescents in a constructive way. Larger social projects like city planning and slum clearance have already demonstrated their value in modifying the attitudes of youth towards deprivation, and in so doing bear directly on crime prevention.

One vital recent development in judicial practice initiated by the trend toward preventive treatment of young delinquents, has been the establishment of Adolescent Courts. Here the stigma of "felony" offense in a young man is removed by handling the offender as a wayward minor before the court. Adolescent courts are thus enabled to utilize psychiatric and social work facilities with youths indicted for major offenses, without bringing them into contact with older, more experienced lawbreakers in detention jails. The records are impounded, and no opportunity is permitted to brand the youth as a criminal. The Adolescent Court embodies one of the prime considerations of the Youth Correction Authority Act: removal of youth offenders from an environment that emphasizes the punitive treatment of social misbehavior and substitution of an individual treatment approach.

PSYCHOTHERAPY OF THE INDIVIDUAL OFFENDER

The psychotherapist's work in the field of criminology embraces two general fields of activity. In one, the psychiatrist acts as counselor, both to trained social workers who deal with cases on probation and parole extramurally and to guards within institutional walls. In the second instance, the psychotherapist works directly with the offender on probation or in confinement. Psychiatric therapy pursued through the agency of social workers has been discussed in Chapter 3, and the intramural involvement of prison guards in the treatment of offenders will be covered in a later section of this chapter. Direct, individual psychiatric treatment of offenders has been described by means of a detailed case report of a larcenist in Chapter 3, under the subtitle, Present-Day Use of Criminologic Psychiatry, and in sections on sexual psychopaths, larceny and military offenders. The basic principles underlying psychotherapy of offenders are the same whether administered in the juvenile court clinic or in the penitentiary, with due regard to psychological complications introduced by the fact of confinement. For the sake of clarity, a generalized picture of the therapeutic problems encountered in treating criminal offenders will be presented first.

In embarking upon psychotherapy of individual offenders, the special emotional situation of the person convicted of crime requires consideration. The public's participation in the offender, traced in an earlier chapter, is of considerable significance in the therapist-offender relationship. A series of psychological defenses arising out of the complicated interrelation between the offender and society must be dealt with preliminarily by the therapist. In the first place, whether the treatment be carried out in prison, reformatory or probation clinic, the patient comes to treatment after the crime has allegedly been committed, and the law has already made up its mind to the fact of disposition and punishment. This is a serious obstacle to treatment and has the profoundest psychological repercussions. One of these resides in the fact that in the eyes of the offender the psychiatrist cannot help but be a carrier of social censure. The offender reads rightly society's twin convictions that crime must be punished and that antisocial conduct will inevitably repeat itself, since criminals are born "bad." As pointed out in an earlier chapter, psychiatry itself has tended to aid this feeling by memorializing this concept in the diagnostic phrase "criminal psychopath." Since the criminal law embodies much of what the public has felt about the criminal, the therapist among criminal offenders must reckon with this piece of social psychology. In this respect the psychiatrist is under a handicap compared to the doctor who treats a private patient. Although the general physician entertains no moral feeling toward the illness of his patient, the doctor working with criminals as a member of society necessarily participates, albeit unconsciously, in the negative social feeling surrounding criminal acts.

Anxieties evoked in the convicted offender by the special emotional situation into which his crime projects him require special attention. From the viewpoint of the offender, the reality situation which stimulates these defensive reactions is far from negligible as an anxiety-producing factor. By the time he has reached the therapist, the offender has been under much pressure. The noncriminal world is a hostile one to him. At the time of his arrest police officers questioned him superficially; later detectives interrogate him persuasively. In the police line-up he is questioned publicly; at the time of the indictment in the lower court another investigation is held. In the District Attorney's office, before the grand jury, before the bar, questioning goes on relentlessly about his crime and record, his life, antisocial tendencies and danger to society. His lawyer demands the truth, his relatives bewail his actions, well-wishers address him with curiosity. Until he reaches the investigating social worker, who consults the offender as to his social background, little solace has been given the criminal. He receives courtesy at most, more often contempt and hatred. It is no secret that many police officials believe that any kind of therapy amounts to the dreaded coddling of prisoners. But it is not until the offender reaches the therapist that he hears talk of the "why" of his crime, and this with no promise of freedom or mitigation of the dreaded oncoming punishment.

The defensiveness of the criminal toward persons in the legalistic environment stems from emotional conflicts as well as from reality situations. Fruitless efforts within the offender to control his impulses combine with feelings of self-recrimination to be represented by complaints against society. The criminal's true foe is his own ineffective conscience, but he is unaware of this state of affairs at the time he is brought to face a legal environment. All his unconscious feelings of self-recrimination are projected outwardly. Neurotic currents thus stimulated lead to a formidable group of reaction-formations and attitudes which immediately greet the psychiatrist in his first therapeutic contact with the convicted offender. Anxiety, irritability or evasion, blocking, mutism and at times outright fear-panics, develop at the approach of a psychiatrist. Success in handling these situational anxieties at the outset often determines the efficacy of psychotherapy of criminals.

Usually the offender shows openly by his attitude that he identifies the psychiatrist with the legal authorities as parts of the same antagonistic, condemnatory element. Especially is this observable in young offenders, who take the position of being injured by a cruel parent. Fear that exposure through psychological probing of inferiority feelings would injure them leads to a characteristic defensive attitude, in which the examiner is placed in a parental position. To immature offenders, psychiatric examination and treatment is a refined type of psychological torture invented by a cunning District Attorney and subtly calculated to increase their punishment. As the offender retreats through his defensiveness into the strategic position of being the aggrieved party, he swings the psychiatrist into the psychological position of a prosecutor whose implied motive of punishment is paramount. This is psychologically desirable to the offender because it allows him to project onto the psychiatrist (parent) the responsibility for his own misdeeds.

The rationalization that adults who exercise domination over young persons enjoy their authority, makes delinquency a virtue and attempts to modify the offender's attitude, an unwarranted interference with "personal" liberty. This "inverse" bullying attitude presents itself very frequently in practice at the start of therapy as a negative phase of the emotional relationship between offender-patient and doctor. Painstaking work is necessary, just as with sensitive, neurotic patients, in pushing back the defenses while offering the young offender emotional support and the possibility of help. Most important is the need to convince the patient that there is no belittlement of his feelings implied in the therapeutic process, only sympathy and the wish to explore his conflicts for his own benefit. This primary therapeutic problem is met almost universally among youths of limited intellectual endowment whose sullen, defiant attitude has a dynamic basis in strong feelings of inferiority. Distrust of public officers, attitudes resulting from insularity of family life and the difficulty of convincingly relating inner emotional problems to outward behavior are commonly met with in immature personalities. Not only the adolescent but adult offenders also express anxieties regarding the capacity of the psychiatrist to injure them by probing into their emotional conflicts. This defensive awareness of censure in the atmosphere about the offender, to which he has been sensitized by society's age-old attitudes, tends to neutralize the psychotherapist's accent on a psychological substratum for criminal behavior. With behavior problems as with neurosis, one of the most important requirements in the therapeutic process is the overt recognition by the patient that something is wrong with him.

From the offender's viewpoint, the therapist has one aim which might conceivably appeal to the former, namely, the promise to help the latter withstand future temptations. In other respects the psychiatrist can do little to relieve the tension developing out of forthcoming punishment. The psychiatrist's other goals, the wish to build up a body of knowledge to aid future culprits and the aim to understand the offender's personality, will not at first impress the average prisoner. Nevertheless, one of the most important functions of a court or penitentiary psychiatrist is the mental hygiene teaching function. The prisoner himself, once he apprehends the mental hygiene idea, becomes a disciple for psychiatry, for he himself has witnessed the makeshift nature of prison and the reformlessness of the reformatory. Preparation of society and criminals alike by thorough dissemination of psychological information is a prerequisite for therapy that cannot be overemphasized.

The primary task of psychotherapy among prisoners in any type of legalistic environment is to put the offender at his ease by understanding him in terms of his own anxieties, particularly those relating to the fear of social punishment for his offense. The therapist should know the attitudes and goals of the offender's social and cultural group, whence he draws his prestige values. The advantages as well as the disadvantages of misbehavior to the offender in terms of the code of his social group should be appreciated by the therapist. As a consequence of this appreciation, the result of a counter-transference relationship, the prisoner will achieve a certain emotional latitude toward his antisocial impulses in the presence of the psychiatrist. Thus fortified against his inner social sensitivity, the patient can be brought to perceive the practical weaknesses of his antisocial attitudes.

The primary phase of softening the defenses of the offender marks the end of the mental hygiene function of the psychiatrist and the beginning of direct psychotherapy. The therapist's willingness to consider the offender an individual who responded to emotional pressure in the commission of his crime, rather than an incurable criminal, comes to have a deep effect on the criminal's life attitudes. The prisoner-psychiatrist relationship gradually develops an emotional meaning for the wrongdoer. The prisoner thaws out to the point of an inner acceptance of his criminal aggression. He will, in a word, be made comfortable with those criminal impulses which his defensive tactics and mechanisms have struggled to hide from his own and society's consciousness.

An example of this type of direct psychotherapy occurred in Briggs, a dull, psychopathic youth of eighteen, who had developed rages of antagonism to rules while in the naval service. His early civilian record was marked by incorrigibility, thefts and other juvenile delinquencies. His military history featured desertion, breaking arrest and theft. In the naval prison where Briggs was confined he was unmanageable and invited other prisoners to mutiny. In one period of rage he tore the fixtures from the wall of his cell, destroyed the bed and became so wild as to require physical restraint. After the rages subsided, Briggs was amnesic about his periods of destructive excitement.

Under therapy, in order to familiarize him with his impulses, he was encouraged to describe the feelings preceding his outbreak. After several sessions the prisoner was able to describe the sudden flood of sensation which accompanied the rage reactions and which moved up from his ankles to his chest and then to his head. As the feeling mounted, his hands trembled and he was seized by an overwhelming wish to break everything in his cell, to choke the guards and to smash his fists against the wall. These impulses arose especially when he meditated on his punishment. During the rages, while the impulse to destroy swept over him, a voice inside him said, "Get up, wreck everything." Immediately it was answered, "Don't break the bed, you have to sleep in it." Then he became aware that he could not rise or move his arms. "It was like a big man holding me down, like a vacuum. I felt about five times as strong as I did before, but I couldn't move."

With repeated therapeutic contacts Briggs began to regard his episodes as less inexplicable and more as objective signs of temper. The prisoner was encouraged to describe and to reproduce his feelings and "watch" the wave of impulse sweep over his legs, body and head as he sat with the doctor.

During the interviews he actually experienced sensations accompanying the impulses and learned that they need not result in activity. Slowly, simple suggestions to him were made to indicate both the inappropriateness and impractibility of these reactions in confinement. Gradually Briggs began to remark that there was no sense in what he was doing and that "smarter men than I have tried it and got fouled up." The sessions were conducted in simple language with much repetition, and explanations were made without reference to technical terms.

The type of treatment outlined here can be described as *attitude therapy*. It is aimed particularly at the unreasonable antagonism manifested among immature youths and psychopathic individuals in offenses of increasing severity. This group of offenders seem untouched by their continual trouble with authority, constant appearances in law courts and punishment through confinement. The therapeutic goal in these cases is to arrest the headlong flight toward continued rebelliousness and to modify antisocial attitudes which impel the offender. An active factor operative in attempts to modify antisocial attitudes is the contribution of emotional support by the therapist. The pattern of early emotional deprivations, from which the immature and psychopathic characters develop their rebelliousness, tends to be replaced by the stabilizing emotional influence of the doctor.

The emotional support given by the therapist is the element which allows the offender to face the fact that there exist emotional conflicts behind his seemingly inexplicable behavior. If the intelligence and the willingness of the offender suffices, further work can be done along these lines. If not, only as much probing is to be done as the patient can tolerate. In this attitude-treatment situation, where a moderate length of time can be given to each offender, the deeper unconscious levels need not be disturbed. Improvement in attitudes is effected by the work of bringing the patient into relation with the fact that his crime was due to a neurotic conflict, assuaging the guilt arising out of society's punitive attitude toward his crime and demonstrating the possibilities of adjusting to acceptable social form on the basis of emotional security provided by the therapist.

The therapeutic principles adduced in the treatment of individual offenders can conveniently be utilized in group therapy also. Within the past decade, and especially in the military services during World War II, group therapy of neurotic cases and acute emotional reactions has been developed widely. The objective of group therapy is to show the offender that his troubles are common to others and that he is not singled out for punishment. The sense of isolation, so characteristic of criminals, is effectively dealt with in order that the offender can then be approached as an individual. Group contacts tend to reduce the incredulity of the offender that his predicament as a lawbreaker can excite anyone's sympathetic interest. The average young offender is struck by the fact that his attitude towards the things of moment in his life—the police, the gang, women, homosexuals, drugs, movies, clothes or the activities of the barroom—are listened to with respect by his associates and the psychiatrist. An amused tolerance of the therapist's interest merges with genuine gratification that his (the offender's) problems are worth listening to.

The group therapy method adopted is the usual one in which the therapist sits with several offenders and guides the three-way or four-way conversation from impersonal to personal topics. A setting of conviviality and sociality may be developed by employing card games, offering cigarettes and encouraging jokes about local occurrences. The psychiatrist has to be in free social contact with his patients to the point of speaking their own idiom and siding with their complaints of privation. The therapist's attitude in this situation differs from that of the passivity of the psychoanalyst. This active approach allows the psychiatrist to more clearly approximate the hospitable and human parent-figure which counterbalances the anxiety-inspiring position imputed to him because he is a psychiatrist attached to a legal agency.

What has been described as "attitude therapy" among groups or in individuals soften defensive reactions expressed in aggressive attitudes to individuals and in antagonism to society. The next step is to provide insight into the formation of these defensive traits through detailed study of the patient's emotional history. This merges into the technic typically employed in psychoanalysis. The neurotic offender of good intelligence in whom the motive for mental health is strong is particularly suited for prolonged, intensive analytic therapy.

There have been a few pioneer efforts (Foxe, Lehrman, Karpman, Zilboorg) at treatment of criminals in penal institutions by psychologic investigation and the psychoanalytic method. Recently Lindner has treated criminals in a penal institution through the use of hypnotherapy, a shortened analytic method which employs deep hypnosis. It is clear, however, that the present status of psychotherapy in criminology does not allow detailed individual treatment of any but an occasional selected case. Since serious offenders must be confined in prisons, it is impractical to treat psychologically murderers, robbers or other criminals with long sentences. Offenders of the younger groups with short prison terms present the most promising material for group or individual therapy within institutional walls.

TREATMENT IN THE PENAL INSTITUTION

The application of psychotherapeutic principles to offenders in prison has already been implied in Chapter 2 in the discussion of management problems occurring in prison—disciplinary violations and homosexuality. The handling of disciplinary violators in institutions reflects the theoretical background of psychiatric treatment for all prisoners and hence will be discussed here.

The psychology of discipline violation is directly related to the effect on convicted criminals of punishment by confinement. Punishment for the prisoner is avowedly the first step in society's plan for his treatment. As has been noted, the wish to punish wrongdoers is a logical result of the doctrine of free will, that those who choose to inflict evil on their fellowmen should suffer in a measure to balance their wrongdoing. In theory, retribution has a preventive aspect, for although injury inflicted in crime cannot be undone, punishment is expected to deter the criminal from further evil-doing. Present-day law conceives three objectives in the theory of punishment: a check on the criminal's activity through incarceration, deterrence of crime in others through the example of imprisonment, and reform and possible rehabilitation of the criminal resulting from the curb on his antisocial tendencies.

Experience with chronic criminals, however, proves that punishment does not prevent the occurrence of future crime. The deterring effect of punishment on a given offender does not spread to others who come after him, as is attested by the irreducible number of inmates confined in penitentiaries and prisons at all times. Punishment by confinement does not influence antisocial impulses that arise from the core of ego, especially in those whose growth of conscience has been inhibited. Indeed, it has been seen that in some neurotic offenders punishment acts as an unconscious gratification of feelings of guilt. The chief value of punishment by imprisonment is in segregation of criminal individuals from society. Confinement may be necessary, but of itself, punishment without treatment has no permanent effect on the ego of the wrongdoer.

Punishment through imprisonment sets up a psychological cycle which develops further antagonism in psychopathic persons. The psychological basis of the behavior of the rebellious prisoner is the wish to gain ascendency over those who control him. The inmate utilizes his contacts with officers and guards to stimulate further punishment which he then perceives as discriminatory against himself. The rebellious prisoner is hence in the position of constantly being forced to work against his will or to undergo further deprivations or segregation. Continued punishment is capitalized as legitimate reason for further rebelliousness. Both the inmate's behavior and his open charges of discrimination focus the attention of the authorities on him and serve to keep the inmate's psychological problems constantly before prison officials.

This cycle of complaint, punishment, rebelliousness and claims of discrimination, has a meaning to the ego of the discipline violator. The psychological strategy of these maneuvers in the prisoner is to stave off the acceptance of punishment with the hope that the punishing parent-figure will relent or soften. This cycle of emotional movements serves to stimulate the ambivalence of the authorities themselves. Parent-figures, represented by officers in authority, tend to decrease their anger when ambivalent feelings are aroused, much as a parent relents after punishing a child. The rebellious inmate, whose unconscious wish for ascendency initiated the emotional interplay, has succeeded in his maneuver when the acknowledgment is made by authority that the prisoner is "incorrigible." It is not unusual to see passing signs of elation in the psychopathic disciplinary problem as he is sent again and again into isolation for unmanageable behavior.

There are times when the conflict between the rebellious prisoner and authority is resolved by the development of hysterical or malingered symptoms in the inmate. Symptoms of neurotic nature call for medical attention, which, when administered, is perceived by the prisoner's ego to contain the elements of affection and protection. Although in reality the result of neurotic headaches, attacks of dizziness or nausea may be a diminution of punishment or a decrease in attitude of severity, the more important result is that of unconscious gratification to the prisoner's ego following the authority's change in its emotional attitude toward him. The fundamental psychological situation of the incorrigible prison violator is that of a dependent, infantile character.

Antagonism among young offenders in prison, particularly among those in a military prison, demonstrates clearly that the roots of the problem of unreasonable antagonism lie in the early home environment and the relationship between the father and son. Those who do not accept authority are emotionally immature and show by their behavior that they cannot relinquish their infantile relationships.

The "bad" behavior seen on the surface is scarcely recognizable as the continual neurotic preoccupation of the individual with his early conflict over affection from the parent. The striving toward dependence on the parent takes the form of provocative behavior; provocative behavior is interpreted as aggression and brings forth firmness or punishment on the part of the parent-figure. At this point the situation cannot be recognized as anything but wishful misbehavior and open conflict between the parent (authority) and the child (prisoner). The individual offender rationalizes his control of parent-figures as demanded by a sense of justice or due to the unappreciated strength of his indomitable will.

The basic emotional meaning of this type of persistent infantile antagonism becomes apparent in the analysis of suicidal attempts by resistant prisoners under incarceration. The case of X illustrates the emotional dynamics of rebelliousness and its expression in behavior.

X was a nineteen-year-old, married seaman who was brought to the disciplinary barracks for the offense of being absent without leave for five days. He stated that he "hated the Navy" and "hated gold braid." He had been in the Navy more than two years and had served at sea most of the time. He had committed twelve offenses in the Navy, some of them of a serious nature. At one time he was said to have struck a warrant officer and another time he attacked and beat up a commissioned officer while on shore. Although no prison sentence had been served, in civilian life he was arrested six times for offenses ranging from vagrancy to suspicion of felony. On admission the man stated clearly that he wished to be discharged from the Navy and therefore went out of his way to disobey regulations. He gave a story which, even if exaggerated, indicated a severe psychopath in whom sadistic elements were prominent. He said his time was spent in thinking, plotting and planning to kill people with whom he had had even petty misunderstandings. He had a particular dislike for officers and had already beaten up two of them unmercifully. The subject had numerous contacts with homosexuals in which he robbed them of their money. He said that he felt like murdering anyone whose blood he saw shed. When he tried to stop the bleeding nose of his brother he became infuriated and a relative watching the episode pulled him away in alarm. There was a possibility that considerable fantasy admixture was present in his story.

In his daily contact with the examiner he showed more anger as it became clear to him that his wish to be discharged from the Navy by breaking rules would not be countenanced. This realization increased his insolence so that he refused to work and from time to time was reprimanded and placed in the blockhouse. At the same time he showed signs of depression and spoke about crushing his foot under a truck or cutting off his fingers so that he would be disabled and hence discharged from the Navy.

He said that while he had been on his last absence without leave he wandered around the streets, sleeping in railroad stations and playing with the idea of jumping under a train to end his life. He wrote his mother saying she would hear from him no more and he planned never to see his wife again. Shortly before he was apprehended, he met a girl who said she had syphilis and he purposely had intercourse with her in order to develop the disease. During our later contacts he expressed strong feelings of debasement, refusing to be treated for a penile lesion in the hope that it was syphilis and that it would invade his blood stream. He said he wanted to live a reckless life, devoted to doing what he pleased without regard to civil authority. He would rather lose a hand than stay in the service and obey the naval authorities. His attitude toward work in the Navy was fixed: he refused to perform his duties.

The suicidal ideas and self-mutilation tendencies in this case indicate the introjected anger of the prisoner. Direct expression of anger against authority was also present. The emotional depression observed appeared to depend basically on the same mechanisms seen in depressive patients whose destructive impulses toward the external world and subsequent guilty feelings eventuate in self-depreciation and despondency. The prisoner's entire reaction was in response to feeling frustrated by naval discipline during his two years in the service.

The antagonism of the subject prevented much psychological study, but enough material was obtained to indicate his identification with his father and unconscious dependence on the latter. The father had been something of a local racketeer, beloved by his cronies and political friends. A happy-go-lucky individual, the father earned a reputation outside the home of being generous and lovable; yet he never provided for his large family, of which X was the youngest. It was the ambition of the prisoner to live recklessly like his father.

The discussion of psychological undercurrents in extreme rebelliousness leads to an assay of treatment methods. Incorrigible criminals require the same careful therapeutic handling as described in this chapter for immature offenders. An additional factor of prime importance in treating incorrigible offenders is the influence of the guards who are in daily contact with the prisoners. A not inconsiderable factor in the frustrating environment of the prison can be the emotional attitude of the guards toward the inmate. Appreciation by the prison guard for emotional currents in resentful prisoners is vital; for example, among military prisoners it was found that sensitivity to guards, often of an age close to that of the prisoner, is derived from strong sibling-rivalry reactions. Since, in the process of sensitization to norms of social conduct, reactions to sibling-authority conduct play an important role, education of the guards as well as the administrative officers is vital to a therapeutic program. This would provide insight into the psychological changes occurring in the prisoner and blend the therapeutic results obtained by the psychiatrist with the daily handling of the prisoner by the guards.

An important function of the psychiatric group in a penal institution is the education of the prison guard through precept, demonstration and discussion of the meaning of the various types of rebellious reactions. The military services during World War II and the Federal Bureau of Prisons prior to that time made a definite start in the education of prison guards by providing orientation courses which discussed elementary facts of emotional reaction and its representations in symptoms and behavior. As psychiatric information modifies the feelings of guards toward a prisoner, the latter gradually learns that neither the guard nor the institution is solely punitive in function.

TREATMENT OF THE PSYCHOPATHIC OFFENDER

In considering psychotherapy of chronic offenders, difficulties in handling the psychopathic personality immediately come to mind. Experiences with this group coincide with the commonly held view that the psychopath suffers from distortions of character structure which are unmodifiable. As the discussion in Chapter 4 indicated, patient study of these cases during the last two decades has shown that there is a possibility of modifying the ostensibly rigid behavior patterns of the psychopath through psychological means. On the other hand, a basic consideration in this therapeutic attempt is society's conviction, shared by some psychiatrists, that the psychopath is unchangeable. This underlying sociopsychological reaction, also discussed in the early part of Chapter 2, should be understood fully in entering upon therapy of psychopaths.

The psychopathic personality is sensitive to the unconscious hostility which lies behind efforts to reform or "treat" him. He distrusts his analyst or psychotherapist as he distrusts society. He senses that society controls its anxiety about its own aggressive antisocial tendencies by projecting them to certain individuals who are viewed as structural or constitutional deviates. These reciprocal reactive feelings on the part of society and the psychopath are related to an intricate psychological situation which is the crux of the therapeutic problem of the chronic offender. The analysis of this situation, a prerequisite for successful treatment of these individuals, justifies an extended discussion.

The view that the antisocial character structure is immutable is shared by psychopaths themselves. Extensive experience with psychopaths indicates that no explanation of their unwillingness to undergo treatment is

plausible other than that they read the meaning of treatment as a reaction formation to unconscious hostilities within the social body. The difficulties of
converting the condition to a transference neurosis, described by analysts in
the treatment of psychopathic personalities, provide further attestation of
this clinical finding. Whether attempts at treatment are in the form of
active humanitarian management or the relative passivity of psychoanalytic
approach, psychopaths react to the unconscious prejudices which society entertains toward them. The psychopath acts throughout life as society unconsciously wishes him to, by remaining irretrievably maladjusted, the carrier of
society's antisocial feelings. He reacts to therapy similarly by defying an
approach of psychological type.

This psychological situation existing between the psychopath and society
imparts a characteristic clinical tone to the therapeutic relationship. As
anyone who has attempted superficial or deep therapy with these cases
can testify, the psychopath, if he co-operates at all, approaches the relationship in a spirit of play which often contains elements of grimness. Whether
the prospective patient be openly antagonistic, apparently submissive and
co-operative, or even courteous, his expression and verbal productions indicate he is not "in" the situation. He plays at being treated for a short
time, losing interest quickly. Even this infantile impulse to play seems
weighted by the inner conviction that sooner of later the play must be
given up—the game has long since been lost. The play attitude is a testing maneuver directed toward the therapist. The threat of a transference development stimulates anxiety which the play aims to quiet through
re-enactment of an earlier anxiety-laden situation. But the psychopath
cannot tolerate the affective tensions developing in the approaching re-enactment. Because of the psychopath's intolerance to his own instinctual strivings, he feels the therapist represents a source of security denied him. The
psychopath reacts to the yearning for security through dependence on a
parent-figure by impulsive flight or aggressive manner and behavior. In
actual practice the psychopath leaves the therapeutic situation abruptly
after one or two sessions or becomes unproductive and hostile if he is under
compulsion to be treated, as in an institution.

Clinical demonstration of these mechanisms is seen in two types of
behavior. (1) If the psychiatrist remains passive in attitude, the patient
flees from the anticipated danger of security through transference development. (2) If the psychiatrist acts as a member of society by virtue of his
official position in court, prison or a welfare agency, this implies moral judgment, and the patient becomes aggressive and un-co-operative.

The intolerance of the psychopath to treatment and hence to transference development requires emphasis in a somewhat different direction. The unconscious perception that a figure in the environment might serve as a father-figure arouses anxiety lest the patient be deprived of his right to remain antagonistic. The only defense the psychopath has in the face of his unconscious acceptance of his position as society's scapegoat is to maintain antagonism to society. His society is and always was a hostile one; it could never have helped but could only have injured him.

The universally antagonistic attitude of antisocial psychopaths is essentially masochistic in its dynamic function. Feelings of insecurity and unconscious masochistic urges contribute to the expectation of social ostracism in the psychopath. His emotional insecurity is, of course, covered from superficial view by a disdainful, truculent attitude and alliance with an asocial viewpoint. The *Weltanschauung* of antisocial persons, which is characterized by rebelliousness and reversal of standards of mature adjustment, supports the individual's self-esteem, allays his anxiety and provides masochistic gratification through identification with the "evil" life.

Defenses against masochistic feelings outlined above and the inner fear of endangering essential narcissistic supplies prove too strong a psychological reality to the patient who is approaching a therapy based on the utilization of transference phenomena. The crux of the therapeutic problem in psychopathic personality lies in the patient's inability to enter into a transference relationship. Transference development depends upon a capacity for object-love formed on the pattern of early love relationships with parents, which tends to repeat itself throughout life. Individuals with strongly developed narcissism have a somewhat limited capacity for object-relations, a clinical fact readily seen in many psychopaths. The influence that probably reduces transference activities in this group is that of inadequate receipts of narcissistic supplies in the oral phase of ego organization. The sensitivity of this group of individuals to lowered self-esteem (although hidden from superficial view) is based on the fact that they invest persons in authority with the prototype image of the denying mother. A denying society is necessarily a hostile one!

The eternal hostility toward society in the psychopath, with its unconscious masochistic influence, is in reality related to the unconscious need for punishment. These analytic findings, which can be verified in therapeutic contact with psychopathic offenders, indicate the need for developing a technic which will foster a rapport of such a nature as to allow deep therapy with this group of individuals. Such a technic has several theoretical requirements. One is that the therapist be neither completely identified with society and its moral evaluations nor completely passive in relation to the affective tensions of the patient. Another is that authority must be exerted to keep the patient under treatment, while the emotional atmosphere in which the analysis is conducted is made as comfortable as possible for the psychopath.

A passive attitude disturbs the patient to the point of flight. On the other hand, an attitude of authority in the analyst paradoxically decreases feelings of insecurity, especially in the youthful psychopath. Deliberate identification of the analyst with authority allows the reinvocation of feelings of dependency, which hitherto have been denied by the patient, and gives an affective meaning to the therapeutic relationship. The fusion of the figure of the analyst as authority with the image of society as a punitive agent relieves guilt feelings in the patient and paves the way for acceptance of security through masochistic mechanisms. The approach suggested then is one in which the analyst deliberately participates in an authoritative position.

Inasmuch as the invocation of authority on the part of a psychotherapist constitutes a fresh approach to the treatment of criminals, a few remarks on its application are in order. Although authority provides emotional security, reactions of a negative nature do occur. The treatment process almost always starts with a negative transference. In a surprisingly short time, however, the delinquent accepts the therapist as a real parent-figure. His acceptance depends for its fullness on the depth of the dependency needs in the individual delinquent. As the therapist demonstrates himself to be a living figure, expressing pleasure or displeasure with the delinquents' behavior, he becomes the standard by which the delinquent tests reality. Therefore, in his role of parent-figure the therapist must have a conscious appreciation of his participation in authority. Before accepting the therapist as a parent-figure, the delinquent frequently tests the therapist's potency as an authoritarian by misbehavior and disciplinary infractions. It is common knowledge that the psychopath or emotionally immature person in confinement frequently tests the authorities by infractions of rules. The lay expression that the psychopath is constantly "looking for trouble" has psychological validity. Only through experiencing trouble with its resultant punishment by paternalistic authority can the delinquent gratify his dependency needs and simultaneously express denial of these needs. This is the common psychic mechanism of removal of anxiety-producing objects by denying them.

This technic produces a figure for the patient that combines the possibility of punishment and the opportunity for understanding and love. The attitude of this figure, new in the psychological experience of the patient, permits gratification of security yearnings and, simultaneously, quiets guilty feelings. The antagonistic psychopath wants to submit to authority and thus reach a source of security, but the anxiety aroused by his masochism must be calmed and his instinctual aggression tolerated. Firmness on the part of the therapist absorbs the projected hostility, which may at times become serious, and eventually allows identification with authority to proceed. The possibility of development of new ego ideals then comes into existence. Simultaneously, greatly needed narcissistic supplies are brought to the ego of the patient through the transference development.

The findings on which psychotherapy of psychopaths has been based in this exposition indicate the similarity, if not the identity, of basic ego disturbances in response to early libidinous frustrations in this group with those of the neurotic individual. Viewed in this dynamic light, psychopathy may be considered as basically a remedial condition. However, the complexities introduced by the peculiar sociopsychological relations of the psychopath to his society make therapy difficult or even hazardous. Social defenses are so strongly intrenched, reality circumstances are so infiltrated with negative attitudes, and such infinite patience and resourcefulness are required of the therapist that spectacular results cannot be expected in the treatment of this socially destructive group of neurotically ill persons.

*　　*　　*

The future of psychotherapy for criminal offenders is bright, but this sanguine statement must be tempered by practical limitations. Individual psychoanalytic therapy is expensive and time-consuming and can be used only in selected cases. In its investigative function lies the greatest present value of psychoanalysis of criminal offenders. It will shed light on psychological mechanisms in criminals. It will find the relationship existing between neurosis and criminal activity. It will contribute knowledge to help fashion psychotherapeutic methods of less intensive type.

Much more investigation into mental conflicts is needed to establish the findings of pioneers in this field on a more secure basis. The greatest promise in the treatment of crime comes from unremitting work with juvenile, youthful and young adult offenders and from the spread of the mental hygiene program which emphasizes the individual psychological nature of criminal acts. What mental hygiene has done during the past forty years in preparing a psychological environment for the understanding and treatment of the mentally ill, psychiatry and especially criminologic psychiatry can now do for the criminal offender.

Such a program, though tedious and costly, will prove its own worth in allowing the ideal of democracy to be realized in the personal life of law-abiding citizen and offender alike. Such an ideal states broadly that only through the hard-won freedom which we wrest from our outmoded infantile impulses may we enjoy in full measure life, liberty and the pursuit of happiness.

THE END

Bibliography

For the convenience of the reader this bibliography has been divided into three sections. Only references which were deemed significant in the development of concepts in psychiatric criminology are listed. The compilation presented herewith, therefore, is by no means exhaustive. A large number of descriptive or controversial articles and treatises in all languages covering criminal anthropology, sociologic aspects of crime, popular accounts of famous criminals or trials, etc., have been excluded. The vast literature of formal, descriptive psychiatry which concerns subject matter now included in criminologic psychiatry has also been omitted.

SECTION I

HISTORICAL AND LEGAL

Alexander, Harriet C. B.: The degenerate and crime, Woman's M. J. 25: December, 1915.

Barnes, Harry E.: Criminology, Encyclopedia of the Social Sciences, vol. 4, New York, Macmillan, 1936.

Benedikt, M.: Anatomical Studies Upon Brains of Criminals: A Contribution to Anthropology, Medicine, Jurisprudence and Psychology., Trans. by E. P. Fowler, New York, Wood, 1881.

Boies, Henry M.: The Science of Penology, New York, Putnam, 1901.

Briggs, L. B.: Prevention of crime, New England J. Med. 210: 955, 1934.

Brigham, A.: Am. J. Insanity 4: 67, 1847.

Cardoza, Benjamin: What medicine can do for law, Bull. New York Acad. Med. 5: July, 1929.

Channing, Walter: A case of murder—Amos D. Palmer, Am. J. Insanity 56: April, 1900.

Cherry, R. R.: Lectures on the Growth of Criminal Law in Ancient Communities, London, Macmillan, 1890.

Collins, Cornelius P.: Treatment of criminals in the court of General Sessions of the County of New York, J. Criminal Law and Criminology, 24: November, 1933.

Cox, J. H.: Practical Observations on Insanity, C. & R. Baldwin, ed. 2, London, Murray, 1806.

Dembitz, Lewis N.: Crime, Jewish Encyclopedia, New York, Funk, 1903, p. 357.

Dugdale, R. L.: The Jukes, A Study of Crime, Pauperism, Disease and Heredity, New York, Putnam, 1877.

East, W. Norwood: Moral imbecility, Lancet 2: 1117, 1921.

Eberstaller, ————: American Neurological Association Meeting, Reprint, J. Nerv. & Ment. Dis. 17: June 3, 1890.

Ellis, Havelock: The Criminal, New York, Scribner and Welford, 1890.

Ferguson, W. S.: Greek Law, Encyclopedia Britannica, ed. 14, vol. 10, 828.

Fink, Arthur E.: Causes of Crime, Philadelphia, Univ. Penn. Press, 1938.

Glueck, Bernard: Sing Sing Prison: Report of the Activities of the Psychiatric Clinic, New York, 1917.

Glueck, Sheldon S.: Mental Disorder and the Criminal Law, Boston, Little, 1925.

Goring, Charles: The English Convict, London, His Majesty's Stat. Off., 1913.

Gregory, M. S.: Prejudices regarding expert testimony in mental diseases, Am. J. Psychiat. 3: 211-217, 1923-1924.

Gray, John P.: Editorial, Am. J. Insanity, vol. 14, April 1858.

Hooton, Earnest Albert: Crime and the Man, Cambridge, Harvard, 1939.

Lecky, William E. H.: History of European Morals, vol. 1, New York, Appleton, 1897.

Lombroso, Cesare: Crime, Its Causes and Remedies, Trans. by H. P. Horton, Boston, Little, 1911.

Maine, Sir H. J. S.: Ancient Law, Edited by Sir Frederick Pollock, 10th London Edition, New York, Holt, 1906.

Mercier, Charles: Moral Imbecility, Practitioner 99: 301, 1917.

Meyer, Adolph: A review of the signs of degeneration and of methods of registration, Am. J. Insanity 52: January, 1896.

Michael, Jerome, and Wechsler, Herbert: Criminal Law and Its Administration, Chicago, The Foundation Press, 1940.

Mills, Charles H.: Presidential address, American Neurological Association, J. Nerv. & Ment. Dis. 13: 523, 1886.

Morel, B. A.: Traité des dégénérescences, physiques, intellectuelles et morales de l'espèce humaine, Paris, Baillière, 1857.

New York Law Journal: Insanity as a defense to homicide in New York, (an editorial), October 5, 1937.

Overholser, Winfred: The place of psychiatry in the criminal law, Boston University Law Review 16: April, 1936.

New York Criminal Reports: People vs. Coleman, vol. 1, December, 1881, p. 1.
————: People vs. McElvaine, vol. 125, p. 604.
————: People vs. Robert Irwin, vol. 166, 1938, p. 751.

Pinel, Phillippe: A Treatise on Insanity In Which are Contained the Principles of a New and More Practical Nosology of Maniacal Disorders than has yet been Offered the Public, Trans. from the French, Sheffield, England, 1806.

Pritchard, James C.: A Treatise on Insanity, Philadelphia, Haswell, Barrington and Haswell, 1835.

Proceedings of the Governor's Conference on Crime: The Criminal and Society, Albany, New York, September, 1935.

Robertson, Frank W.: Sterilization for the criminal unfit, American Medicine, 5: p. 349, 1910.

Sellin, Thorsten: Crime, Encyclopedia of the Social Sciences, vol. 4, New York, Macmillan, 1936.

Spitzka, E. C.: Political assassins: are they all insane?, J. of Ment. Path. 2: No. 2, 69, 1902.

Staff of the Citizen's Committee on the Control of Crime in New York.: Sex Crimes in New York City, A Report, 1937 (1938).

Stephen, Sir James F.: History of the Criminal Law of England, London, Macmillan Company, 1883.

Stevenson, William G.: Criminality, Medico-Legal Journal, September, 1877.

Talbot, Eugene S.: Study of stigmata of degeneracy among criminal youth, J. A. M. A. 30: 849, 1898.

Tredgold, A. F.: Moral imbecility, Practitioner 99: 43, 1917.

Weihofen, Henry: Insanity as a Defense in Criminal Law, New York, Commonwealth Fund, 1933.

Wharton, Francis and Stilles, Moreton: Medical Jurisprudence, ed. 5, Rochester, E. R. Andrews Printing Co., 1905.

White, William A.: Insanity and criminal responsibility, J. Criminal Law and Criminology, 1911.

———: Insanity and crime, Ment. Hyg. 10: 265, 1926.

Yawger, N. S.: Is there a moral center in the brain? Am. J. M. Sc. February, 1935.

SECTION II

SOCIOLOGIC AND CRIMINOLOGIC

Asbury, Herbert: The Gangs of New York: An Informal History of the Underworld, New York, Knopf, 1929.

Barnes, Harry E., and others, etc.: Contemporary Social Theory, London, Appleton-Century, 1940.

Barnes, Harry E., and Teeters, N. G.: New Horizons in Criminology, New York, Prentice-Hall, 1943.

Brace, C. L.: The Dangerous Classes of New York, Wynkoop & Hallenbeck, New York, 1872.

Birnbaum, K.: Der psychopathischen Verbrecher, ed. 2, Leipzig, Thieme, 1926.

Blanchard, Paul, and Lukas, Edwin J.: Probation and Psychiatric Care for Adolescent Offenders, Society for the Prevention of Crime, New York, January, 1942.

Brown, Fred.: Social maturity and stability of non-delinquents, proto-delinquents and delinquents, Am. J. Orthopsychiat. 8: 214-219, 1938.

Burrow, Trigant: Crime and the social reaction of right and wrong, J. Criminal Law and Criminology 24: No. 2, November-December, 1933.

Burt, Cyril L.: The Young Delinquent, London, Univ. London Press, 1944.

Cantor, Nathaniel F.: Crime, Criminals and Criminal Justice, New York, Holt, 1932.

Carriere, Jean: Degeneration in the Great French Masters, Trans. by McCabe, New York, Brentano, 1922.

Coghill, H. DeJ.: The proposed Youth Correction Authority Act, Psychiatry, 1943.

Cooper, Courtney R.: Here's to Crime, Boston, Little, 1937.

Crime Commission of New York State, the Sub-Commission on Causes and Effects of Crime: A Study of Problem Boys and Their Brothers, Albany, Lyon, 1929.

De Fleury, Maurice: The Criminal Mind, (trans. from the French), London, Downey and Co., 1901.

Doll, Edgar A.: Vineland Social Maturity Scale, Public Training School, Vineland, New Jersey, No. 3, 1936.

Faris, E.: Attitude and behavior, Am. J. Sociology 34: 271-281, 1928.

Ferri, Enrico: Criminal Sociology, Trans. by Kelly, Joseph I. and Lisle, John, Boston, Little, 1917.

Ferries, J. Kenneth: Crooks and Crime, Describing the Methods of Criminals from Area Sneak to the Professional Card-sharper, Forger or Murderer, London, Seeley Service & Co., 1928.

Glueck, Sheldon and Glueck, Eleanor J.: 500 Criminal Careers, New York, Knopf, 1930.

Glueck, Sheldon, and Glueck, Eleanor J.: Criminal Careers In Retrospect, New York, Commonwealth Fund, 1943.

Hake, Alfred Egmont: Regeneration, New York, Putnam, 1896.

Halpern, Irving W., and Stanislaus, John N. and Botein, Bernard: The Slum and Crime, New York Housing Authority, New York, 1934.

Harrison, L. V., and Grant, P. M.: Youth in the Toils, New York, MacMillan, 1938.

Hill, Frederic: Crime. Its Amount, Causes and Remedies, London, Murray, 1853.

Kopp, Marie E.: Surgical treatment as sex crime prevention measure, J. Criminal Law and Criminology 28: 692, 1938.

Michael, Jerome, and Adler, Mortimer J.: An Institute of Criminology and of Criminal Justice, A report of survey, Bureau of Social Hygiene and School of Law, New York, Columbia Univ. Press, 1932.

———: Crime, Law and Social Science, New York, Harcourt, 1933.

Reckless, Walter C.: Criminal Behavior, New York, McGraw, 1940.

Rosenbaum, Betty B.: The sociological basis of the laws, relating to women sex offenders in Massachusetts, J. Criminal Law and Criminology 28: 815-846, 1938.

Rusche, George, and Kirchheimer, Otto: Punishment and Social Structure, New York, Columbia Univ. Press, 1939.

Saleilles, Raymond: Individualization of Punishment, Trans. by R. S. Jastrow, Boston, Little, 1911.

Sanford, Nevitt R.: A psychoanalytic study of three types of criminals, J. Crim. Psychopath. 5: 57-69, 1943.

Sapir, Edward: Cultural anthropology and psychology, J. Abnorm. & Social Psychol. 27: 229-242, 1932.

Shaw, C. R., and McKay, Henry D.: Social factors in juvenile delinquency, J. Abnormal & Social Psychol. 22: 1928.

Slawson, John: The Delinquent Boy, Boston, The Gorham Press, 1926.

Southard, E. E., and Jarret, M. C.: The Kingdom of Evils, Psychiatric Social Work; Presented in 100 Case Histories with a Classification of Social Divisions of Evil, New York, Macmillan, 1921.

Sutherland, Edwin H.: Principles of Criminology, Philadelphia, Lippincott, 1939.

Tannenbaum, Frank: Crime and the Community, Boston, Ginn, 1938.

Thompson, C., and Raymond, A.: Gang Rule in New York; The Story of a Lawless Era, New York, Dial Press, 1940.

Thrasher, Frederic M.: The Gang, Chicago, Univ. Chicago Press, 1927, (1936).

Wickersham, G. W.: National Commission on Law Observance and Enforcement, Report on Causes of Crime, Washington, D. C., U. S. Government Printing Office, 1931.

SECTION III

PSYCHOLOGICAL AND PSYCHIATRIC

Abraham, Karl: The history of an imposter in the light of psychoanalytical knowledge, trans. by A. Strachey, Psychoanalyt Quart. 4: 1935.

Aichorn, August: Wayward Youth, Trans. Viking Press, New York, 1936.

Alexander, Franz: Mental Hygiene and Crime (Germ.) Imago, vol. 17, 1931.

———: The relation of structural and instinctual conflicts, Psychoanalyt. Quart., 2: 181, 1933.

———: A double murder committed by a 19-year-old boy, Psychoanalyt. Rev. 24: 113, 1937.

Alexander, Franz and Staub, Hugo: The Criminal, the Judge and the Public: A Psychological Analysis, New York, Macmillan, 1931.

Alexander, F. and Healy, W.: Victim of Criminal Morality (Germ.) Imago vol. 21, 1935.

———: Roots of Crime: Psychoanalytic Studies, New York, Knopf, 1935.

Von Baeyer, Walter: Zur Genealogischer Psychopathische bei Schwindler und Lugner, Leipzig, Thieme.

Banay, Ralph S.: Immaturity and crime, Am. J. Psychiat. 100: 170, 1943.

———: Study of murder for revenge, J. Crim. Psychopath, 3: 1, 1941.

Bender, L. and Blau, A.: The reaction of children to sexual relations with adults, Am. J. Orthopsychiat. 7: 500-518, 1937.

Bender, Lauretta, Keiser, Sylvan, and Schilder, Paul: Studies in aggressiveness, Genet. Psychol. Monogr. 18: Nos. 5-6, October-December, 1936.

Bender, Lauretta: Psychiatry mechanisms in child murderers, J. Nerv. & Ment. Dis. 80: 32-47, 1934.

———: Psychopathic Behavior Disorders in Children, Handbook of Correctional Psychology, New York, Philosoph. Library, 1947, chap. 26.

Bergler, Edmund: The psychological interrelation between alcoholism and genital sexuality, J. Crim. Psychopath. 4: 1943.

———: Applications of the Mechanics of Orality in Neurosis & Criminosis, Handbook of Correctional Psychology, New York, Philosophical Library, Inc., 1947, chap. 44, p. 611.

Bingham, Anna: Determinants of sex delinquency in adolescent girls based on intensive studies of 500 cases, J. Criminal Law and Criminology 13: February, 1923.

Blackman, Nathan: Psychotherapy in a Prison Setting, Handbook of Correctional Psychology, New York, Philosoph. Library, 1947, chap. 41.

Bowman, Karl M.: Challenge of the sex offenders—Psychiatric aspects of the problem, Ment. Hyg. 22: 10-20, 1938.

Branham, V. C.: Classification of defective delinquents, Psychiatric Quart. 1: 59, 1927.

Brasol, Boris: Elements of Crime, London, Oxford, 1927.

Brill, A. A.: Necrophilia, J. Crim. Psychopath. 2: 433, 1941; and 3: 50, 1941.

Brill, N. Q., et al.: Electroencephalographic studies in delinquent behavior problem children, Am. J. Psychiat. 98: 494-498, 1942.

Bromberg, W., and Abeles, Milton: Psychogenic amnesias in criminal cases, J. Nerv. & Ment. Dis. 85: 456, 1937.

Bromberg, W., Apuzzo, Anthony A., Locke, Bernard, Psychological study of desertion and overleave in the Navy, U. S. Nav. M. Bull. 44: No. 3, 558-568, 1945.

Bromberg, W., and Frosch, J.: The sex offender: A psychiatric study, Am. J. Orthopsychiat. 9: No. 4, 761, 1939.

Bromberg, W., and Keiser, S.: A psychologic study of the swindler, Am. J. Psychiat. 94: No. 6, 1441-1456, 1938.

Bromberg, W., and Rodgers, Terry C.: Marihuana and aggressive crime, Am. J. Psychiat. 102: No. 6, 825, 1946.

Bromberg, W., and Thompson, C. B.: Relation of psychoses, mental defect and personality types of crime, J. Criminal Law and Criminology, 28: 1, 1937.

Bromberg, Walter: Marihuana, intoxication: a clinical study of cannabis sativa intoxication, Am. J. Psychiat. 91: 303, 1934.

————: Psychologic motives in tattooing, Arch. Neurol. & Psychiat. 33: 228, 1935.

————: A Psychiatric Study of the Adolescent Offender, Nat. Probation A., Year Book, 1935, p. 71.

————: The Liar in Delinquency and Crime, The Nervous Child, no. 4, 1942.

————: The effects of the war on crime, Am. Sociological Review 8: 685, 1943.

————: Antagonism to Authority Among Young Offenders, Handbook of Correctional Medicine, Phil. Library, New York, 1947, chap. 33, pp. 452-462.

Cason, Hulsey: The psychopath & the psychopathic, J. Crim. Psychopath. 4: 522-527, 1943.

Cassity, John H.: Personality study of 200 murderers, J. Crim. Psychopath. 2: 296-304, 1941.

————: Socio-psychiatric aspects of female felons, J. Crim. Psychopath. 3: 597-604, 1942.

Charnyak, J.: Some remarks on the diagnosis of psychopathic delinquents, Am. J. Psychiat. 97: 1326-1340, 1941.

Christie, T., Richman, John, and Glover, Edward: Symposium, Brit. J. M. Psychol. 12: 234, 1932.

Christie, T.: Criminal lunatics and crime of arson, Brit. M. J. 1: 162, 1930.

Cleckley, Hervey: Mask of Sanity, St. Louis, Mosby, 1941.

————: The psychosis that psychiatry refuses to face, J. Clin. Psychopath. **6:** 117, 1944.

Clark, L. P.: Psychologic study of stealing in delinquents, Arch. Neurol. & Psychiat. **1:** 535, 1919.

Crounse, D.: Dementia praecox and crime, Ment. Hyg. **9:** January, 1925.

Crowley, Ralph M.: Psychoanalytic literature on drug addiction and alcoholism, Psychoanalyt. Rev. **26:** 39-54, 1939.

Curran, Frank J.: Specific trends in criminality of women, J. Crim. Psychopath. **3:** 605-624, 1942.

————: Group Treatment in Rehabilitation of Offenders, Handbook of Correctional Psychology, Phil. Library, New York, 1947, chap. 42.

Doll, Edgar A., and Fitch, K. A.: Social competence of juvenile delinquents, J. Criminal Law and Criminology **30:** May, 1939.

Dunn, William H.: The psychopath in the armed forces, Psychiatry **4:** 251, 1941.

East, W. N.: Alcoholism & crime in relation to manic depressive disorder, Lancet **1:** 161-163, 1936.

East, W. N., and Hubert, W. H. DeB.: The Psychological Treatment of Crime, London, His Majesty's Stat. Off., 1939.

Ellis, Havelock: Psychology of Sex, Philadelphia, Davis, 1923.

Ferrald, M. R., Hayes, M. H., and Dawley, A.: A Study of Women Delinquency in New York State Public Bureau of Social Hygiene, New York, Century, 1920.

————: Poison as the Weapon of Women Criminals, New York Times, p. 12, April 26, 1925.

Foxe, A. N.: Resistance to understanding criminotic behavior, Psychoanalyt. Rev. **24:** 389, 1937.

————: Crime and Sexual Development, Monograph Editions, New York, 1936.

Freud, Sigmund: Criminality from a Sense of Guilt, Collected Papers, vol. 4, London, Hogarth Press, 1924.

Freud, S.: Certain neurotic mechanisms in jealousy, paranoia and homosexuality, Collected Papers, vol. 2, London, Hogarth Press, 1933, p. 232.

————: Psychoanalysis and the ascertaining of truth in courts of law, Collected Papers, vol. 2, London, Hogarth Press, 1933, p. 13.

————: The economic problems in masochism, Collected Papers, vol. 2, London, Hogarth Press, 1933, p. 255.

Ganser: Ueber einen eigenartigen hysterischen Dammerzustand, Arch. f. Psychiat. **30:** No. 2, 633, 1898.

Gibbs, Fred A., Bloomberg, Wilfred, and Bagchi, B. K.: An electroencephalographic study on adult criminals, Tr. Am. Neurol. A. **68:** 87, 1942.

————: Electroencephalographic study of criminals, Am. J. Psychiat. **102:** 294, 1945.

Glueck, Bernard: A study of 608 admissions to Sing Sing Prison, Ment. Hyg. **2:** 85, 1918.

Glueck, Sheldon: Psychiatric examination of persons accused of crime, Ment. Hyg. **11:** 287, 1927.

Goddard, Henry H.: Feeblemindedness, Its Cause and Consequence, New York, Macmillan, 1914.

Goldfarb, William: Psychological privation in infancy and subsequent adjustment, Am. J. Orthopsychiat. **15:** 247, 1945.

Goldwyn, Jacob: Impulses to incendiarism and theft, Am. J. Psychiat. **9:** 1093-1099, 1930.

Gray, M. G., and Moore, Merrill: The incidence and significance of alcoholism in the history of criminals, Am. J. Psychiat. **98:** 347, 1941.

Gregory, M. S.: Psychiatry and the problem of delinquency, Am. J. Psychiat. **91:** 773, 1935.

Greenacre, Phyllis: Conscience in the psychopath, Am. J. Orthopsychiat. **15:** 495, 1945.

Gross, Hans: Criminal Psychology, 4th German ed., trans. by Horace M. Kallen, Boston, Little, 1911.

Hacker, Frederick J., and Geleerd, Elizabeth R.: Freedom and authority in adolescence, Am. J. Orthopsychiat. **15:** 621, 1945.

Haire, Norman: Encyclopedia of Sexual Knowledge, London, F. Aldor, 1934.

Healy, W.: Pathological Lying, Accusation and Swindling, A Study in Forensic Psychology, Boston, Little, 1926.

———: The Individual Delinquent, Boston, Little, 1915, reprint, 1929.

———: Mental factors in crime, Ment. Hyg. **12:** 761-767, 1928.

———: Psychoanalysis of older offenders, Am. J. Orthopsychiat. **4:** January, 1934.

Healy, W., and Bronner, Augusta: Delinquents & Criminals: Their Making and Unmaking, New York, MacMillan, 1926.

———: New Light on Delinquency and its Treatment, New Haven, Yale, 1936.

Henderson, D. K.: Psychopathic States, New York, Norton, 1939.

Henderson, D. K., Patrie, A. A., and Durran, D.: A symposium on psychopathic states, Ment. Sc. **88:** 485, 1942.

Henniger, James M.: The senile sex offender, Ment. Hyg., **23:** 436, 1939.

Henry, G. W., Sex Variants, 2 vols., New York, Hoeber, 1941.

Henry, G. W., and Gross, Alfred.: Social factors in the case histories of one hundred underprivileged homosexuals, Ment. Hyg., **22:** 591, 1938.

Hollander, Bernard: The Psychology of Misconduct, Vice and Crime, London, G. Allen Unwin Ltd., 1922.

Hopwood, T. S., and Snell, Albert C.: Amnesia in relation to crime, Ment. Sc. **79:** 27-41, 1933.

Humphreys, E. J.: Psychopathic personality among the mentally defective, Psychiatric Quart. **14:** 231, 1940.

Kahn, Eugene: Psychopathic Personalities, New Haven, Yale, 1931.

Karpman, Ben: Perversions as neuroses—their relation to psychopathy and criminality, J. Crim. Psychopath. **3:** 180-199, 1941.

———: Psychoses in criminals, studies in the psychopathology of crime, J. Nerv. & Ment. Dis. **64:** 331, 482; **67:** 224, 355, 478, 599; **68:** 39, 1926.

———: Case Studies in the Psychopathology of Crime, vols. 1 and 2, New York, Ment. Science Pub. Co., 1939.

———: New criminology, Am. J. Psychiat. **1:** 687-722, 1931.

———: Problem of psychopathics, Psychiatric Quart. **3:** 495, 1929.

———: The mental roots of crime, a critique, J. Nerv. & Ment. Dis. **90:** 89, 1939.

————: The myth of the psychopathic personality, Am. J. Psychiat.: **104,** No. 9, 523-534, 1948.

Klein, Melaine: Criminal tendencies in normal children, Brit. J. M. Psychol. **7:** July, 1927.

Krafft-Ebing, Richard: Psychopathia Sexualis, trans. from 12th German ed., London, Heinemann, 1939.

Lambert, Alexander: Therapeutic of drug habits, New England J. Med. **215:** 72, 1936.

Lehrman, Philip R.: Some unconscious determinants in homicide, Psychiatric Quart. **13:** 605, 1939.

Levine, Maurice: Normality and Immaturity, The Family March, 1940.

Levy, David M.: Primary affect hunger, Am. J. Psychiat. **94:** 643-652, 1937.

————: Attitude therapy, Am. J. Orthopsychiat. **7:** 103-113, 1937.

Lindner, Robert W.: Experimental studies in constitutional psychopathic inferiority, J. Crim. Psychopath. **4:** 252-484, 1942.

————: Rebel Without a Cause, New York, Grune & Stratton, 1944.

Lippman, H. S.: The Neurotic Delinquent, Am. J. Orthopsychiat. **7:** 114-121, 1937.

Locke, Bernard: Intellectual, educational, personal and occupational status as factors in a penal group, Abstract in J. Crim. Law and Criminology, December-January, 1941.

Lorand, Sandor: Compulsive Stealing, J. Crim. Psychopath. **1:** 247-253, 1940.

————: Crime in fantasy, dreams and the neurotic Criminal, Psychoanalyt. Rev. **17:** 183-194, 1930.

Lowrey, Lawson G.: Problems of Aggression and Hostility in the Exceptional Child, Proc. 5th Inst. Child Research Clinic, Woods School, Langhorne, Pennsylvania, October, 1938.

————: Personality distortion and early institutional care, Am. J. Orthopsychiat. **10:** 576-585, 1940.

MacDonald, Martha W.: Criminally aggressive behavior in passive, effeminate boys, J. Orthopsychiat. **8:** 70-78, 1938.

Mangun, Clarke W.: The Psychopathic Criminal, J. Crim. Psychopath. **4:** 117-127, 1942.

Maskin, Meyer H., and Altman, Leon L.: Military psychodynamics: psychological factors in the transition from civilian to soldier, Psychiatry. **1:** 263-269, 1943.

Maughs, Sidney: A concept of psychopathy and psychopathic personality: its evolution and historical development, J. Crim. Psychopath. **2:** 329-356, 465-499, 1941.

Menaker, Esther: A contribution in the study of the neurotic stealing symptom, J. Orthopsychiat. **9:** 368-378, 1939.

Meyer, Adolf: Our Children, A Handbook for Parents, Fisher & Gruenberg, edit., New York, Viking, Chap. XV, p. 155, 1933.

Murchison, Carl A.: Criminal Intelligence, Worcester, Clark Univ. Press, 1926.

Noyes, A. P.: Modern Clinical Psychiatry, ed. 2, Philadelphia, Saunders, 1939, chap. 28, p. 504.

210   Bibliography

Oltman, Jane E., and Friedman, S.: A psychiatric study of one hundred criminals, J. Nerv. & Ment. Dis. **93:** 16-41, 1941.

Partridge, G. E.: A study of 50 cases of psychopathic personality, Am. J. Psychiat. **7:** 593-673, 1928.

———: Current conceptions of psychopathic personality, Am. J. Psychiat. **10:** 53, 1930.

Preston, Mary I.: Children's reaction to movie horrors and radio crime, J. Pediat. **19:** 147-168, 1941.

Rapaport, Jack: A case of necrophilia, J. Crim. Psychopath. **4:** 277-289, 1942.

Reik, Theodore: The Unknown Murderer, New York, Prentice-Hall, 1945.

Reynolds, Walter B.: District attorney association of the state of New York: The new youthful offender laws, New York (a report), June, 1943; also Chapter 549, Laws of 1943, New York.

Roche, Philip Q.: Masochistic motivations in criminal behavior, J. Crim. Psychopath. **4:** 431-444, 1942.

Root, William T.: A Psychological and Educational Survey of 1910 Prisoners in the Western Penitentiary of Penna. Publ., Pittsburgh, Pa., 1927.

Rosenzweig, M., Simon, B., and Ballou, M.: The psychodynamics of an uxoricide, Am. J. Orthopsychiat. **12:** 283-293, 1942.

Ruggles, A. H.: Ganser's Symptom, Am. J. Insanity, pp. 307-311, October, 1905.

Schilder, Paul: Attitudes of murderers towards death, J. Abnorm. Social Psychol. **31:** 348, 1936.

———: The analysis of ideologies as psychotherapeutic method in group treatment, Am. J. Psychiat. **93:** 601-607, 1936.

———: Results and problems of group psychotherapy in neuroses, Ment. Hyg. **23:** 87-98, 1939.

Schilder, Paul, and Keiser, Sylvan: A study in criminal aggressiveness, Genet. Psychol. Monogr. **18:** Nos. 5 and 6.

Schneider, Kurt: Psychopathic personality, Rev. J. Nerv. & Ment. Dis. **81:** 103-104, 1935.

Schroeder, P. L.: Criminal behavior in later period of life, Am. J. Psychiat. **92:** 915, 1936.

Selling, Lowell S.: Diagnostic Criminology, Ann Arbor, Edwards Bros., 1938.

———: Types of behavior manifested by feebleminded sex offenders, Proc. Am. A. Ment. Def. **63:** 178-186, 1939.

———: The psychiatric findings in cases of 500 traffic offenders and accident prone drivers, Am. J. Psychiat. **97:** 68-97, 1940.

Silverman, Daniel: Clinical and electroencephalographic studies in criminal psychopaths, Arch. Neurol. & Psychiat. **50:** 18-33, 1943.

———: The electroencephalograph and therapy of criminal psychopaths, J. Crim. Psychopath. **5:** 439-466, 1944.

Spaulding, Edith: An Experimental Study of Psychopathic Delinquent Women, Published for Bureau of Soc. Hygiene, New York, Rand-McNally, 1923.

———: Emotional episodes among psychopathic delinquent women, J. Nerv. & Ment. Dis. **54:** 298-323, 1921.

Sprague, George S.: The psychopathology of psychopathic personality, Bull. New York Acad. Med. **17:** 911-921, 1941.

Stern, Adolph: Psychoanalytic therapy in the borderline neuroses, Psychoanalyt. Quart. **14:** 190-198, 1938.

Terman, Lewis: The Measurement of Intelligence, Boston, Houghton, 1916.

Thompson, C. B.: A psychiatric study of recidivists, Am. J. Psychiat. **94:** No. 3, November, 1937.

Tulchin, Simon H.: Intelligence and Crime, A Study of Penitentiary and Reformatory Offenders, Chicago, Univ. Chicago Press, 1939.

Walton, Robert P.: Marihuana, America's New Drug Problem, Philadelphia, Lippincott, 1938.

Webster, Blakely R.: Psychoses among criminals, Psychiatric Quart. **2:** 136-143, 1928.

Wechsler, David: The Measurements of Adult Intelligence, Baltimore, Williams & Wilkins, 1939.

Wender, Louis: The dynamics of group psychotherapy and its application, J. Nerv. & Ment. Dis. **84:** 54, 1936.

Wertham, Frederic: The catathymic crisis, Arch. Neurol. & Psychiat. **37:** 974-978, 1937.

White, W. A.: Crime and Criminals, New York, Farrar & Rinehart, 1933.

Wittels, F.: The criminal psychopath in the psychoanalytic system, Psychoanalyt. Rev. **24:** 276-291, 1937.

Yarnell, Helen: Firesetting children, J. Orthopsychiat. **10:** 272, 1940.

Yoakum, C. S., and Yerkes, Robert M.: Army Mental Tests, New York, Holt, 1929.

Young, H. T. P.: Incendiarism in adult males, Lancet **1:** 1334, 1925.

Zeleny, L. D.: Feeblemindedness and Criminal Conduct, Am. J. Soc. **38:** January, 1933.

Zilboorg, G.: Some sidelights on the psychology of murder, J. Nerv. & Ment. Dis. **81:** 442, 1935.

————: Dynamics of schizophrenic reactions related to pregnancy and childbirth, Am. J. Psychiat. **8:** 733, 1929.

————: Murder and justice, J. Crim. Psychopath. **5:** 1, 1943.

Index

213